# THE FUTURE OF EUROPEAN WELFARE

*Also by Martin Rhodes*

CRISIS AND TRANSITION IN ITALIAN POLITICS
(*with Martin Bull*)

DEVELOPMENTS IN WEST EUROPEAN POLITICS (*editor with Paul Heywood and Vincent Wright*)

SOUTHERN EUROPEAN WELFARE STATES (*editor*)

THE REGIONS AND THE NEW EUROPE (*editor*)


*Also by Yves Mény*

ADJUSTING TO EUROPE (*editor with P. Muller and J. L. Quermonne*)

DEMOCRACY AND CORRUPTION IN EUROPE (*editor with D. della Porta*)

GOVERNMENT AND POLITICS IN WESTERN EUROPE
(*with A. Knapp*)

IL CONSIGLIO DI STATO IN FRANCIA E IN ITALIA (*editor*)

# The Future of European Welfare

## A New Social Contract?

Edited by

**Martin Rhodes**
*Senior Research Fellow*
*Robert Schuman Centre*
*European University Institute*
*Florence*

and

**Yves Mény**
*Professor, Institut d'Etudes Politiques, Paris*
*Director, Robert Schuman Centre*
*European University Institute*
*Florence*

First published in Great Britain 1998 by
**MACMILLAN PRESS LTD**
Houndmills, Basingstoke, Hampshire RG21 6XS and London
Companies and representatives throughout the world

A catalogue record for this book is available from the British Library.

ISBN 0–333–67824–9

First published in the United States of America 1998 by
**ST. MARTIN'S PRESS, INC.,**
Scholarly and Reference Division,
175 Fifth Avenue, New York, N.Y. 10010

ISBN 0–312–21195–3

Library of Congress Cataloging-in-Publication Data
The future of European welfare : a new social contract? / edited by
Martin Rhodes and Yves Mény.
p. cm.
Includes bibliographical references and index.
ISBN 0–312–21195–3 (cloth)
1. Europe—Social policy.   2. Public welfare—Europe.   3. Welfare
state.   I. Rhodes, Martin.   II. Mény, Yves.
HN380.5.A8F87  1997
361.6'5'094—dc21
                                                         97–38223
                                                              CIP

This book is printed on paper suitable for recycling and made from fully managed and
sustained forest sources.

10   9   8   7   6   5   4   3   2   1
07  06  05  04  03  02  01  00  99  98

Printed in Great Britain by
The Ipswich Book Company Ltd
Ipswich, Suffolk

# Contents

## Contents

# Acknowledgements

The editors would like to thank the Ministry of Science Policy and Infrastructure of the Belgian government for its invaluable financial support for the conference on which this book is based.

# Notes on the Contributors

**Carlos Closa** is Assistant Professor in the Department of Political Science and Administration at the Complutense University of Madrid. He has written on citizenship and European and Spanish politics and his recent publications include 'Citizenship of the Union and Nationality of Member States', *Common Market Law Review*, 32, (1995)' 'National Interest and Convergence of Preferences: A Changing role for Spain in the EU?', in C. Rhodes and S. Mazey (eds) *The State of the European Union Vol. 3: Building a European polity?* (Boulder: Lynne Rienner, 1995) and *Sistema Político de la Unión Europea* (Madrid: Ed. Complutense, 1997).

**Colin Crouch** is Professor of Political and Social Science at the European University Institute, Florence, Italy. He has written extensively on European and British politics and industrial relations and his recent publications include *Industrial Relations and European State Traditions* (Oxford: Clarendon Press, 1993), with F. Traxler (eds), *Organized Industrial Relations in Western Europe: What Future?* (Aldershot: Avebury, 1995) and, with W. Streeck (eds), *Les capitalismes en Europe* (Paris: La Découverte, 1996).

**Bob Deacon** is Professor of Social Policy and Director of the International Social Policy Research Unit based at Leeds Metropolitan University. He has written extensively on social policy in Eastern Europe and his recent publications include *The New Eastern Europe: Social Policy Past, Present and Future* (London: Sage, 1992), *Social Policy, Social Justice and Citizenship in Eastern Europe* (ed.) (London: Sage, 1992) and *Globalism and Social Policy* (London: Sage, 1997).

**Maurizio Ferrera** is Professor of Public Policy and Administration at the University of Pavia. He also teaches Political Science at the Bocconi University in Milan, where he co-directs the Centre for Comparative Political Research. He has written extensively on Italian and comparative social policy and his publications include *Il Welfare State in Italia* (Bologna: Il Mulino, 1984), *Modelli di solidarietà. Politica e riforme sociale nelle democrazie* (Bologna: Il Mulino, 1993) and *Stato sociale e mercato* (ed.) (Turin: Edizione della Fondazione Giovanni Agnelli, 1993).

**Ulrike Götting** has been Research Fellow at the Centre for Social Policy Research, University of Bremen, since 1991 and completed her dissertation on the politics of welfare state reform in Eastern Europe in 1997. Her recent publications include 'Destruction, Adjustment and Innovation: Social Policy Transformation in Eastern and Central Europe', *Journal of European Social Policy*, 4, (1994) and (co-authored with Karl Hinrichs and Karin Haug), 'The Long Road to Long-Term Care Insurance in Germany', *Journal of Public Policy*, 14, (1994).

**Bill Jordan** is Professor of Social Policy in the Department of Social Work and Probation Studies at the University of Exeter and visiting professor at the Department of Political Science, Cornelius University, Bratislava, Slovakia. His publications include *The Common Good: Citizenship, Morality and Self-Interest* (Oxford: Blackwell, 1989), *Trapped in Poverty? Labour-Market Decisions in Low-Income Households* (with S. James, H. Kay and M. Redley) (London: Routledge, 1992), *Putting the Family First: Identities, Decisions and Citizenship* (with M. Redley and S. James) (London: UCL Press, 1994) and *A Theory of Poverty and Social Exclusion* (Cambridge: Polity, 1996).

**Yves Mény** is director of the Robert Schuman Centre, European University Institute, Florence, Italy and professor at the Institut d'Études Politiques, Paris. He has written extensively on European politics and public policy, and his recent publications include *Il Consiglio di Stato in Francia e in Italia* (ed.) (Bologna: Il Mulino, 1994), *Government and Politics in Western Europe* (with A. Knapp), 2nd edition (Oxford: Oxford University Press, 1994), *Adjusting to Europe* (co-edited with P. Muller and J-L. Quermonne) (London: Routledge, 1996) and *Democracy and Corruption in Europe* (edited with D. Della Porta) (London: Cassel, 1996).

**Paul Ormerod** is chairman of Post-Orthodox Economics, London and Visiting Professor of Economics, University of Manchester. In 1994 he published the *Death of Economics* (London: Faber and Faber) which has been translated into nine languages. Recent and forthcoming articles cover the topics of unemployment, the statistical distribution of recessions in capitalism, post-Keynesian econometrics, and the topological dimension of macroeconomic data series.

**Serge Paugam** is a sociologist at the CNRS and works in the Observatoire sociologique du changement (FNSP/CNRS) and at the Laboratoire de sociologie quantitative (CREST/INSEE). He teaches at l'École des hautes études en sciences sociales and at the Institut d'études politiques in Paris. His main publications include *La disqualification sociale, essai sur la nouvelle pauvreté* (Paris: Presses Universitaires de France, 1991), *La société* *française et ses pauvres, l'expérience du revenu minimum d'insertion* (Paris: Presses Universitaires de France, 1993) and, as editor, *L'exclusion. L'état des savoirs* (Paris: La Découverte, 1996).

**Giovanna Procacci** is Research Director in the Department of Sociology, University of Milan. Her publications include *Gouverner la misère. La question sociale en France* (Paris: Seuil, 1993) (published in Italian as *Governare la povertà*, Bologna: Il Mulino, 1997), 'La naissance d'une rationalité moderne de la pauvreté' in S. Paugam (ed.), *L'exclusion. L'état des savoirs* (Paris: La Decouverte, 1996), 'Le grondement de la bataille' in R. Rotmann (ed.), *Au risque de Foucault* (Paris: Centre Georges Pompidou, 1997) and was guest editor of the special issue of *Rassegna Italiana di Sociologia*, 1, 1997 on 'Inequality Today'.

**Martin Rhodes** is Senior Research Fellow in the Robert Schuman Centre, European University Institute, Florence, Italy. He has written extensively on Italian politics, European social policy and the welfare state and his recent edited books include *The Regions and the New Europe* (Manchester University Press, 1995), *Developments in West European Politics* (with Paul Heywood and Vincent Wright) (Macmillan Press, 1997), *Crisis and Transition in Italian Politics* (with M. Bull) (London: Frank Cass, 1997) and *Southern European Welfare States* (London: Frank Cass, 1997).

**Fritz Scharpf** is Professor of Political Science at the Max Planck Institute für Gesellschaftsforschung, Cologne, Germany. He has written extensively on democratic theory and European and German public policy and is the author, among many other publications, of *Crisis and Choice in European Social Democracy* (Ithaca: Cornell University Press, 1991), *Horizontale Politikverflechtung: Zur Theorie von Verhandlungssystem* (with A. Benz and R. Zintl) (Frankfurt-am-Main: Campus Verlgag, 1992) and *Optionen den Föderalismus in Deutschland und Europa* (Frankfurt-am-Main: Campus Verlag, 1994).

**Karel Van Den Bosch** works at the Centre for Social Policy at the University of Antwerp and has written extensively in the area of poverty analysis. His publications include 'Poverty Measures in Comparative Research', in J. Berghman and B. Cantillon (eds), *The European Face of Social Security: Essays in Honour of Herman Deleeck* (Aldershot: Avebury) and (with T. Callan, J. Estivill, P. Hausman, B. Jeandidier, R. Muffels and J. Yfantopoulos), 'A Comparison of Poverty in Seven European Countries and Regions using Subjective and Relative Measures', *Journal of Population Economics*, 6, (1993).

# List of Figures and Tables

# 1 Europe's Social Contract Under Stress
## Martin Rhodes and Yves Mény

## INTRODUCTION

We are currently living in an era of welfare pessimism. While extensive welfare programmes and high levels of social transfers remain central to the political economy of western – and, to a lesser extent, eastern – European countries, the traditional 'social contract' between states and their citizens is simultaneously failing to fulfil its original objectives while also being eroded by stealth or, in some cases, directly attacked. Older notions of solidarity are breaking down as structural changes in western societies render political and economic identities more individualistic and group oriented and the changing balance between the generations (the ageing of western societies) threatens the contract that was originally struck between them. Globalization, although of contested significance, has reduced the autonomy of governments to pursue 'market-correcting' policies and preserve their own idiosyncratic forms of 'social contract'. Although their existence is not in jeopardy, the western welfare states are clearly at an impasse. There appear to be few viable alternatives available to a shift towards 'more market' and the acceptance of greater inequalities, as revealed by the convergence of major party political programmes on an agenda of reregulation and 'neo-liberal' reform.

Understanding the nature of this impasse is far from straightforward, because objective problems and constraints merge with ideological opposition in the current economic and political climate. Thus, while in many countries escalating health and pension costs have become an economic liability (as in the case of certain pension-biased welfare states in continental Europe, whose public sector deficits or reliance on employer and employees' contributions pose major policy problems), in others, the attack on welfare is more politically motivated. By the same token, while the call by employers (especially small and medium-sized firms) for cut backs in welfare in the interests of lower social charges is dictated by self-interest (and exploits the current weakness of pro-welfare coalitions), high

1

labour costs are posing genuine problems in certain countries and have led firms to rationalize production and/or relocate in lower cost countries. Globalization is increasingly viewed as the core of the problem; yet globalization is itself a controversial and contested term, and has both an objective reality and a strong ideological bias, as revealed by the role of international organizations such as the Organization for Economic Co-operation and Development (OECD), World Bank and the International Monetary Fund (IMF) as the international mediators and purveyors of institutional 'best practice' in social policy (see Chapter 10 by Bob Deacon).

None of this means that welfare states are changing dramatically or that welfare programmes are being fully dismantled. For as some of the leading analysts of western welfare states have pointed out, the politics of welfare is still, by and large, the 'politics of the status quo' (Pierson, 1996; Esping-Andersen, 1996a). This is certainly the case in eastern Europe where, as Götting shows (Chapter 7), welfare state institutions have remained remarkably stable during the transition to democracy, and have consequently failed to respond adequately to the social costs of rapid economic change. In the west, where Esping-Andersen (1996a: 24) talks of a 'frozen' institutional landscape, the slow process of accretion whereby welfare programmes have expanded in the post-war period is far from easy to modify or reverse, even where there is the political will, as in Reagan's America or Thatcher's Britain. Bureaucratic sclerosis, the complex institutional nature of welfare arrangements, popular opposition and the adverse electoral consequences of assaults on welfare all militate against either rapid and far-reaching retrenchment (as sought by the anti-welfare New Right) or gradual and more moderate reform, as attempted in countries seeking a more equitable recasting of well-entrenched institutional arrangements. Thus, while adjustments to welfare programmes have occurred since the 1970s, when fiscal strains began to erode welfare commitments in most advanced industrial states, these involved cuts at the margins, alongside a decentralization and rationalization of welfare bureaucracies, while the major programmes of health, pensions and social security were, by and large, maintained. Indeed, contrary to certain predictions of the imminent demise of the welfare state, the 'old social contract' still appears to be standing its ground in most western European countries, at least in terms of income protection, and social security transfers are as important as ever in fighting or preventing poverty (Van Den Bosch, Chapter 6).

But this does not mean that the status quo is safe, for even marginal cuts may affect profoundly certain segments of the population; and their cumulative impact can be great. Nor is it necessarily easy to defend via institutional tinkering and marginal adjustments to established rights or programme revenue and spending. Moreover, the 1980s and 1990s arguably have seen the emergence of a new set of contradictions and challenges, as well as more serious attempts to scale back welfare spending and commitments. Welfare states today are in trouble, because of both ideological opposition and objective problems (deficits, perceived inefficiencies, benefits disequilibria, legitimacy deficits) and are engaged in a difficult process of crisis management. In many countries this may require if not the breaking of the social contract between the state and citizens, then at least its reformulation.

This book seeks to examine several dimensions of the current welfare state impasse. Part I looks at how we should interpret the contemporary shortfalls of European welfare states (the persistence of unemployment, poverty and social exclusion); Part II discusses whether and to what extent existing systems of social protection are under stress from domestic pressures; Part III considers how global pressures and constraints are affecting the process of change and limiting options for reform; and finally, the problems of reforming Europe's social contract are examined in Part IV. The aim of this Introduction is to briefly consider the nature of this 'social contract', the reasons why it is presently under stress and the prospects for a positive and equitable revision of its terms.

## THE NATURE OF EUROPE'S SOCIAL CONTRACT

As Rosanvallon (1995: 52) remarks, the modern welfare state owes more to Rousseau (and, one could add, Hobbes) than it does to Marx, in that its basis does not lie in attempts to liberate the proletariat from its chains but rather in a more paternalist effort to protect the weak and poor and associate all within a protective community – often for nationalistic ends. For while class struggle – or rather its attenuation – was clearly important (the fear of revolution and of the *classes dangereuses* was certainly instrumental in many countries, beginning with Bismarck's Germany), the origins of the welfare state also reveal a strong patriotic dimension and were linked to the consolidation and defence of notions of nationhood. Wars were often instrumental in developing a sense of trade-off between the suffering that people had to endure during the conflict and their potential entitlements in times of peace and renewed growth. Because international conflicts imply a total dedication of the people to the objectives of the national government, unity and solidarity became the catch words and the key values. In the name of the defence of the nation, taxes were raised, women were put to work and men were sent to the front line at the risk of being wounded or killed. After the war, it was felt both by citizens and politicians that those who had contributed to this collective effort had to be compensated.

Theda Skocpol has shown in *Protecting Soldiers and Mothers* (1992) the decisiveness of the financial contribution provided to the widows and the pensions paid to the soldiers of the American war of secession in the construction of a nascent social policy. Beveridge himself based the ambitious reforms that he promised to the British population on the fundamental opposition between the warfare states of the fascist and Nazi dictatorships and the welfare states of the democratic regimes. The same account could be made of the history of the welfare state in France at the end of both World War I and World War II. The claims were more nationalistic in tone after 1918 and more class-based in 1945–6, but on both occasions the idea of national solidarity was a key element in the rhetoric and the principles guiding reform. Social policies were conceived as the modern basis of a new contract: to civil and political rights, western democracies were compelled to add social rights.

Ideology and ideas were clearly also important in differentiating the subsequent trajectories of welfare states. The political debate and actual policies in Europe were strongly influenced by both the church and socialist reformers to a greater extent than in either the USA or the UK. And when a growing opposition to the post-war consensus on welfare began to emerge in various quarters in the late 1970s and early 1980s after Mrs Thatcher and Ronald Reagan came to power, such opposition was muted in continental Europe by the absence of conservative right-wing parties and the dominance of Christian Democracy. This is partly why the notions of 'social contract' and 'solidarity', which are pervasive in the welfare state discourse of continental Europe, sound strange – and even alien and threatening – to Anglo-Saxon ears. It also explains why the British – regardless of political complexion – find it so difficult to accept 'continental European' notions such as the 'social dimension' of the European Union (EU) and its 1989 'Social Charter'. The cross-party commitment to the notion of a 'contract' in continental Europe, with its emphasis on a mutual set of commitments and obligations between state and citizen, employer and worker, contrasts with the more residual character of social security provision in the UK, as provided under the original Beveridge model, and with its more 'voluntarist' system of industrial relations. Thus, while poverty in France is interpreted as a failure of society, producing a debate on how best to increase solidarity via social spending, in the

UK – where a jump in inequality since the late 1970s has put more adults and children below the poverty line of 50 per cent of median income than in any other European country – poverty has revived the nineteenth-century discourse about the possible negative consequences of helping the poor (Paugam, Chapter 3). And as Ferrera demonstrates (Chapter 5), the policy legacy of selectivity (rather than 'universalistic maintenance'), handed down from the time of the Poor Laws in the UK, has facilitated an erosion of 'solidarity' in that country via a remarkable growth in targeted, means-tested services – an innovation much harder to introduce in continental Europe, given the greater institutional and symbolic commitment to 'contract-based' solidarities.

However, although the welfare state systems of continental Europe were rooted in a similar ideological and political background, the policy variations among them have also been great. Even leaving aside the UK 'liberal' system, this makes it difficult to talk of a 'European Social Model' as such, beyond certain common general characteristics such as trade union rights to collective bargaining, extensive systems of work force protection and redistributive policies. As Ferrera (Chapter 5) points out, although there is a strong affinity among European systems at a high level of abstraction, seen from below, the European Social Model 'shatters into a kaleidoscope of historical sediment and national specificity'. For the nature of the social contract, in spite of its transnational commonalities, was national in form and style. It was framed very much by the political and social movements of the past, by its initial developments, by the time of its birth and expansion. According to the country, it was universalistic or piecemeal in its scope and organization, pluralistic, authoritarian or corporatist in its management. Most welfare state experts, such as Esping-Andersen (1990) and Ferrera (1993), have recognized this fragmentation in their attempts to build up 'families' and acknowledge that these ideal-types or models pay less than full justice to the internal variety and heterogeneity of each group. This diversity remains a strong and persistent feature of the welfare state systems amongst the western democracies. The differentiation is even greater when the former socialist countries are brought into the picture, both in terms of their existing institutional structures and plausible future trajectories (Götting and Deacon, chapters 7 and 10).

It is this fundamental feature – together with the financial and political dimension – which justifies the view that welfare states are, by definition, national states and that they should remain so: as Carlos Closa argues in his analysis of the relationship between citizenship and nationality, if it is difficult to create solidarity between fellow citizens with a common identity, the development of citizenship rights at the

European level is even more so; and it may be quite utopian to imagine supranational or multinational boundaries allowing for financial redistribution on a significant scale. As the French writer Renan (the founding father of the national citizenship concept after the French defeat by Prussia in 1870) put it: 'A Zollverein is not a polity' (Renan 1992), although the EU has certainly had ambitions in that direction; a point we return to below.

## THE SOCIAL CONTRACT UNDER STRESS

Given the diversity of the 'social contract' among Europe's 'welfare families', it is unsurprising that they face rather different challenges in the contemporary period. As Esping-Andersen (1990) has demonstrated, welfare states emerged with quite different institutional structures and modes of operation: because of the nature of its domestic social compact, among the 'three worlds of welfare', the Scandinavian model achieved a high degree of decommodification (distancing the citizen from market dictates) and a cross-class commitment to high levels of welfare spending and taxation; the 'Germanic' continental model had a lower level of decommodification and a more status-or occupational-basis for welfare provision, but, nevertheless, there was a political consensus on an extensive and comprehensive social contract; meanwhile, the Anglo-Saxon model has always been less generous, providing flat-rate benefits based on taxation and a general social insurance system, and was built on a much narrower class coalition. A distinctive, and unevenly institutionalized variant of the continental 'social contract' emerged in the countries of southern Europe after the 1960s, dependent on a combination of state programmes and traditional (charity and family-based) welfare to provide a functional equivalent of the more 'state interventionist' forms of welfare found among its northern neighbours (Ferrera, 1996; Rhodes, 1997a).

Several chapters in this book reveal the implications of these distinctions for reform. While Van Den Bosch (Chapter 6) shows that different countries are more resistant than others to the appearance of new types of poverty, Paugam (Chapter 3) demonstrates how groupings of countries (corresponding roughly to the above schema) have quite different interpretations of and treatments for poverty. Ferrera, meanwhile, shows in Chapter 5 how these welfare families confront quite diverse solidarity dilemmas and political and institutional constraints on reform, suggesting that while they are responding to common problems, the policy outcomes are unlikely to produce any straightforward form of convergence. Others, suggest that there may be a certain form of convergence, at least at the level of policy design, suggesting that an understanding of welfare states based on past trajectories may be less than useful for comprehending their present development and future directions: while Jordan (Chapter 12) fears a convergence on a neo-Hobbesian order and the emergence of an 'enforcement state' as traditional solidarities break down and become more and more difficult to repair, Rhodes and Deacon (Chapters 9 and 10) are less pessimistic, suggesting, although from rather different standpoints, the emergence of hybrid forms of social policy which attempt to strike a new balance between state and market. What Rhodes calls 'competitive corporatism' and Deacon 'social liberalism' are both suggestive of a possible convergence in policy design (if not outcomes) in an era where both neo-liberal reform and the post-Fordist deconstruction of work and security challenge the arrangements underpinning traditional solidarities and communities.

What seems to be increasingly clear is that the different welfare state regimes generate different contradictions and face different problems at a time when the external constraints and pressures deriving from globalization are the same. These diverse contradictions and problems, rather than any general incompatibility between competitiveness and the welfare state, will determine the stress lines in different systems and stimulate the policy responses to them (Gough, 1996; Rhodes, 1996). The issue of employment reveals how different national systems have to face the consequences of the past social contract, which in most cases result from an accretion of policies and institutional structures rather than explicit policy choices. In his contribution to this book, Paul Ormerod argues that unemployment is for the most part a distributional phenomenon, or in other words, that 'the average rate of unemployment that prevails over the course of the business cycle is a result of the particular form of social contract which exists'. He stresses that flexibility in the USA labour market has been achieved thanks to the pressure of immigrant workers ready to accept jobs even with very low pay, obliging the employed to adjust to the situation, that is, to lower their salary claims. Instead, in the Scandinavian countries, the distributional costs were met by an explicit social contract by those in employment. They pay high taxes for an over-developed public sector which has to share a large proportion of the unemployed labour force. In Japan, the price for full employment was paid, until recently, in the form of a costly and low-productivity service sector. In continental Europe, governments, employers and labour unions have more or less agreed that the price of adjustment had to be put on the shoulders of the unemployed (see also Esping-Andersen, 1996b). In short, unemployment is less a matter of differentiated growth than a matter of often implicit and undebated political choice.

In responding to such problems, what is problematic today in these countries is not the option of which of these 'welfare futures' they should choose (for, as Maurizio Ferrera explains, social policy innovation is heavily constrained by institutional traditions), but rather the persistence over time of a social contract that is proving inadequate for facing the problems of the day. The old social contract in new circumstances may itself generate solidarity dilemmas, with unemployment, once again, revealing the negative consequences of the social achievements of the past. In continental Europe, a general consensus has emerged that if labour market 'outsiders' – especially the young unemployed – are to become insiders, then changes to the regulations that cover both employment and the funding of welfare (especially in the social insurance countries) will have to be made, alongside other innovations such as the work-sharing alternative suggested by Ormerod in Chapter 2. The paradox of this situation is that in order to resolve their solidarity dilemmas, the European states – which usually differentiate themselves by a high level of development of their welfare systems – have lost part of their margin for manoeuvre. The general feeling is that any change is a zero sum game which encounters the fierce resistance of the political losers. The status quo is itself beginning to undermine the legitimacy of the social contract (from the viewpoint of young people, the unemployed or women, for example), while its evolution and adaptation are resented as an unacceptable attack on the entitlements and *droits acquis* of the beneficiaries of the present situation.

Rightly or wrongly, globalization is perceived as the core of the problem; it obliges certain reactions and constrains the range of political action. As already noted, the past, present and future prospects of the European social contract are closely linked to the relationship between domestic and international economies. As Scharpf and Rhodes discuss in Chapters 8 and 9, external constraints on domestic welfare states, deriving either from globalization or Europeanization, have grown in importance and heavily reduce the policy options available to governments. For the 'old' social contract – and its diverse institutionalization in these welfare states was very much part of the 'golden age' of western economic development, during which the preservation of national sovereignty, uninterrupted growth and the Keynesian welfare state all went hand in hand. National autonomy (referred to by Scharpf as 'boundary control') was preserved in the era of 'embedded liberalism' (Ruggie, 1982) with the help of exchange and trade controls, even if economies became increasingly open after the 1950s. This 'relative autonomy' allowed the construction of rather different types of welfare state and social contract, each with its own approach to the provision of public goods and the institutionalization of solidarity. But in the post-1970s era of 'disembedded liberalism', the ability of governments to fulfil their side of the welfare compact is beginning to wear thin, due to the loss of government control in a global economy over employment and other broad economic policy objectives as the flow of goods and capital have steadily been liberalized (Ruggie, 1994; Rhodes, 1996).

This has compounded an internal contradiction in the operation of European welfare states that was analyzed in the 1970s in terms of a trade off between legitimacy and accumulation. In the writings of O'Connor (1973), Gough (1979) and Offe (1984), the welfare state 'crisis' was understood to derive from the ultimate incompatibility of continued capitalist accumulation and the legitimation of capitalism via expanded social spending. Fiscal crisis – an unmanageable tax burden on the state, resisted increasingly by the firms paying a large part of the welfare bill – would be the result. While the extent of the crisis in the 1970s was probably exaggerated – and due in part to the long recession triggered by the twin oil shocks – the legitimacy of welfare programmes did decline during this period, the result of a loss of faith in the capacity of large bureaucracies to manage welfare programmes efficiently and effectively deal with problems of poverty and social exclusion. For as internal problems were increasingly exposed by external constraints, the former pro-welfare coalitions were also being weakened – and it is the interaction between internationalization and what Offe (1996) has called 'the destructuration of collectivities' that poses the greatest threat to the integrative' universalist norms of west European welfare states. At the same time, governments began to lose faith in their capacity for intervention, due to the budgetary strains caused by past mismanagement or uncontrolled expansion, and the 'objective support' this has given to the anti-welfare lobby. Everywhere, the 'welfare jeopardy thesis' – the idea that high levels of welfare spending and growth are incompatible – has gained ground, despite inconclusive evidence that this really is the case (see Hirschman, 1991 and Gough, 1996, for a survey of the arguments). In the process, the 'old' social contract is being constantly reneged on as governments seek ways off trimming costs and reducing 'welfare dependency' (see Rhodes, 1995; 1997b). Such measures include:

- the modification of funding arrangements (so as to reduce the burden of social charges on firms);

- more stringent regulations and qualifying conditions (increasing the age of retirement, restricting access to unemployment benefits);
- increased targeting, which has been most extensively employed in the UK, but also introduced in Germany, the Netherlands and Italy (where income limits have been set for the receipt of certain benefits) and Spain (where family allowances have been linked to income);
- a shift from passive to active measures (for instance, transforming entitlements into incentives, which can range from schemes linking unemployment benefits to training schemes to more draconian forms of 'workfare');
- and privatization or the introduction of quasi-markets (in the UK an explicit policy of encouraging personal, private pension schemes, and elsewhere a form of 'creeping' privatization in health care – such as a transfer of costs to individuals through so-called 'co-payments' – and the introduction of 'market' principles into health care management).

These measures have taken different forms in different institutional contexts, but all aim to tackle common problems created by:

- demographic change (the ageing of the European population poses a major challenge due to the shift in the ratio of active citizens to passive welfare recipients);
- the rising cost of health care (due in some part to 'demand-side' factors such as ageing, higher disposable incomes and greater insurance coverage, but much more importantly to 'supply-side' effects, such as technological improvements, a growth in medical personnel and facilities and rising real health care prices, creating their own inflationary dynamic);
- low economic growth and high unemployment (implying higher spending on income support for the growing number, especially of younger people, unable to find work and on devising new forms of active labour market policy to improve their employability);
- and the changing nature of the labour market. The growing proportion of non-standard forms of employment, such as fixed-term and part-time work, and the increasing participation of women in the work-force both pose challenges to traditional arrangements: the former because such workers may be denied access to entitlements devised for permanent, full-time workers and employees; the latter because social protection is generally geared to male breadwinners and tends to penalize female careers which are often interrupted for family reasons, causing pension losses in many countries. One can add that females are often heavily

concentrated in areas of non-standard work, which means they may be doubly penalized.

The consequence of these developments, which is more acute in some contexts (notably the Anglo-Saxon one) than others, is a meaner (although not necessarily leaner or less expensive) welfare state. Meaner because two adverse trends have ensued: a process of 'explicit disentitlement' as the access of various categories to welfare provision is either restricted or denied altogether (the proliferation of the homeless on the streets of many European capitals is one symptom of this); or 'implicit disentitlement' as the changing nature of work itself modifies entitlements to benefits in systems where social security is geared to standard life-work cycles (Standing, 1995). These changes may have contributed to the sharply rising trends in poverty identified by Van Den Bosch in Ireland and the UK and the more modest increases measured in Germany, France and Sweden.

High levels of unemployment, of course, interact with these developments, exacerbating existing social problems and creating news forms of poverty. This problem is especially acute in the eastern welfare states where an inadequate pre-transition status quo has depended on a full-employment economy for its limited effectiveness. As economic reform has proceeded, and the artificiality of eastern 'full employment' has been exposed, the burden of new demands threatens the sustainability of this weak welfare infrastructure. In the west, unemployment has been described as the 'Achilles' heel' of the welfare state because of its short-term and long-term effects on welfare (while initially creating new levels of dependency, it also creates longer-term problems of disentitlement and greater strains on welfare budgets) (Jallade, 1992). This is not just because of the impact of sustained levels of unemployment on welfare costs (higher unemployment benefits, the exposure of the unemployed to greater general 'social risk') but because of the apparent inability of European countries to deal with unemployment, and the growing perception that their welfare states may have something to do with this. This is certainly the view of many firms and growing numbers of middle-class voters in Europe who are becoming increasingly intolerant of what the critics of the welfare state call a 'dependency culture'. It is also the view of a number of intellectual critics – and not only from the New Right – who have identified a number of impediments in welfare state arrangements to employment creation. For example, Esping-Andersen (1994) and Jessop (1994) have both identified the relationship between traditional welfare states and Fordist constituencies, bureaucracies and forms of industrial

development as a major obstacle in the way of transition to a more
flexible, service-employment-based, post-Fordist era. Their more liberal
counterparts (for example Lindbeck 1993; 1994) advocate a major overhaul of the traditional European social contract to counteract its negative
consequences – primarily the destruction of incentives, the generation
of employment-reducing social costs, and the expansion of welfare
dependency ('moral hazard').

## CHALLENGES TO THE WELFARE STATUS QUO

Summarizing the above, we can specify a number of major challenges to
the welfare status quo:

*An on-going contradiction between the economic and social spheres.*
As indicated, nation-states are still appropriate entities for the design and
implementation of social policies in spite of present challenges. But they
are less and less well adapted to the internationalization of goods and services and flows of all kinds. Individual states can attempt to slow down, to
impede or to mitigate the process. They are unable to resist it even when
they are authoritarian and still pretend to be socialist countries. The capacity of states to deliver welfare benefits is limited by their inability to
control these transnational developments. As Crouch (Chapter 11), puts it,
'globalization makes possible a certain amount of "régime shopping"'
which, as Scharpf, argues, poses particularly difficult problems in building
a new European social dimension to reinforce or replace those under stress
at the domestic level. But as Rhodes argues in Chapter 9, mediating external pressures and controlling transnational developments may be possible
through the construction of new class compromises, institutionalized
through pragmatic social pacts. These will help buffer the impact of external pressures and allow a more variable and equitable set of trade-offs than
is often suggested by those who see a straight forward choice between the
USA and the European model – in other words between more inequality
and more jobs, or the preservation of solidarity alongside high rates of
unemployment.

*The progressive hollowing-out of the state as a mediator between the
firm and the individual.* In Europe, at least, the relationship between the
employee/citizen and the company was instigated by state intervention.
Individual firms had to pay taxes of all kinds in order to match the needs
of social protection provided through systems run or controlled by public
authorities. In most European countries, social benefits, health insurance,
pensions, family allowances were provided through public channels, in

contrast to the USA where state intervention was limited to basic needs or to social assistance. In this case, the firm was and is crucial in deciding on and providing the extent and the amount of benefits the employees are entitled to. Before being national, USA welfare is company welfare. What used to be 'American exceptionalism' tends to apply more and more to some segments of European welfare systems. It is not so much a matter of the speed or magnitude of the process but more a problem of legitimacy. 'Because firms are increasingly the central institutions of our societies', writes Crouch, 'their forms and practices are coming to be seen as almost the only acceptable ones for running organizations of many different kinds' (Chapter 11). Once again, however, their may be ways of embedding firms within new or modified social arrangements, as suggested by the social pacts analyzed by Rhodes in Chapter 9.

*The ideological challenge to the state as a legitimate redistributive actor at the individual level.* Welfare systems are under strain not only because of the financial problems they have to face, particularly in some countries and/or sectors. The problem is just as much ideological: the 'rolling back of the state' can be read as 'rolling back the welfare state'. Rather than define the relationship between the individual and the welfare state in the Marshallian term of 'social citizenship', social policies – at least in the USA and increasingly in the UK since the 1980s – are often perceived as detrimental to the personal responsibility of the human being. Not only does the welfare state not contribute to solving the problems, but it exacerbates the propensity of the poor to rely on social benefits rather than take care of themselves. Just as 150 years ago, the purpose is to bring back to work the unemployed poor by avoiding the perverse effects of blind redistribution and by 'reinforcing the moral and subjective structure of the interpretation of poverty' (see Procacci, Chapter 4). Redistribution, in most radical liberal views, is not only wrong for practical or financial reasons. It is morally destructive. By emphasizing the individual rather than the collective dimension of citizenship, the liberal approach paves the way for a welfare state retreat; by emphasizing 'workfare' rather than welfare, the policy response to unemployment and social exclusion in the USA and the UK risks increasing the divisions between the employed and the unemployed, and between those citizens included in society and those rendered marginal (King, 1995: 214). As Jordan (chapter 12) argues, this state-directed 'destructuration of collectivities' creates optimal conditions for 'cultures of resistance' (covert, risk-sharing, informal clubs or semi-legal and illegal activities) and drives up the cost of rebuilding lost solidarities.

*The ideological challenge to the state as a legitimate redistributive actor at the territorial level.* The discussion of the role of the state *vis-à-vis* the individual has also had an impact on one other form of redistribution: what can be called the 'territorial welfare state'. The principles which motivated the redistributive policies of the welfare states in Europe were extended *mutatis mutandis* to the territorial components of the state. This evolution began in the 1950s but became important and visible in the 1960s and 1970s: Germany, France, the UK and Italy all pursued active policies of equalization at the local/regional level through multiple instruments, for example, industrial and procurement policies, public investment, financial subsidies, tax rebates. To say the least, the results were very uneven but, nevertheless, the principles at the roots of the redistributive mechanisms were not seriously challenged. Furthermore, they were extended at the European level: the deepening of the common market was sold to some reluctant countries (the less developed south) and to hesitant public opinions with a commitment to help and protect the weakest; mechanisms of social cohesion were put in place and the regional structural funds were an instrument amongst several to equalize economies and social cohesion while strengthening the legitimacy of the European enterprise. But what was considered a few years ago as a necessary condition of the European integration process is seen today by many as an inefficient and unacceptable way of using public money (see Hooghe, 1997). The solidarity principle which was extended at the territorial level as one more way of reinforcing social bonds (both nationally and Europe-wide) is more and more considered as an obsolete, costly and inefficient way of guaranteeing prosperity. Several cases illustrate that trend to date: the *Lega* movement in Italy, the reallocation of income tax (favouring wealthy regions in Spain), the claims of Flanders in favour of a regionalization of the Belgian social security system. In the former socialist countries, the break up of Czechoslovakia and of Yugoslavia meant the refusal of territorial solidarity. The wealthier parts of these countries thought they would be better off by keeping for themselves their relative advantages.

## NEGOTIATING A NEW SOCIAL CONTRACT

These recent developments are troublesome: they clearly indicate that solidarity as a concept and as a value in many instances is insufficient to maintain social bonds. Beyond the problem of the social contract there emerges the wider question of the state. If it is unable to control the economy and its legitimacy as a builder of the social fabric is challenged, one might doubt its future, at least in the form it has taken during the twentieth century. However, the proposal for a 'new' social contract does not necessarily entail a far-reaching dismantling of welfare but rather a well-thought out process of restructuring. Such ideas are now on the agenda of most European countries – because all governments are facing budgetary problems in a climate in which higher taxes are hard to impose (because of voter disenchantment and the disapproving view of the financial markets) and costs are still by and large increasing. Social demo-cratic parties – such as the British Labour party – have asked its policy advisors to 'think the unthinkable' in searching ways out of the contempo-rary welfare state impasse. A high degree of imagination – and caution – is clearly warranted in pushing this enterprise forward.

For, as Sigg *et al.* (1996) point out, European welfare states all face difficult dilemmas in maintaining their legitimacy by adjusting political expectations and maintaining or rebuilding supportive domestic coalitions. While coping with pressures from the international economy (including the deflationary, cost-cutting impact of moves towards economic and mon-etary union for members of the EU), they must also maintain a balance between the three basic components of the traditional social contract – insurance against risk, the welfare safety net and the principle of solidarity (achieved through income redistribution). Prioritizing the insurance com-ponent (by basing a greater proportion of entitlements on employment-linked social contributions, as is occurring, for example, in the Scandinavian countries) risks penalizing the poorer and inactive members of society. Moreover, this form of 'recommodification' endangers the ideal of solidarity on which the higher-spending, more consensual welfare states have been based and undermines less complete notions of social cit-izenship that have been central to other, less comprehensive welfare systems. But prioritizing social assistance and income redistribution would threaten the support given to welfare programmes by the electorally, and resource-important middle classes which, in any case, are increasingly predisposed towards individualist solutions to social security, health and pensions. A loss of support from this quarter also threatens to undercut social solidarity. Welfare state reform must of necessity negotiate a course between these options if the European version of the 'social contract' is to be defended and the neo-Hobbesian order projected by Jordan (Chapter 12) avoided.

Negotiate is the key word, for consensus is the most critical of the pillars that underpin the European social model. Although the level at which this should occur is still unclear, it seems increasingly unlikely that it will be at the European level, even if European policy will play a key role in underpinning certain minimal standards, especially in the labour market but also in the wider social field. For although much faith and investment has been put into European-level social policy, for the reasons mentioned by Scharpf (Chapter 8) and Closa (Chapter 13), there are formidable difficulties in negotiating a social compact between member states with different levels of social policy standards and in putting in place a pan-European form of social citizenship, even though this was the original aim of the maximalist proponents of the 'European social dimension'. The failure of this 'maximalist' programme can be explained in terms of the 'nation-state paradox' described by Wolfgang Streeck (1995: 33): 'While losing more and more of their internal sovereignty over their economies, nation-states have retained *external* sovereignty over international relations; the nation-state is still the dominant wielder of power at this level, despite the fact that it has lost the ability to apply such power domestically for purposes which are not market-supporting or market-conforming.'

For the resistance of nation-states to the transfer of social policy authority to the EU is not based just on ideological antagonism towards a federal system but on the strong existing links between social policy development and political legitimacy. This means that multi-tiered systems such as the EU remain vulnerable to the dynamics of 'competitive state building' – the competition between tiers of authority for credit for social provision – and, as Scharpf (chapter 8) argues, their incompletely co-ordinated social systems vulnerable to the danger of 'regime shopping' by firms and, once European Monetary Union (EMU) is in place, of 'social devaluation' by governments. For regardless of certain advances being made in Europe's embryonic 'social dimension' (in the areas of labour market rights and entitlements) social policy and social relations will be exposed more and more to market forces as a result of market integration. 'Negative integration' thereby triumphs over 'positive integration', unless complex new arrangements for European decision making are put in place, as suggested in chapter 8 by Fritz Scharpf. But this is a development which the preoccupation since Maastricht with subsidiarity would appear to forestall. Moreover EMU – or, for the time being, meeting the convergence criteria for EMU membership – poses major problems for those member states with substantial public sector deficits, while also exerting significant deflationary pressures on the economies of Europe as a whole. And given the problems facing tax increases (above all political hostility), in many countries there is only one option if these criteria are to be met – cuts and rationalization in social welfare provision.

As Rhodes (Chapter 9) argues, recent developments suggest not only that social policy options constrained by these developments will continue to be negotiated at the national level, but that, contrary to a major theme in European political economy–'Europessimism' (Streeck, 1995) – nation states may still retain considerable capacity for a positive reinterpretation of their domestic social contracts. This will depend, of course, on the political capacity of their governments and social partners to renegotiate the details of the class compromises that underpinned their 'golden age' welfare states. In addition (and also in contrast to the Europessimist position), the failure to constitute a pan-European corporatist response to the challenges to the social contract may not mean that domestic compacts will be impossible to sustain. At present, many European countries are engaged in an agonizing reappraisal of their welfare state arrangements, and many governments are beginning to negotiate a new social contract which, as the southern European case suggests (Rhodes 1997a), may in certain ways be more equitable than the old. The outcome is as yet unclear, and the models competing for attention at the global level (and sponsored by international agencies) still offer multiple rather than single-path trajectories into the future. And while as Bob Deacon argues, 'any new social contract in the welfare field will have to be struck at the global level between agencies and social movements', the national level – and domestic politics – will remain critical in determining its shape.

## REFERENCES

Esping-Andersen, G. (1990) *The Three Worlds of Welfare Capitalism*, Cambridge: Polity Press.

Esping-Andersen, G. (1994) 'Equality and Work in the Post-Industrial Life Cycle', in D. Miliband (ed.), *Reinventing the Left*, Cambridge: Polity Press, pp. 167–185.

Esping-Andersen, G. (1996a) 'After the Golden Age? Welfare State Dilemmas in a Global Economy', in G. Esping-Andersen, *Welfare States in Transition: National Adaptations in Global Economies*, London: Sage, pp. 1–31.

Esping-Andersen, G. (1996b) 'Welfare States without Work: The Impasse of Labour Shedding and Familialism in Continental European Social Society', in G. Esping-Andersen, *Welfare States in Transition: National Adaptations in Global Economies*, London: Sage, pp. 66–87.

Ferrera, M. (1993) *Modelli di solidarietà: politica e riforme sociale nelle democrazie*, Bologna: Il Mulino.

Ferrera, M. (1996) 'The "Southern Model" of Welfare in Social Europe', *Journal of European Social Policy*, 6, 1, pp. 17–37.

Gough, I. (1979) *The Political Economy of the Welfare State*, London: Macmillan.

Gough, I. (1996) 'Social Welfare and Competitiveness', *New Political Economy*, 1, 2, pp. 209–32.

Hirschman, A.O. (1991) *The Rhetoric of Reaction: Perversity, Futility, Jeopardy*, Cambridge, Mass. and London: The Belknap Press of Harvard University Press.

Hooghe, L. (1997) 'The Structural Funds and Competing Models of European Capitalism', paper presented at the conference on 'Territorial Politics in Europe:

A Zero-Sum Game?', European University Institute, Robert Schuman Centre, Florence, April 21–2.

Jallade, J-P. (1992) 'Is the Crisis Behind Us? Issues Facing Social Security Systems in Western Europe', in Z. Ferge and J.E. Kolberg (eds.) *Social Policy in a Changing Europe*, Frankfurt: Campus Verlag and Boulder, Colorado: Westview Press, pp. 37–56.

Jessop, R. (1994) 'The Transition to post-Fordism and the Schumpeterian Workfare State', in R. Burrows and B. Loader (eds.), *Towards a Post-Fordist Welfare State?*, London: Routledge, pp. 13–37.

King, D. (1995) *Actively Seeking Work? The Politics of Unemployment and Welfare Policy in the United States and Great Britain*, Chicago and London: The University of Chicago Press.

Lindbeck, A. (1993) *Overshooting, Reform and Retreat of the Welfare State*, Institute for International Economic Studies, Seminar Paper No. 552, Stockholm.

Lindbeck, A. (1994) *Uncertainty Under the Welfare State: Policy Induced Risk*, Institute for International Economic Studies, Seminar Paper No. 576, Stockholm.

Offe, C. (1984) *The Contradictions of the Welfare State*, London: Hutchinson.

Offe, C. (1996) *Modernity and the State, East and West*, Cambridge: Polity Press.

O'Connor, J. (1973) *The Fiscal Crisis of the State*, New York: St James Press.

Pierson, P. (1996) 'The New Politics of the Welfare State', *World Politics*, 48, 2, pp. 143–79.

Renan, E. (1992) *Qu'est-ce que'une nation?: Et autres essais politiques*, Paris: Presses-Pocket.

Rhodes, M. (1995) '"Subversive Liberalism": Market Integration, Globalization and the European Welfare State', *Journal of European Public Policy*, 2, 3, pp. 384–406.

Rhodes, M. (1996) 'Globalization and West European Welfare States: A Critical Review of Recent Debates', *Journal of European Social Policy*, 6, 4, pp. 305–27.

Rhodes, M. (1997a) 'Southern European Welfare States: Identity, Problems and Prospects for Reform', in M. Rhodes (ed.), *Southern European Welfare States: Between Crisis and Reform*, London: Frank Cass, pp. 1–22.

Rhodes, M. (1997b) 'The Welfare State: Internal Challenges, External Constraints', in M. Rhodes, P. Heywood and V. Wright (eds.), *Developments in West European Politics*, London: Macmillan, pp. 57–74.

Rosanvallon, P. (1995) *La nouvelle question sociale: repenser l'état-providence*, Paris: Éditions du Seuil.

Ruggie, J.G. (1982) 'International Regimes, Transactions and Change: Embedded Liberalism in the Postwar Economic Order', *International Organization*, 36, 2, pp. 379–415.

Ruggie, J.G. (1994) 'Trade, Protectionism and the Future of Welfare Capitalism', *Journal of International Affairs*, 48, 1, pp. 1–11.

Sigg, R., Zeitzer, I., Scheil-Adlung, X., Kuptsch, C. and Tracy, M. (1996) 'Developments and Trends in Social Security, 1993–1995', *International Social Security Review*, 49, 2, pp. 5–126.

Skocpol, T. (1992) *Protecting Soldiers and Mothers: The Political Origins of Social Policy in the United States*, Cambridge: Harvard University Press.

Standing, G. (1995) 'Labor Insecurity through Market Regulation: Legacy of the 1980s, Challenge for the 1990s', in K. McFate, R. Lawson and W.J. Wilson (eds.), *Poverty, Inequality and the Future of Social Policy: Western States in the New World Order*, New York: Russell Sage Foundation, pp. 153–96.
Streeck, W. (1995) 'From Market-Making to State-Building? Some Reflections on the Political Economy of European Social Policy', in S. Leibfried and P. Pierson (eds.), *Fragmented Social Policy: The European Union's Social Dimension in Comparative Perspective*, Washington D.C.: Brookings Institution, pp. 389–431.

# I Interpretations

# 2 Unemployment and Social Exclusion: An Economic View

Paul Ormerod

## INTRODUCTION

A large range of problems within the EU can be thought of as arising from the separation of the relevant population into two groups: the included and the excluded. There are obvious examples, such as the employed and the unemployed, poor regions and rich regions, poor and rich areas of the same city, single parents without access to child care and two-income households. Of course, in practice the two blend into each other at the margins, but it is helpful to keep them conceptually distinct.

More generally, the distinction between the excluded and included groups can operate in one or more of three dimensions. The *social dimension*, embracing questions of class, gender and race; the *spatial dimension*, covering the geographic aspect of prosperity; and the *structural dimension* of the distinction between the macro, meso and micro levels. The concept of social exclusion embraces a wide range of apparently unrelated examples. The spatial exclusion, for example, of the poorer areas of a city at first sight has little in common with, say, the social exclusion of ethnic minority groups.

But there are three stylized facts which emerge from many of these seemingly disparate areas, including that of unemployment. First, there is a marked tendency for exclusion, once it arises, to persist for long periods of time. At the extreme, for example, the areas of Manchester noted by Engels (1892; 1977) in the 1840s as suffering the most acute deprivation have scarcely changed in their relative status over a period of 150 years, with many of them remaining the poorest parts of the city today. Of course, not every example of social exclusion persists for such a long period of time, but, once established, patterns of behaviour are difficult to change.

Second, as a corollary of the point 1, self-equilibrating mechanisms beloved of conventional economics appear to be weak in the context of social exclusion. In economic theory, for example, imbalances between supply and demand are corrected by movements in the price of the product in question. The system contains negative feedback, in that the system operates to dampen rather than to amplify any disturbances which might occur. Yet in the labour market, following the sharp upward rise in unemployment in the early 1980s, in countries of the EU unemployment has persisted above 7 per cent for 15 years, the sole exception being (West) Germany, where even here unemployment has persisted at historically high levels for the same length of time.

Over very long periods of time, non-trivial unemployment rates have persisted in the western economies. For example, over the last 140 years – the longest period for which data of any remote degree of reliability exist – the unemployment rate in the UK has averaged 5 per cent. In the peace time years this century, unemployment has averaged 6 per cent in the USA. Even in Germany, the peace time years since 1920 have seen an average unemployment rate of over 4 per cent, whilst in Belgium the figure is almost 6 per cent. These may seem small percentages, but they represent many millions of individuals – in today's terms, for example, the USA unemployment rate mentioned above amounts to 8 million people.

Kenneth Arrow (1994), who placed free market economic theory onto a modern mathematical basis in the early 1950s, has recently stated that he now regards general equilibrium theory in economics as being empirically falsified, with the single most important fact being the failure of labour markets to clear over long periods of time.

Third, there is a widespread failure of conventional policies of targeting public resources on specific exclusion problems to bring about a permanent improvement in the relative position of the excluded group. This is not, of course, to say that such policies never have beneficial results. But there are many examples of conventional policy failure.

The purpose of this chapter is to discuss European unemployment from this general perspective, and to propose ways in which the problem might be tackled in the context of a new social contract.


UNEMPLOYMENT IN EUROPE: THE EVIDENCE

The long-run persistence of European unemployment, and the implied failure of conventional policies to solve the problem, can be seen very clearly using graphs. The conventional way of doing this in economics is to plot the series over time. Figure 2.1 does this, showing the unemployment rate in Belgium (using OECD data throughout) from 1960 to 1994.

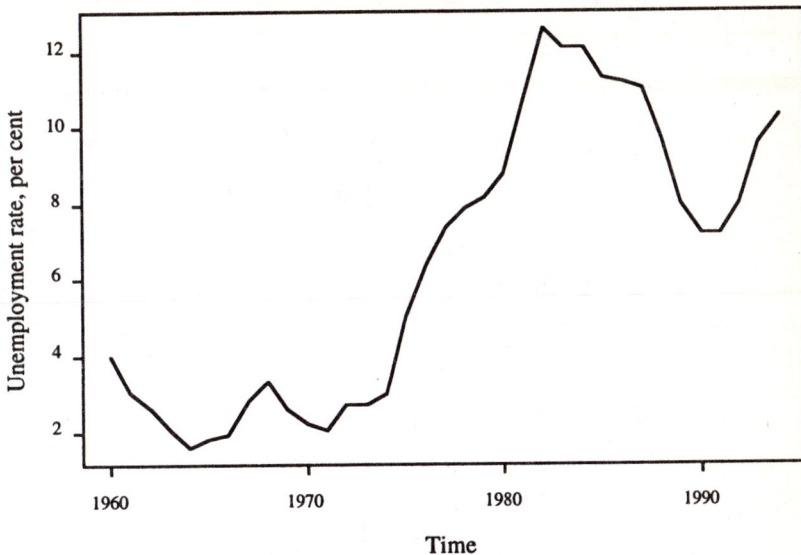

*Figure 2.1*   Unemployment rate in Belgium 1960–94

Unemployment was very low from 1960 to 1973, rose sharply to the early 1980s, and since then has fluctuated around a high average level.

An alternative way is to use a connected scatter plot, which is widely used in non-linear systems analysis. Figure 2.2 constructs a scatter plot of unemployment in Belgium in any particular year against unemployment in the previous year. The resulting points are then connected together in sequence. Such charts can provide three technical pieces of information. First, whether the data tends to exhibit cycles over time. If so, the data in a connected scatter plot will appear in the shape of an ellipse. Second, the average value around which the series fluctuates. This is the point in the centre of any ellipse which, applying technical jargon, we can call the attractor point of the data. The data in the series is attracted around this point. Third, the chart shows the magnitude of the cycles around the attractor point. An ellipse which was very tightly drawn, for example, would imply that the data showed only small fluctuations over time. The sequence of points in the bottom left of the chart show the economic cycles in the 1960s and early 1970s. Unemployment showed only small fluctuations around a low average. There was then a large, continuous rise until the peak of 1982, but since then a new pattern has been established, of large fluctuations around a high average level.

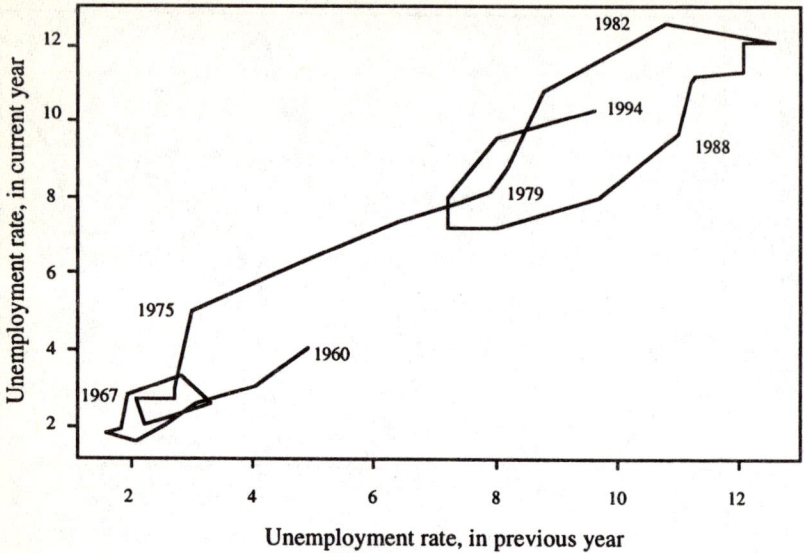

*Figure 2.2*   Connected scatter plot of Belgian unemployment rate 1960–94

The connected scatter plot of unemployment in Belgium reveals a pattern which is qualitatively similar in a majority of the countries of the EU. For interest, Figure 2.3 and Figure 2.4 show (West) German and UK unemployment, but the pattern is typical of countries such as the Netherlands, Italy, Denmark and Austria. France and Spain exhibit different behaviour in that unemployment rose more or less continuously from the mid-1960s to the mid-1980s, but since then the same pattern of large fluctuations around a high level attractor point has become established in both these countries. Figure 2.5 plots the connected scatter plot of unemployment in France.

In general, the behaviour of unemployment in Europe over time is characterized by two features. First, the existence of reasonably regular cycles of similar amplitude which can persist for considerable periods of time. Second, abrupt shifts away from any given attractor point of the cycles, followed by a short period of time before a new attractor point emerges, which itself then persists with no self-regulating factors moving it back to its initial position. In other words, the average rate of unemployment is moved sharply up or down by major shocks to the economy, but once the shift has occurred, the new average level itself persists for long periods of time.

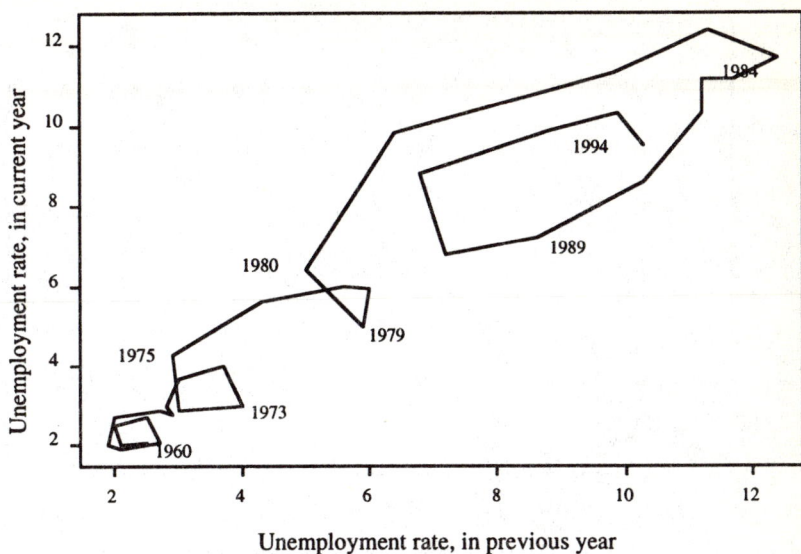

*Figure 2.3* Connected scatter plot of British unemployment rate 1960–94

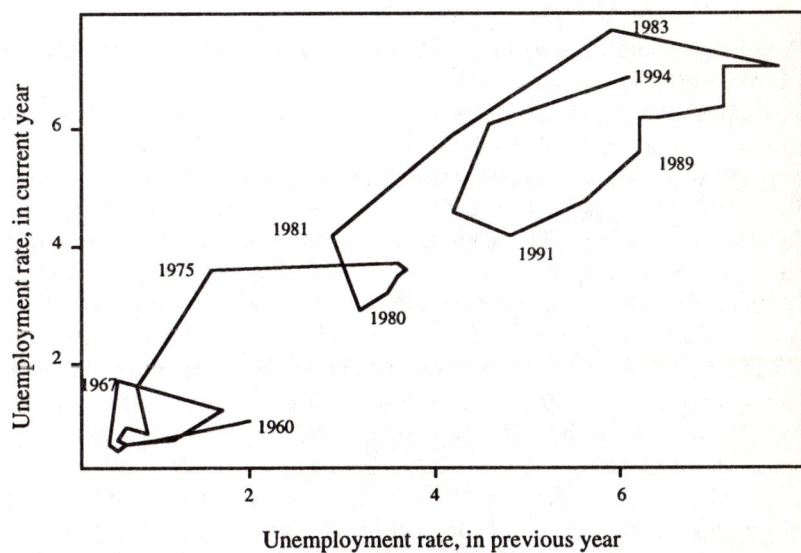

*Figure 2.4* Connected scatter plot of German unemployment rate 1960–94

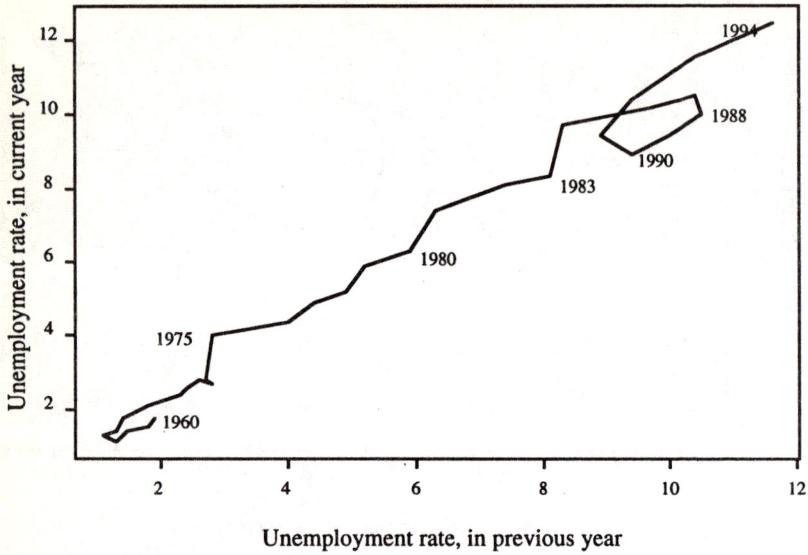

*Figure 2.5*   Connected scatter plot of French unemployment rate 1960–94

## A THEORETICAL APPROACH TO SOCIAL EXCLUSION

A theoretical model must be able to account for the key stylized facts of persistence of exclusion and of the widespread failure of conventional policies to solve such problems. Such an analytical framework is in fact available, which generalizes the principles of the amplification of disturbances through positive feedback and 'lock-in' which have been developed in recent years in the areas of the choice of technology and of the regional location of industry. The sources of persistence, and the consequent difficulty of altering the relative position of the excluded by targeted expenditure, are increasing returns through positive feedback. This latter term is used here not in a normative sense, but in its technical sense of meaning that the dynamic processes at work reinforce each other, and lock the system strongly into whatever direction it is moving. The original insights into increasing returns and the choice of technology were provided by Brian Arthur (1983; 1989), using non-linear probability theory.

In essence, the model is as follows. Two new technologies have been developed which are about to compete with each other. For example, the market for video recorders in the 1980s or the nuclear reactor market in the 1950s. The population of potential adopters is assumed to be divided equally in its preferences between the two. One group is more likely to choose one technology, and the other group its competitor. The key assumption now is that each of the technologies enjoys increasing returns with adoption. The choice of technology by any agent alters the probability that all subsequent agents will choose this rather than its rival. It is easy to think of reasons why this is the case. For example, with video recorders the lead in market share which VHS obtained encouraged retailers to stock tapes for these machines rather than for its rival Betamax, which in turn gave an incentive for new purchasers to choose a VHS machine. The final assumption in the technology model is that adopters come forward to buy the technologies in a random sequence. As a theorem, in such a model, no matter how small the change in the probabilities following each individual adoption, one technology will eventually gain 100 per cent market share and its rival will be eliminated. It is not possible to predict in advance which technology will succeed, for by construction the outcome is a matter of the random process of initial adoption. A technology which in an objective sense was inferior to its rival could therefore achieve 'lock-in' under these processes.

The assumption of increasing returns – positive feedback – means that the market does not automatically 'know best'. Indeed, Betamax was technically superior to its VHS rival; the QWERTY keyboard was deliberately developed 120 years ago to be inefficient, because the transmission of words by telegraph at that time could not cope with a faster input. Yet, because people are trained on this keyboard, it has not proved possible for more efficient keyboards to break the lock over the market of this inefficient design, despite numerous attempts to do so.

The above is a particular example of the more general analytical problem, which involves the question of how to exit from a local minimum/maximum in a non-linear system when searching for a superior local or even the global minimum/maximum. There are many such examples in the social sciences. Dasgupta (1995), for example, has recently set out a system of positive feedback with lock-in solutions in a model of poverty, population and environmental degradation in the Third World. In such systems, it is known that 'nearest neighbour' strategies, involving a series of small movements in the immediate neighbourhood or locality often work poorly. These strategies can be thought of in the context of social exclusion as a programme of targeted expenditure designed to improve the position of the excluded group gradually.

Perhaps the best way to think of the problem is geometrically, visualizing it in three dimensions. A surface exists with many peaks and troughs. The map of the surface which we have is incomplete, for in contrast to the assumptions of orthodox economics, either we have incomplete information or we lack the ability to process efficiently all the information which we have. The task is to move out of a local minimum to a local maximum. In other words, from a trough to a peak. Intuitively, if the topology is in some sense well-behaved – rolling hills rather than sharp peaks and deep valleys – a 'nearest neighbour' strategy might work quite well. Even with imperfect knowledge of the terrain, a series of small moves may well succeed in taking us towards the top of a hill. But in a terrain with sharp peaks and valleys, such a strategy has only a low chance of success.

The two topographies can be thought of as representing the two types of model discussed above, namely a model in which increasing returns/positive feedback is essentially unbounded, and a model in which their impact is bounded. If the terrain is rugged, the conventional response of spending money or subsidizing the excluded in some way may well not work very well at all. The trough which they are in is fairly steep and deep, so even a large effort to get them out may simply result in them rolling back down again. Or, even worse, our imperfect knowledge of the terrain may lead them to fall into an even deeper, unexpected trough.

The prevalence of increasing returns in capitalist economies can be seen by asking the question: when a shock to the system takes place and unemployment rises, why do not the newly unemployed simply set up production on their own account at the prevailing wage rate? If they were able to do this, Say's law would operate, with supply creating its own demand, and an underemployed equilibrium could not persist.

At the micro-level, the existence of increasing returns to production is an important reason why such behaviour is not widely observed (Weitzman, 1982). Whilst it may well be possible for a skilled professional, such as a lawyer or accountant, to set up on his or her own account with a minimum of capital outlay, it is not open to a steel worker or miner, say, to operate in the same way because of increasing returns to production. Even where small-scale production might be technically feasible, imperfect capital markets often prevent individuals from borrowing the amount needed to set up production, which is simply another manifestation of increasing returns. The existence of increasing returns to production is a necessary condition for the persistence of high unemployment. An implication of this is that policies which address explicitly the inability of the unemployed to produce on their own account – for example, assistance to SMEs – may help. But in general, a permanent and substantial reduction in unemployment will require an increase in employment in existing organizations.

## GROWTH AND UNEMPLOYMENT

The idea that higher rates of economic growth are a solution to unemployment permeates policy thinking within the EU, both at a national and European level. A higher rate of growth, it is argued, will increase employment, mainly in existing companies, and hence reduce unemployment. There are disagreements as to whether this is best achieved by policies of demand management or by the newly-fashionable supply side polices, and there are doubts about how successful such policies can be. But despite reservations, higher growth is seen as an important contributor to the problem of European unemployment.

*Prima facie* there is apparently a strong relationship between growth and employment/unemployment. During the course of any particular economic cycle, there is usually a strong correlation between changes in output and changes in employment and unemployment. But the connection between movements in output and employment over the course of the economic cycle misleads people into believing that this relationship necessarily persists over the course of several cycles. In most European countries, the proceeds of economic growth in the past 20 years have not been used to generate new jobs (in net terms), but have been appropriated by those who have remained in employment. More precisely, a system of social relationships has arisen which has allowed the appropriation to take place.

Spain provides the most striking example of this. Since 1970, in real terms the Spanish economy has essentially doubled in size. Yet employment is actually lower now than it was over 20 years ago. More generally, the output of most western European economies has increased by around three-quarters over the past 20 years, yet the percentage increase in net employment can be measured in single figures. The lack of connection between output growth and the labour market extends to unemployment as well. The growth rate in many western economies from the late 1970s, once the initial impact of the oil price shock had been absorbed, has been very similar, at around 2 per cent a year on average. Yet against the background of similar growth rates over a period of some 15 years, unemployment rates vary substantially across countries. France, (West) Germany, Italy, Austria and Spain have all grown at an average annual rate of around $2\frac{1}{4}$ per cent in the past 15 years. Yet unemployment has averaged 9 per cent in France, 6 per cent in Germany, 9 per cent in Italy, only 3 per cent in Austria and 16 per cent in Spain. The UK, Sweden and Switzerland – countries with governments of quite diverse attitudes to economic policy – all grew at just under 2 per cent over the same period.

Unemployment averaged 9 per cent in the UK, almost 3 per cent in Sweden and less than 1 per cent in Switzerland.

The experience of the 20-odd years following World War II misled people into believing that a rapid rate of growth was necessary to bring about low unemployment. During this period, growth was higher and unemployment lower than the two decades following the 1973/74 oil shock. But even in the earlier period, low unemployment was preserved with markedly different growth rates. In both Germany and the UK unemployment averaged around 2 per cent, but growth in Germany averaged over 5 per cent compared to just under 3 per cent in the UK. Whilst, despite an average growth rate of 3.5 per cent, USA unemployment averaged almost 5 per cent.

The share of wages in national income (broadly defined to include, for example, employers' contributions to public and private pension schemes) in the main European economies is very similar in the first half of the 1990s to its value in the early 1970s. In the UK and the Netherlands it has fallen slightly, but in France, Italy, Germany and Belgium the wage share is almost identical in the two periods. Employment has risen very little in percentage terms, and unemployment has increased sharply. In other words, the average real wage of those in employment has gone up broadly in line with the growth in real GDP. Those in work have appropriated the benefits of growth, whilst the unemployed have been excluded.

## UNEMPLOYMENT: A DISTRIBUTIONAL PHENOMENON

In terms of our model of social exclusion, we can think of the European experience as follows. A system of social and economic relationships has been built up which strongly reinforces the micro-economic basis of exclusion through increasing returns discussed above. A potential way of overcoming this and of changing the topography of the system is discussed below.

The main point addressed in this section, however, is the proposition that unemployment is essentially a distributional phenomenon. In other words, the average rate of unemployment which prevails over the course of the business cycle is a result of the particular form of social contract, whether explicit or implicit, which exists. Europe in the past 20 years offers but one particular outcome, one particular type of social contract, from a wide variety of possibilities. The aggregate model of Goodwin (1969) offers a wide range of possibilities as to why the unemployed may remain locked out. Goodwin's original formulation of a system linking profits and unemployment has been extended mathematically in a number of ways. But an extension of the economics of the model illustrates the point.

The long-term rate of growth depends upon the share of investment in total output, in its broadest sense to embrace human as well as physical capital. In turn, investment depends upon the state of long-term expectations and the share of profits in national income. Over the course of the cycle, the profit share and unemployment interact in the system. But the average rate of unemployment around which the limit cycle moves in profit/unemployment space is indeterminate. In other words, in order to sustain a given rate of growth in any given state of long-term expectations, a particular share of profits in national income is implied. The share of labour is then implied as the residual (in practice, there are of course some minor elements in national income in addition to the main ones of wages and profits). But the division of labour's share of national income between the employed and the unemployed is indeterminate. This indeterminacy removes any automatic link between output growth and employment, and is entirely consistent with the empirical evidence discussed above.

The North American experience during the past 20 years has been different from that of Europe. Unemployment in the USA has averaged just under 7 per cent over this period. This is slightly higher than the German average, and distinctly higher than in a number of the smaller European countries which remained outside the EU. At the present time, unemployment in the USA is markedly lower than it is in major European countries such as France, but in terms of unemployment in the past 20 years, the American labour market has not performed that much more effectively than have such markets in Europe. But there has been a dramatic difference in the rate of job creation in the USA. And it is this which raises issues in Europe about the desirability or otherwise of deregulating labour markets and reducing the level of involvement by the state. Much of the conventional wisdom of economics ascribes the apparently poor European performance to a lack of 'flexibility' in the labour market.

The USA economy has indeed created many more jobs than the EU economies. But it has needed to do so, for the supply of labour has expanded more rapidly in the USA. The two points are linked analytically. Essentially, the USA operates a policy of open borders for the migration of labour. From time to time political pressures arise which lead to efforts of varying degrees to keep immigrants out. But for all practical purposes, anyone who wishes to enter the USA and work there can do so. Almost all of this inflow of labour is from Third World economies – the USA has a major border with Mexico. Such people are willing to work for what are, by western standards, very low wages, and it is low wage employment which makes up much of the increase in employment in America. The willingness to work for low wages drives down the wages elsewhere in the economy of the relatively unskilled.

The supply of millions of workers from Third World countries has an impact on the 'flexibility' of the labour market in the USA which makes arguments about the Social Chapter in Europe very much a second order issue. By far the most effective way to bring about flexibility in the USA sense in European labour markets would be to open the borders to migration from Eastern Europe and North Africa. But such a policy hardly commends itself, least of all, ironically, to those politicians who speak most fervently in support of flexibility and free markets.

USA labour markets of the past 15–20 years offer one particular solution to the distribution of labour's share of national income. By driving down the wage rates of substantial sections of the labour force, employment opportunities are created. But this approach necessitates a dramatic widening of the distribution of income. Unemployment is kept relatively low, and the distributional consequences are carried by those whose real wage rates are forced down. As in Europe, the share of wages in national income is now very similar to the levels of the early 1970s. But in the USA, employment has increased substantially. The topography of the economic system, with its inherent tendency to lock out the unemployed, has been altered in the USA by the application of powerful market forces. The change has not taken place with the consent of the included, but they have been compelled to alter their behaviour.

The Scandinavian economies have, until very recently, offered yet another answer to the distributional question. Public expenditure and taxation have been used, not in a Keynesian short-term sense, but structurally to allow the public sector to operate as an employer of last resort. Adverse shocks to the system are met by job creation in the public sector. The distributional costs here are met, in an open and explicit social contract, by those in employment who pay higher taxes than they would otherwise have done. Growing resistance to higher tax rates coupled with shocks particular to these economies (in Finland, the collapse of the Soviet Union and in Sweden the collapse of the banking system following the abolition of exchange controls), have caused problems for this approach. But the opposition to paying tax is not a matter of technical economic policy, but a question of social values.

Yet another solution has been provided by Japan. There are a number of dimensions to this, the most important of which is the very low productivity levels of the domestic service sector in Japan. Large numbers of people are employed, at decent wage rates, carrying out tasks which to westerners often appear incomprehensible. But although the economic productivity of the sector is low, its social productivity is high in the important sense that unemployment is kept low and social cohesion preserved. The costs in this case are met by Japanese consumers, who pay much higher prices for services than they would do if the sector were run on grounds of narrow economic efficiency alone.

The final model to mention is that of the West in general in the 25 years or so following World War II. Economic prosperity grew dramatically, but in a framework in which the benefits were spread equally. The low skilled were not excluded from employment, and real wages rose at approximately similar rates across the income distribution. The specific historical background of the privations of the 1930s followed by the co-operative spirit of the war were obviously very important in allowing the model to operate successfully. As the impact of these values faded over time, the USA moved to a different answer to the distributional question – forcing down real wage rates – and Europe to another, namely the social exclusion of the unemployed.

The above three examples, whilst seemingly disparate in a number of respects, are in an analytical sense very similar. In terms of the geometric representation of our general model of social exclusion, we can think of the landscape as being one of gentle, rolling hills rather than the forbidding terrain of Europe in the past 20 years. The socially included behaved in such a way as to facilitate the absorption of the less skilled and potentially unemployed members of society. In different ways, the included accepted the costs of such behaviour.

## EUROPEAN UNEMPLOYMENT: A WAY FORWARD

Whatever solutions to the problem of unemployment might have worked in different countries or at different times, it is not really meaningful as a policy prescription to think of borrowing or transferring social and cultural values. In particular, no amount of nostalgia can restore the past. One way of creating jobs in Europe has already been noted. Namely, by opening the borders to immigration from the poor countries which surround the EU, and thereby force a change in the topography of the labour market. But this, as the USA experience shows, brings with it a different set of exclusion problems arising from the associated widening of the distribution of income. Thoughtful ways of assisting SMEs, and particularly assisting the unemployed to set up production on their own account, can help overcome the impact of increasing returns and the inherent tendency for unemployment to persist. But, even if successful, such policies would not be suitable for everyone.

The central issue is that the employed in Europe need to be given incentives to modify their behaviour in a way which facilitates the re-entry of the unemployed to employment, rather than operating as a cartel and reinforcing the microeconomic tendency to lock-out. One such possibility is given by work sharing, using the phrase to encompass a wide range of options from literal sharing of a job by two people, to reductions in the total number of hours supplied by a worker over his or her lifetime, whether in the form of a shorter working life, longer holidays or a shorter working week. Of course, this must be accompanied by pro rata reductions in pay. But this is matched by an increase in leisure time. An explicit trade-off is made between work and leisure.

The idea of work sharing is attacked by economists on the grounds that the idea is derived from the lump of labour fallacy, from the mistaken idea that there is only a fixed number of jobs available. But on the contrary, the number of jobs can grow over time: it is not the number of jobs which is fixed, but the share of labour in national income (for any given growth rate, institutions and expectations). The growing real value of this share can be taken up entirely by those in employment, leaving the number of jobs constant, or, at the other extreme, entirely by new jobs leaving the level of real wages constant.

Keynes considered the question of worksharing as a solution to the unemployment of the 1930s in a little-remembered section of the *General Theory*. He rejected the idea, but only on the grounds that 'A point comes where every individual weighs the advantages of increased leisure against increased income. But at present the evidence is, I think, strong that the great majority of individuals would prefer increased income to increased leisure' (Keynes, 1978: 326). In other words, Keynes's only objection was that at the levels of income which were obtained in the 1930s, the solution was 'premature'.

It is now nearly 60 years since the publication of the *General Theory*, and the world has moved on. A striking feature of this period, and in particular of most recent 30-odd years, is the enormous appetite for increased leisure over the course of a working lifetime which people in the West have shown. In the memory of many people alive today, a working life consisted of what may be termed 'the three 50s'. Almost everyone left school at 14 or 15, and was expected to work into their 60s, or for some 50 years. The working week was typically close to 50 hours a week. And people worked for 50 weeks a year, with just two weeks of holiday. Today, a large and rising number of young people remain in full-time education until their early 20s, and many people retire well before the statutory retirement age. For most of the population, the expected number of years in a working life has fallen to under 40. In terms of hours per week, the majority of full-time employees work under 40 hours a week. And whilst holiday entitlement has not yet increased so markedly as to ensure less than 40 weeks a year at work – except for a small number of privileged groups – many workers now take five or six weeks' total holiday a year.

Under the regime of the 'three 50s', just a few decades ago, the average worker who remained in full-time work throughout his or her lifetime would work for (50 × 50 × 50) = 125 000 hours during a lifetime. Even for a 'full-time' worker, in the mid-1990s this figure has fallen to some 65–70 000 hours. In other words, during the second half of our century alone, the amount of work which a 'full-time' worker is expected to do in the course of a lifetime has fallen by almost a half. So, in an important sense, by the standards of the 1930s and 1940s, almost every single worker today is part-time rather than full-time, and worksharing in its general sense is already both highly popular and practised very widely. As the economy grows and productivity rises, those in employment can take the benefits in two ways. At one extreme, all the increase is received in the form of a higher level of real income. At the other, real income can be kept constant, and the benefit taken in the form of doing less work for this level of income. In practice, of course, a mixture of the two occurs. As a broad approximation, in the first half of the twentieth century, at the low levels of real income which prevailed, most of the benefits of growth were seen in the form of increases in real income rather than of leisure. In the second half, a much greater proportion of the total surplus generated by growth has been taken in the form of more leisure.

In short, during the past 40 years, most people have expressed a clear desire to increase the amount of leisure time over the course of a lifetime. At the levels of real income which prevail in Europe, many people prefer to take a substantial proportion of the benefits created by higher productivity in the form of more leisure time. The policy of work sharing simply articulates this clearly expressed consumer preference, and endeavours to use it positively to reduce unemployment. It is difficult to legislate specifically to restrict hours, increase holidays or whatever. To succeed, such moves must command the underlying support of the workforce. But governments can encourage such shifts in a variety of ways. Gregg (1994), for example, argues for a marginal employment subsidy combined with a shorter working week, so that employers received for a limited period a proportion of the wages of any job created from hours released.

In the UK, a very successful policy to reduce unemployment by increasing leisure time was actually implemented by the government in the early 1980s, known as the Job Release Scheme. For a short time, anyone certified as suffering from a disability could retire early on full benefits, provided that his or her employer took on an unemployed person, not necessarily to fill the same position, but anywhere in the organization. In the areas of high unemployment, doctors were only too willing to assist, and certified people with the most minor disabilities as being unfit for work. This in a sense was the undoing of the scheme, in that the government came to believe that skilled workers who were perfectly capable of work were retiring early, and that this was not the intention. But while it lasted, it was both very popular with the beneficiaries and very effective.

But, although work sharing in its broad sense is the clearly revealed preference of most of the workforce, active measures to promote it are often resisted. The apparent paradox between the clear desire to have more leisure time and the resistance to proposals to encourage this, is perhaps understandable in the climate of uncertainty which has been created in recent years. There are two dimensions to this. First, the fact that a switch away from work towards leisure may involve not just a loss of income but a loss of rights. Second, the speed of technological innovation combined with a new culture of management mean that there is a high level of worry about losing one's job completely, and so individuals have an incentive to extract as much money from it as they can in the short-term.

It is hardly surprising that, in such circumstances, it is difficult to create a climate in which co-operative solutions to unemployment can prevail. But it is essential that they do, for a system of economic relationships has been built up in the EU economies, deriving from the response of social institutions and of the general social fabric to major economic shocks, which now prevents the achievement of full employment through conventional economic policies, whether Keynesian, monetarist, or supply-side.

## CONCLUSION

Unemployment can be thought of as a very important but nevertheless special case of the more general phenomenon of social exclusion. Three stylized facts characterize exclusion. First, the tendency for exclusion, once it arises, to persist for long periods of time. Second, self-equilibrating mechanisms appear to be weak or non-existent. Third, policies targeted at excluded groups have a long history of failure. Unemployment itself exhibits all these factors. Mathematically, this can be thought of as a non-linear system in which positive feedback takes place. This latter term is used not in a normative sense, but in its technical sense of meaning that the dynamic processes at work re-inforce each other. The system becomes locked into a particular solution, from which it is difficult to exit.

'Nearest neighbour' strategies, which involve relatively small steps in the immediate locality of the solution path to try to escape from it, are known not to be very effective. This result accounts for the fact that many conventional policies of targeting expenditure on excluded groups to improve their position gradually have not really succeeded. An illustration of this is macro-economic policy, whether of a Keynesian or monetarist kind. In general, such policies merely alter the shape of the particular cycle of unemployment and do not shift the average rate of unemployment around which such cycles take place.

The current widespread belief that higher rates of economic growth will reduce unemployment often fails to make the distinction between fluctuations in the growth rate around the underlying trend, and the trend itself. But even if this latter variable could in some way be increased, there is no guarantee that unemployment will be lower in the medium term. In the West in general, and particularly within Western Europe, there is little or no correlation over the course of several economic cycles between the rate of economic growth and either the growth of employment or the average rate of unemployment.

Unemployment is essentially a distributional question. For any given set of long-term expectations, any particular growth path for an economy requires a particular share of profits in national income for it to be sustained. In the medium term, this implies a particular share of wages, defined in a broad sense, in national income. But the share of this latter factor either between the employed or between the employed and unemployed is not related to the underlying rate of economic growth.

A variety of empirical solutions can be observed to the share of labour in national income. In Western Europe in the past 20 years, the proceeds of economic growth have been appropriated by those in employment, to the exclusion of the unemployed. Any permanent solution to unemployment requires a change in behaviour by the employed. In terms of the general model of social exclusion, this can be thought of as altering the topography of the system, by modifying those forces which lead to lock-in and exclusion.

One such policy is that of work sharing, using the phrase to encompass a wide range of options and not just literally the sharing of a job by two people. The past 40 years have seen a massive increase in effective job sharing, with the number of hours which an individual can expect to work during the course of his or her lifetime falling by a half. By the standards of the 1930s, almost everyone in employment today is a part-time worker. This trend of increased leisure over a lifetime is very popular but, paradoxically, explicit measures to promote various forms of sharing work are often resisted by the labour force. The challenge facing Europe's politicians is to find ways of overcoming such resistance in a new social contract to bring about a sustained and substantial fall in unemployment.

## REFERENCES

Arrow, K. (1994) 'Problems Mount in Application of Free Market Economic Theory', *The Guardian*, London, 3 January 1994.

Arthur, W.B. (1989) 'Competing Technologies, Increasing Returns and Lock-In by Historical Events', *Economic Journal*, 99, 394, pp. 116–31.

Arthur, W.B., Ermoliev, Y. and Kaniovski, Y. (1983) 'On Generalized Urn Schemes of the Polya Kind', *Cybernetics*, 19, pp. 61–71.

Dasgupta, P.S. (1995) 'Population, Poverty and the Local Environment', *Scientific American*, 272, 2, pp. 26–31.

Engels, F. (1977) *The Condition of the Working Class in England*, text of 1892 edition, Moscow: Progress Publishers.

Goodwin, R.M. (1969) 'A Growth Cycle', in C.H. Feinstein (ed.), *Socialism, Capitalism and Economic Growth*, Cambridge: Cambridge University Press, pp. 54–58.

Gregg, P. (1994) 'Creating Jobs through Work Sharing', *New Economy*, 1, 1, pp. 13–19.

Keynes, J.M. (1978) [1936] *The Collected Writings of John Maynard Keynes, Vol. VII: The General Theory of Employment, Interest and Money* London: Macmillan.

Weitzman, M.L. (1982) 'Increasing Returns and the Foundations of Unemployment Theory', *Economic Journal*, 92, 4, pp. 787–804.

# 3 Poverty and Social Exclusion: A Sociological View*

Serge Paugam

## INTRODUCTION

The sociological literature on both poverty and social exclusion is large and varied, and the abundance of references means that providing a review is an arduous task. It becomes even more difficult when trying to compare different nations or cultures. Thus, there is no question of providing an exhaustive study of recent, past and ongoing research; however, it is more realistic to establish the complex linkage between this research, and social and political debate. The main problem for scholars in this field is constructing a research question which, whilst being distinct from contemporary ways of thinking which characterize the social debate (science must distance itself from the subject matter in order to build a conceptual framework) can also stimulate debate. Sociologists will favour studying what appears dysfunctional or anomalous in the social system at any given moment. They must, therefore, partially base their work in social debate. But the science which they aim to develop cannot simply be social criticism or, conversely, an ideological justification of existing norms.

After attempting to explain the equivocal nature of ideas found at the heart of social debate, we will try to operationalize some elements of sociological thought on the evolution and contemporary forms of poverty and exclusion in Europe.

## THE EQUIVOCAL NATURE OF 'EXCLUSION'

It has become popular to juxtapose the question of inequality – a central theme of Europe's so-called 'golden age' of economic growth – with the current (and, for some, new) problem of exclusion. The considerable

41

changes that have occurred in the terms of social debate have been
striking. The worsening of the jobs market and the weakening of social
ties, such as divorce and separation, the atomization of the work force and
suburban strife, are major factors in explaining this evolution. The most
pressing social question is no longer alienation in the workplace and disparities between socio-professional classes, but instead the re-emergence
of a large number of the population who are likely to become increasingly
dependent on social provision. Some see the concept of exclusion as a
means of superseding the concept of poverty – which has become out-
dated because of its static nature and its linkage to inequality and especially income. We do not intend studying in detail the many definitions of
poverty and their relative strengths and weaknesses: but it is clear that
none of them can encompass the great variety of problems experienced by
social actors today.

However, it is far from certain that the concept of exclusion is any
better. In many ways, it is as hazy and equivocal a sociological category as
poverty. Its use in describing diverse situations and populations with little
or nothing in common has rendered it banal in the extreme. Julien Freund
even claims that the notion of being excluded is 'saturated with sense,
nonsense and contradiction and can be used to describe virtually anything'
(Freund, in Xiberras, 1994).

As a result, policies against exclusion often contain as many specific
devices as there are individual problems to be solved. One aspect of their
weakness is a relative lack of understanding of the processes against
which they are meant to work (Paugam, 1996). Equally, they rely too
heavily upon so-called 'common knowledge' which fills the vacuum left
by the lack of serious analysis of the subject.

This common knowledge is nurtured by the media. Journalists are
usually searching for something spectacular, and so do not worry themselves overly about how representative of real life the (often caricatured)
images and examples that they use are. Let us cite three examples which
are widespread in France:

1) French society is made up of two opposed social groups – the
'included' and the 'excluded'.
2) Exclusion can affect anybody in contemporary society.
3) The suburbs are about to become dangerous ghettos like those found in
the USA.

Not only is each of these images false: each prolongs a myth which in the
long term hinders the search for solutions.

The image of French society as a duality lends to the confusion. The 'excluded' are meant to form a new social class which is separated from the rest of society. It is true that the many marginalized groups in society are outside the job market and are forced to live on social security in neglected suburbs. It is also true that social policies such as the minimum income (RMI) indirectly help institutionalize and make more visible the poor members of society, and thus stigmatize them further. That said, the sociological analysis of populations, designed to look at the lowest strata of society, emphasizes the diversity of individual situations. This heterogeneity does not always leap to the eye of observers looking for a sensational news-story. Often suffering from class ethnocentrism, they are sensitive to what distinguishes themselves from those they are talking about; but they are usually unable to recognize the objective differences and the ways in which they might do so. We should remember that even those who receive the minimum income do not form a homogeneous social group. We can distinguish between various types if we look at contrasting backgrounds, advantages and disadvantages in the jobs market, and the strength or weakness of social ties. The image of a dual society is doubtful because it disguises this reality. In over-generalizing situations and then opposing them in such a radical manner, it is common to forget that exclusion is primarily a process which starts from fragility and can sometimes end in the breaking of social ties, but which does not on the surface seem to be the result of deterministic effects or of an inescapable rut. This process, which I have called 'social disqualification', is comprised of various phases which can progressively follow each other into situations of extreme deprivation, but which are not irreversible (Paugam, 1991).

The phrase 'it doesn't only happens to others', is a result of the same error in perception. It supports the currently widespread idea that anybody can be affected by exclusion. This phrase, however, is more the product of collective anxiety in the face of unemployment than a strict analysis of the available statistics. Certainly, charity organizations are making themselves available more and more to people who have undergone a serious class upheaval. Their directors often cite the example of the unemployed senior manager who has to face divorce, the loss of his home, separation from his family and who gradually drops down the social ladder until he finds himself on the street. The strength of this example derives from its challenge to the current depiction of the unemployed or the poor from humble origins. It thus contributes to alerting public opinion and also to putting pressure on public authorities. But we should not think for a moment that the risk of exclusion is equal for all individuals, whatever their social situation. The diverse forms of precariousness may be spread throughout French society, but they do not negatively accumulate in the case of all individuals.

Finally, the general use of the term 'ghetto' as a label for the French suburbs is inappropriate. It does not help resolve the problems to be found there which sustain a collective sense of insecurity in the face of possible 'social upheaval'. Of course, it is not a matter of denying the existence of deprived communities, where a large proportion of the unemployed are to be found, or of minimizing the social effects which result. Rather, it is to encourage a rigorous analysis of the facts. This term 'ghetto' is at the root of many misunderstandings. To equate the poorer parts of the Paris suburbs with the ghettos of Chicago and New York demonstrates a serious misunderstanding of the USA situation (Wacquant, 1992). French suburban areas, including the most hemmed-in ones, are rarely completely sealed off as they are in the USA, due to their geographic positions. Their ethnic composition is highly diverse, and their levels of poverty, the degradation of the quality of life, and the extent of criminality, are incomparable with the USA ghettos. One should not discount the reality of the social horrors of violence, drug-trafficking and confrontations with the law which have become the norm in certain French city districts; but the generalization of these isolated cases encouraged by the media to cover all suburbs makes their inhabitants feel as if they belong to an abandoned world. The danger of being simplistic is a real one and is at least partially responsible for creating bad reputations for certain areas. If policies are to be elaborated and adapted, a detailed understanding of the social relationships and the institutionalized stigmatization of these areas and their inhabitants is essential.

Any representation of French society which tries to oppose the 'excluded' from the rest of the population is not only false, but it also impedes the fight against exclusion. It misdirects efforts towards intervention at too late a stage, when social actors try to implement solutions for groups which they believe are easy to identify, but which are in fact quite indistinct due to their unstable and heterogeneous nature.

## THE NECESSARY DECONSTRUCTION OF CONCEPTS FROM SOCIAL DEBATE

As I have tried to show using France as an example, sociologists are able to point out the incoherences in social debate and thus reformulate the social processes through which public action is taken in their country.

However, I do not feel this is sufficient by itself. Without the deconstruction of concepts which spring from the debate, and a consequent reconstruction of a framework for analysis, sociologists risk being simply experts who provide their opinion, whether it criticizes or justifies current and future public policy. But their ambitions usually hinder this task.

On questions as socially and politically sensitive as poverty and exclusion, sociologists must first of all recognize the impossibility of finding exhaustive definitions. These concepts are relative, and vary according to time and circumstance. It is unreasonable to expect to find a fair and objective definition, which is distinct from social debate, without falling into the trap of putting unclearly defined populations into clumsily defined categories. Defining the 'poor' and the 'excluded' according to precise long-term criteria leads almost to a reification of new social groups, or ones that are similar to the current categories, and gives the impression that the study of poverty and exclusion is an exact science which can divorce them from their social and cultural context.

Poverty and exclusion are, by definition, concepts which come from common parlance and lack any innate contextual framework. This causes problems for those who wish to construct a theory which goes beyond their everyday implications. These concepts are also to be found in the discourse of professional social organizations which, according to short-term institutional interests and considerations, endow them with narrow meanings which may, however, come to be accepted as irreversible definitions. In all modern societies, these concepts formed the core logic of welfare-state construction and the creation of various welfare institutions at the regional and national level.

Because of both the multiple social and institutional uses of these concepts, and the common knowledge which inevitably accompanies them, it seems to me to be fruitful to leave them to one side. 'Exclusion' and 'poverty' should be considered *prénotions* (pre-concepts) in the Durkheimian sense. It is useful to distinguish scientific from social usage, as the latter can prove a major obstacle to the clarity of the former as well as to the development of theory.

Of course, this does not mean that the sociologist should renounce the use of empirical tools, such as statistics, to measure the extent of these phenomena. The cross-national comparison of poverty lines is a helpful way of demonstrating disparities in living standards and income gaps between different social groups. Similarly, we can try to compare non-financial indicators, such as social linkages – family ties, participation in communal life, private aid networks, *inter alia* – with economic indicators, in order to study the accumulation of handicaps amongst the most heavily disadvantaged.

As useful as this approach is, it is not exhaustive at the sociological level. Sociologists should remember that the meaning of such indicators varies according to the cultural context of each society. They should, therefore, aim to apply them to collective organizations and to the history and the measures used by institutions in the fight against poverty and exclusion while remembering that the latter are also conditioned by the context of economic development and the condition of the jobs market.

As early as the beginning of this century, Georg Simmel pointed to the ambiguous nature of poverty as a sociological category. 'The fact that someone is poor does not mean that he belongs to the specific social category of the "poor". He may be a poor shopkeeper, artist, or employee but he remains in this category, which is defined by a specific activity or position.' He concludes, 'It is only from the moment they are assisted – perhaps also when their overall situation would normally require assistance, even though it has not yet been given – that they become part of a group characterized by poverty. This group does not remain united by interaction among its members, but by the collective attitude which society as a whole adopts towards it' (Simmel, 1908). This approach, which today would be labelled 'constructivist', is essential in analysing the issues of poverty or exclusion. It has various theoretical implications. The first is that, from a sociological perspective, the social institutional format of any society at a given moment is what matters, not the definition of poverty or exclusion as such. The second is that these institutions are not static, as they themselves are formed by social processes. The third is that the status of the poor and the excluded depends on the meaning given by each society to criteria such as the standard of living or the degree of participation in economic and social life, and on the position in which 'poor' or 'excluded' groups find themselves *vis-à-vis* those who label them as such.

International comparisons can help construct an appropriate framework for analysis, because they allow the step backwards required to advance beyond the common meanings of these categories.

## SOCIAL ORIENTATION TO POVERTY AND EXCLUSION IN EUROPEAN SOCIETIES

Sociological thought on poverty and exclusion cannot therefore base itself entirely on a substantive analysis of 'the poor' or 'the excluded'.[1] It should also contribute to the understanding of *social orientation* to poverty and exclusion. To define this concept, I propose the consideration of two dimensions.

The first is of a macro-sociological type, using a collective and social representation of this phenomenon and a social explanation of the 'poor' and 'excluded'. It can be seen, at least partially, in the analysis of the institutional forms of social intervention which aim to help the members of these groups. Such forms of social intervention are responsible for shaping the social perception of poverty and exclusion, the importance given to these questions, and the ways in which they aim to address the problems.

The second problem derives more from micro-sociology, considering the importance of these people's own experiences, the attitudes they have towards those who give them these labels and the way they adapt to different situations. 'The poor' and 'the excluded' are not defined and treated in the same way within different European countries, let alone cross-nationally. At similar standards of living, social assistance during one's active life will not necessarily have the same meaning or evoke the same attitudes in a nation of limited unemployment and heavily anti-marginal attitudes as it does in a society experiencing structural unemployment and widespread economic change. In the former case, the individuals concerned are in a minority and face stigmatization by not conforming to general social norms; in the latter, they are less marginalized and have a greater chance of recovering their previous social status through the material and symbolic resources available to them as members of the economic underclass.

These two dimensions of social orientation towards poverty and exclusion are linked to various factors which should be analysed simultaneously: the degree of economic development, the nature of the jobs market, the type and strength of social ties, the welfare-state profile, and more generally, the values and the culture through which individuals' attitudes are shaped.

Without entering into the details of this perspective, I propose to highlight certain elements to illustrate the diversity of social orientation in European societies. To do this, I shall use the classic methodological device of 'ideal types'.

## Three Ideal Types

It is possible to identify three types of social orientation to poverty and exclusion: integrated poverty, marginal poverty, and disabling poverty (see Tables 3.1 and 3.2). These terms link the concept of poverty to its social context. They do not take their point of reference from population groups, but instead from relatively stable groupings which, whilst having a social basis, evolve as they draw members, who are labelled 'poor' or 'excluded', from different social categories. Of course, they do not provide a profile of society at any one given moment, despite following the Weberian scheme of comparing the groups with their ideal types: they are only useful for highlighting convergences and differences and testing the strength of the hypothesis. As useful as this exercise may be, it should be carried out with care. The social construction of poverty and exclusion are never-ending processes. The social debate which accompanies this

*Table 3.1*    Types of social orientation to poverty in Europe: general characteristics

| Types of social orientation to poverty | Collective representation | Identity of 'the poor' |
| --- | --- | --- |
| Integrated poverty | – poverty defined as a social condition affecting a large section of the population<br>– social debate organized around the question of socio-economic and cultural development | – the poor do not form an underclass, but an extensive social group<br>– low stigmatization of the poor |
| Marginal poverty | – 'fighting' poverty<br>– social debate around inequality and the distribution of benefits<br>– visibility of marginalized social group ('4th world') | – people with a 'poor' social status (cf. Simmel) are few, but heavily stigmatized<br>– labelled as 'social problem cases' |
| Disabling poverty | – collective conscience faced with 'new poverty' or 'exclusion'<br>– collective fear of the risk of exclusion | – a growing number of people being labelled as 'poor' or 'excluded'<br>– highly diverse social situations<br>– underclass impossible to define (see above) but still used in social debate |

Table 3.2   Types of social orientation to poverty: factors which contribute to their construction and maintenance

| Types of social orientation to poverty | Jobs market | Social links | System of social protection |
|---|---|---|---|
| Integrated poverty | – weak economic development<br>– parallel economy<br>– hidden unemployment | – strong family solidarity<br>– familial protection | – weak social protection<br>– no guaranteed minimum revenue |
| Marginal poverty | – close to full employment<br>– reduced unemployment | – maintenance or progressive reduction of resorting to family solidarity | – generalized social protection system<br>– guaranteed minimum revenue for the most disadvantaged (limited availability) |
| Disabling poverty | – high increase in unemployment<br>– instability of employment<br>– difficult social re-entry | – weak social ties, in particular amongst the unemployed and disadvantaged groups | – increased claimants of guaranteed minimum revenue<br>– development of assistance for poor |

question, and the policies which target the area are constantly evolving. The social linkages themselves are no less mutable and should be studied dynamically.

*Integrated poverty* refers more to traditional forms of poverty than to social exclusion. Those labelled 'poor' are, from this perspective, extensive in number and relatively indistinguishable from other social strata. Their situation is of such immediacy that it is more likely to be treated as a regional or local problem, rather than one affecting a particular social group. Social debate is organized around issues of socio-economic and cultural development in their broadest sense, and focuses especially on the territorial dimension of social inequality. Poverty in the national population and the entire social system is linked, via collective representation, to that found at the regional level. Because 'the poor' form a broad social class, rather than a strictly defined 'underclass', they are not heavily stigmatized. Their standard of living is low, but they remain part of the social networks which stem from family and the immediate neighbourhood. Moreover, although unemployment may also impinge upon this group, it does not lead to a concomitant loss of status. In fact, its effects are usually compensated for by resources available from the underground economy, and furthermore, such activities play an integrating role for those who participate.

This type of social orientation towards poverty is more likely to develop in traditional, 'under-developed' or 'under-industrialized' societies than in their advanced, modern counterparts. It is often linked to the economic backwardness of pre-industrial societies as against those with more advanced production and social welfare protection.

*Marginal poverty* also refers more to traditional forms of poverty than to social exclusion as such. As opposed to integrated poverty, those who are referred to as 'the poor' or 'the excluded' in this case constitute only a minor part of the population. In the collective consciousness, they are made up of those who cannot adapt to the progress of modern civilization, or conform to the norms of economic development. Even though they are only a residual minority, their existence is disruptive because it demonstrates the presence of 'system drop-outs' and may foster 'disillusionment with progress' (Aron, 1969). It is for this reason that social welfare institutions ensure that they cater for those socially and professionally unable to integrate with society, without the influence of any outside pressure. This social orientation towards poverty is based on the idea that this peripheral minority is unlikely to challenge the economic and social functioning of the system in its entirety. Measures should be taken, but they should not monopolize the efforts of economic, political and trades union actors. In any case, the social debate is organized not so much around this residual group, but rather around the sharing of benefits amongst socioprofessional groups. The social status of those judged unable to integrate is thus badly compromised. Social intervention reinforces the feeling that these people are on the margins of society, and once stigmatized, they are unable to escape fully from the protection of the social organizations who look after them.

This social orientation towards poverty and exclusion is more likely to manifest itself in advanced and developing industrial societies, where unemployment can be controlled to a certain degree, and revenues are sufficiently high to guarantee everyone a high level of social protection – often the result of union demands. Without automatically sweeping away the protection afforded by close ties (such as the family, for example) the welfare state which provides more general security may, in the long term, eventually replace them in their role as social stabilizers.

*Disabling poverty* is concerned more with the question of exclusion than that of actual poverty, although social actors continue to employ both terms. Those who they refer to as 'the poor' or 'the excluded' are becoming steadily more numerous. They exist outside the productive sphere and become more dependent on social welfare institutions as they encounter greater and greater problems. It is not so much a question of abject destitution, spreading more widely every year, but rather a process which can produce sudden changes in daily life. Although we should not generalize, as we noted above, it is nevertheless true that progressively more people are confronted with precarious situations in employment which are liable to increase their burdens: low revenue, unsatisfactory housing and health care, weak familial ties and social networks and unstable position in institutionalized social networks (Paugam, Zoyem and Charbonnel, 1993). Material decline, even if only relative, and dependence upon social benefits – especially financial aid – result in the feeling of an inevitable descent into social hopelessness for those in such a situation. Their self-devaluation is accentuated by the fact that many have not experienced any sort of childhood deprivation.

In contrast to marginal poverty, the scope of this phenomenon affects society as a whole and is turning into the so-called 'new social question', which threatens social order and cohesion. 'Disabling poverty' is a social orientation towards 'the poor' and 'the excluded' which generates collective anxiety, as the membership of this stratum grows, and the number of its potential members similarly increases.

This specific orientation to poverty and exclusion is most likely to develop in societies faced with high unemployment and an unstable jobs market – linked to changes in the productive sphere and the globalization of economies – and manifests itself in what Robert Castel refers to as the 'crisis of the wage society' (*la société salariale*) (Castel, 1995). Normally in this type of society, the role of family ties, although not completely absent, has diminished: far from balancing economic and social inequalities, they may in fact exacerbate them. Furthermore, the parallel, or underground, economy is too regulated by public institutions to offer any stable support for the most disadvantaged. The processes which help soften the effects of unemployment under what we have termed 'integrated poverty' are less effective, and certainly less organized under 'disabling poverty'. As a result, dependence upon social welfare institutions is more evident in the case of the marginal sections of the population.

## NATIONAL AND REGIONAL REALITIES CONTRASTED

Unsurprisingly, national and regional situations do not correspond precisely to these three ideal types of poverty and exclusion. However, we can at least draw comparisons between them.

### European Societies Similar to the First Type: Integrated Poverty

If the standard threshold of 50 per cent of equivalent national mean spending is taken as a statistical definition of poverty in each country, it becomes immediately clear that the economically poorest countries are also those with the highest percentage of poor people. For example, in 1985, more than 30 per cent of the population of Portugal could be considered poor, as against less than 10 per cent in Belgium, Denmark and Germany (Eurostat, 1990). It should be stressed that there are often strong regional disparities in these societies. In 1993, using the same threshold, 20 per cent of families in the south of Italy would merit the label poor, as opposed to 5.4 per cent in the north and 7.8 per cent in the centre (Commisione di indagine sulla povertà, 1994; Sgritta and Innocenzi, 1993). In 1991, 11 out of 43 provinces had from 30 per cent to 41 per cent levels of poor families, whereas the national average is 19.4 per cent (Juarez, 1994).[2] These high levels of poverty are accompanied by differing social representations of the phenomenon and of the status of the unemployed in comparison with those found in economically more developed regions or nations.

According to an opinion poll by Eurobarometer in 1989 (EEC, 1990) the majority of respondents in southern countries see poverty as a permanent condition (Greece: 65 per cent; Portugal: 63 per cent; Italy: 55 per cent; Spain: 50 per cent) whereas in Holland, the proportion of respondents with the same opinion is only 17 per cent; in Denmark, 20 per cent, and in Germany 24 per cent. In the latter countries, the majority of the population feel that poverty is at the end of a 'slope' ('the poor' having 'slipped' into poverty). It is evident that poverty is perceived differently according to the degree of economic development. Collective representations thus partially account for national contrasts found in statistical evidence.

In those regions where the level of poverty is high, 'the poor' or the unemployed are not heavily stigmatized. Social integration seems to be founded principally on belonging to the family unit. Those who are most economically disadvantaged do not lose this security, as is often the case, for example, in France and the UK. In the statistical analysis using correlations of certain variables (Paugam, Prélis and Zoyem, 1994) we could observe a lack of correlation between low standards of living and weakened family cohesion in Spain and in Italy (Portugal and Greece are absent from the study due to a lack of adequate statistical data). In these countries, results obtained from other indicators, such as private aid networks, were similar: even those who were poorest economically were not deprived of contacts or the possibility of help if needed.

In the south of Italy, one can refer to a 'solid base of unemployment' (Pugliese, 1993) linked to the specific way in which the jobs market functions in a region with three identifiable sectors: the public sector, socially the most valuable; the private sector, made up of unstable companies with low salaries and virtually no career prospects; and the informal sector. The ideal situation for any worker looking for a job is to enter the public sector, and complement this position as much as possible with additional work in the informal sector. To secure a place in this sector, one must wait for positions for which demand is greater than supply. Moreover, clientelism determines the distribution of these posts (in much the same way as it regulates the distribution of invalid pensions). In the full knowledge that the system favours those who have been registered unemployed for the longest – it is not inconceivable that a long-term unemployed person will be accepted into the public sector – many will refuse to work in the private sector, instead searching in the meantime for work in the informal sector.[3] The unemployed survive for the most part thanks to work on the black market. In this sense, poverty is evidently not related to unemployment, and these people remain integrated within the social system.

The social orientation to poverty we find in these regions is often a hindrance to new social legislation. Poverty is a component of the social system and might even be said to help regulate it. Institutional and political élites, who are responsible for managing the social aid system, have often taken into account the social and cultural logic of compensation behind the jobs market and collective action against poverty. They also recognize the importance of the family, which often leads them to conclude that it is pointless changing existing policies. In Italy, sociologists openly condemn this attitude because they see it simply as a pretext for inaction (or rather, for action without an institutional framework). In Spain, the situation is very similar, even if the use of clientelism is less evident. The autonomous 'Communidades', with their minimum income policies, have all adopted different principles, according to the types of poverty aid which they see as best adapted to their specific social and cultural context (Aguilar *et al.*, 1995). Most of them have chosen not to weaken family ties.

In these examples, we can see that there has been an advance since the time of kinship aid amongst the peasantry. In describing these societies, Henri Mendras (1976) emphasized that the social relationships which developed 'are all linked together by bilateral relationships which involve a recognition of solidarity and homogeneity and form a stable, interlinked collectivity'. From this perspective, it is clear that Mediterranean societies still have much in common with their peasant predecessors. A society based on wage income, under a modern economy, is evidently less well organized, and its type of development allows the coexistence of various subsystems of production and exchange, be they complementary or conflictual. This heterogeneity partially explains the reason for the maintenance of this specific social orientation to poverty and exclusion. It is even tempting to postulate that, though these informal social systems of action against poverty still exist today, they would disappear were economic development to become more intense. However, we should note that they still exist despite various industrial development programmes in some of these regions. The functioning of the welfare state and the different types of aid distributed amongst certain sections of the population have not dissolved these close ties either. We must, therefore, consider the effects of the social and economic system functioning as a whole, and the force of inertia that these might present to any future reform.

## European Societies Similar to the Second Type: Marginal Poverty

The period of the 'golden age' in Europe closely matches this type, especially in the case of France. It was during the course of this era that the movement 'ATD Quart-Monde' was formed, with the objective of defending the interests of the underclass, stricken by inter-generational poverty, which in the past had simply been disregarded as a 'residue' of economic growth. It is certainly true that the economic climate allowed for optimism for the level of unemployment was still insignificant. Housing problems, which were serious in the 1950s, became progressively less important (Paugam, 1993). However it is also true that 'the poor' were to be found in large numbers during these years of prosperity – indeed, to such an extent that it was normal to consider them as representative of the entire working-class, at least until the early 1970s. Granted, social debate was also organized around the questions of low salaries and unacceptable working conditions, etc. However, using Simmel's terminology, this related more to social inequalities than to social orientations towards poverty. These labourers were integrated in terms of factory employment, social conflict and neighbourhood settings. Their social identity was not primarily that of being poor as such, but was rather defined by their position in the workplace, as opposed to the underclass, who were to be found only on the fringes of the economy. The latter group were targeted by specific social policies, such as halfway housing and supervision, in an attempt to remove their accumulated handicaps. This period was characterized by a dual phenomenon: the worker still involved in social conflict with its roots in nineteenth-century class struggle; and the maintenance of a disinherited social group on the margins of a thriving society. The situation in France today has changed considerably, and thus the social orientation to the problem has also been transformed.

Certain European countries are still close to this model. This is not so much because their socio-economic circumstances have not changed over recent years, but because of the stability of collective representation and modes of intervention in favour of 'poor' groups of the population.

Germany is a case in point. We will not consider the comparatively low level of economic poverty in this country, or its (until recently) low rate of unemployment. Rather, we wish to emphasize that Germany has always nurtured a specific social orientation to the problem, which can be found in its value system and historical traditions. Firstly, debate on poverty and exclusion seems to be virtually non-existent. The German state has always hesitated in participating in any European programmes against poverty. Indeed, it still has not approved the Fourth Programme on Poverty proposed by the European Commission, which may lead it to be scrapped. The German Ministry for Social Affairs follows the argument that poverty is being 'fought' – especially thanks to the quality of German social and legal institutions – and that it is therefore pointless, and even detrimental, to make it a central theme of social debate.

Of course, this does mean that 'poverty' does not exist in Germany. Many German economists and sociologists study this phenomenon in universities, often funded by charity organizations who wish to provide a forum for the expression of the views of the most disadvantaged (Hauser, 1993). Yet, the number of such studies is still limited, and they are less likely to stimulate social introspection, as is often the case in France.

The depiction of poverty in Germany seems to fit this pattern. According to a recent survey, 50 per cent of Germans consider poverty to be extinct in their country, 30 per cent did not express an opinion, and only 20 per cent believe that it has not been totally eradicated (Schultheis, 1996). To understand the meaning of these results, it is evidently necessary to carry out some historical analysis. Franz Schultheis ascribes the specific nature of this social orientation to poverty to a socio-cultural tradition, founded intellectually in the 1950s, when, during the 'German miracle', many authors and political figures believed that social inequality had been overcome and that notions of 'class' and 'poverty' were now redundant. This was the result of a collective suppression of reality, in which the trauma of the war undoubtedly played a significant role. We should not overlook the importance of collective belief in social welfare institutions and the legislation adopted at the beginning of the 1960s to guarantee a minimum income for all. The advantage of this system lies in permitting both the distribution of elementary rights to all those in a situation of poverty, and providing them with supplementary help according to their specific needs.

The Scandinavian countries are equally close to this model of social orientation to poverty. But we should also pay close attention to the differences between the Nordic countries. We will simply note that the concepts of poverty and exclusion are not to be found at the centre of social debate, even if an ever growing number of writers accept that the 'Scandinavian model' has reached its limits and that poverty is an actual problem (Abrahamson, 1994). However, there are still many politicians, especially conservatives and liberals, who try to minimize its importance. As in Germany, poverty is still invisible for many. Researchers agree that it is a minority affliction, whatever the criteria for assessment. One Swedish researcher has stated that, during the 1980s, an average of 6 per cent of the population needed some form of social aid to survive, and that these figures had never been higher in any other period of the twentieth century (Abrahamson, 1994). We can perhaps speak of a form of poverty management which has changed little over the years, despite economic changes. In the Swedish case, it is also worth emphasizing the unique system of labour market regulation, which has strongly limited the extent of unemployment. According to Philippe d'Iribarne, this country 'belongs not only to the large family of countries (sometimes called "corporatist") which are characterized by a search for compromise between groups via codetermination and consensus', but it is distinguished from these others 'by the strength of its agrarian culture implying both a rigorous work ethic and a sense of community. This latter seems far stronger than in countries where urbanization is far older, and where bourgeois individualism is far more important' (d'Iribarne, 1990).

Although the number of 'poor' in Germany and Scandinavia may be limited, their status is quite low. They are made the target of individual social welfare measures which often prove to be highly stigmatizing. The groups which use these services in countries where they are in a minority, risk being perceived as 'social problem cases' or 'social rejects'.

**European Societies Close to the Third Type: Disabling Poverty**

Despite their differences, France and the UK are close to the third model of social orientation to poverty and exclusion. In both cases, we should note that the question of poverty evokes very old debates which have structured the representation of, and help to, disadvantaged groups. The British have had a national system of poverty aid since the sixteenth century and the Elizabethan edicts (Merrien, 1994). The repeal of these laws and attempts to reform the system in line with changes resulting from the industrial revolution provoked fierce and prolonged debate in the nineteenth century – a debate which is surprisingly close to contemporary arguments. The French, for their part, remain favourable to the idea of a national debt to the weakest members of society, originating in the eighteenth century and especially from the Revolutionary 'Comity de Mendicité' (Committee against Begging). This institution stressed the need for a collectively guaranteed minimum level of support for those without resources, power or social status. Two centuries later, the vote on the RMI (see above) evoked once again this principle of national solidarity (Paugam, 1993). So, for different historical reasons in France and the UK, this problem is still a topic for discussion, not just amongst academics, but also amongst the political élites who are often judged on their success in fighting 'poverty' and 'exclusion'.

The economic situation of the two countries are quite comparable: a steady worsening of the jobs market, growing instability of the work force, and increasing unemployment (Schnapper, 1981; Gallie, Marsh and Vogler, 1994; Morris, 1995). We can observe a high correlation between the increasing precariousness of employment, such as the growing risk of redundancy and unemployment, and low standards of living and the weakness of the private aid network, family cohesion and participation in collective activity. The greater the distance from the ideal situation of stable employment, the more economic poverty, and also poverty of social exchange, is noticeable (Paugam, Préles and Zoyem, 1994). Furthermore, the number of those receiving a guaranteed threshold of revenue has been on the increase in both countries over the past few years. The total percentage of the population dependent upon such a guaranteed revenue was around 10 per cent in France, and 17.4 per cent in the UK, in 1993 (Evans, Paugam and Prélis, 1995). The expanding marginal categories of the population, including young people who have never worked, are thus grouped together in an inactive and supported sector. The levels of exit from such sectors are low, and certainly much lower than the levels of entry.

The growing importance of this phenomenon in France and the UK has become a major preoccupation of the public authorities, firstly for financial reasons, due to the growing social costs, but also for social reasons. What will eventually happen to these people, who society can support financially but do little else, especially in terms of employment? They are rejected from the labour market, which can only lower their status, and their existence affects the social system as a whole.

Social orientation to poverty and exclusion can be similar, but the solutions are noticeably different. In the UK, this growth in poverty has not led to an increase in aid to those affected. On the contrary, is has been suggested that the levels of 'income support' should be lowered to provide an incentive for the poor to help themselves. In this context, the gap between rich and poor has widened considerably (Barclay, 1995) and the disadvantaged groups who depend on support, and whose status is already weakened, are often suspected of profiting from social assistance. As a result, social debate still revolves, as in the nineteenth century, around the possible negative side-effects of helping the poor. The logic which seems to guide political thinking on the subject is to try to lessen the social costs on companies. Economic competitiveness is prioritized, which should provide jobs for 'the poor' as long as they possess the will to return to work. It is striking how many studies in the UK are devoted to these mechanisms of 'active interest'. Individuals are supposed to be rational actors, and so the welfare system is designed to benefit those who actively seek employment. This is also the way in which the question of the under-class is treated, especially amongst Conservatives. Once again, this returns to the classic view of the welfare class into which 'the poor have fallen': only policy incentives can lift them out.

In France, the question of poverty is addressed not from the perspective of an underclass, but from a general principle of national solidarity. The dominant view is that the collective nature of society has become weak. Debate on exclusion becomes generalized to include a collective fear of a loss of employment and of social advantages. Political élites or those in charge of social aid rarely use the argument that 'the poor' are taking advantage of the welfare system and that aid should be reduced to encourage them to find work. The current idea is rather to increase social expenditure to increase solidarity. Those who are labelled poor, feel socially disabled, especially in the process of social disqualification. The concept of social integration through the workplace is adopted subconsciously by most people (Schnapper, 1989). There are certain forms of compensation available for those leaving the jobs market which might indicate a type of unemployment or welfare support 'culture'; but it certainly does not indicate that the values organizing society have been put in question, or that those on the margins of society no longer feel disadvantaged. Whatever indications there might be, this process is certainly less advanced than in Mediterranean countries.

This social orientation to poverty and exclusion is not restricted to France and the UK. To a lesser degree, Belgium and the Netherlands are also close to this model.[4] We might also hypothesize that, as this is an ongoing process whose effects have not yet been fully analysed, it is very likely to extend to other countries, including those who currently only experience what we have referred to as 'marginal poverty'.

## CONCLUSION

It is striking that sociologists often criticize current and planned policies designed to fight 'poverty' or 'exclusion' in their countries. Italian sociologists have a tendency to qualify the role of family solidarity, especially in the south, because they believe that this is helping to relieve the state of its social responsibilities. Scandinavian sociologists point out the stigmatizing effect of social intervention towards the marginalized 'poor', as did certain French sociologists in the 1960s and 1970s regarding certain policies directed at the underclass in disadvantaged areas. Contemporary German sociologists, understanding the circumstances of the most socially disabled, help in some ways to discredit the collective view of 'fighting poverty'. Finally, French and UK sociologists try to reveal the gap between the reality of exclusion and the impact of social policies. As we stated in the introduction, sociology, when dealing with sensitive subjects such as 'poverty' and 'exclusion', will inevitably stimulate and play a role in social debate, but it must limit itself in this respect. Its main purpose should be to explain how each society regulates its orientation towards 'the poor' and 'the excluded'.

In democratic societies, 'poverty' and 'exclusion' are almost inevitably to be found at the heart of social debate, although varying according to the time and place. The persistence and renewal of forms of destitution provoke outrage because they turn the concept of equal rights for all citizens on its head. Social impotence in the face of this phenomenon is all the greater in societies where there has been a progressive implementation of social protection which aspired to eradicate the problem once and for all. Even if the standard of living around the world has continued to rise throughout this century, and destitution is now less common than before, it is quite clear that there are still groups living outside the social norm, and that some of these are suffering in conditions of extreme poverty. It is also the case that these inequalities, as Raymond Aron rightly predicted, have not only continued to exist, but have also given birth to new forms of poverty. These can be linked to the social inferiority of certain strata, which depend on social welfare, for example, and which provoke as much dissatisfaction as traditional forms of destitution.

The contradiction between the egalitarian ideal and the inequalities linked to the way the economy functions cannot be totally overcome. The latter can be partially reduced by the identification and application of what are called 'credit rights' – which help especially those who are most economically and socially disadvantaged – but it is impossible to eradicate them completely. This conclusion inevitably leads to frustration. Far from disappearing, these frustrations can only increase in relation to the increased satisfaction of demands for equality and the crumbling of social barriers. Everyone wishes to achieve social betterment; but, because of this, the social mechanisms which hinder individual and familial aspirations are seen as unfair and denounced as undemocratic.

As a result, social debate would seem to be unavoidable: indeed, it is all the more so because of its integral role in the functioning of modern society. Social scientists should try to contribute to this debate without becoming immersed in it. Attempts to distance themselves should occur through a clarification of concepts and a comparison of different nations and cultural systems. Their role is not to provide solutions for the politicians, but is rather more modest: namely, to suggest that they address the real questions, and consider the meanings, the possible drawbacks and the eventual contradictions of their policies. Under these conditions, a sociological perspective on 'poverty' and 'exclusion' can serve a purpose.

## NOTES

\*   Translated by Jocelyn Evans
1   This is why inverted commas are used for the 'social' rather than the scientific meaning of these words.
2   Moreover, this was calculated using 50 per cent of annual mean family income rather than the 50 per cent threshold of equivalent national mean spending.
3   I am relying here on information provided by Nicola Negri in an article entitled 'Politiche di sostegno del reddito in Italia', forthcoming in a collection on minimum incomes in Europe.

4   The stigmatization of the poor seems less salient in the Netherlands, which
    has maintained a high level of social protection towards the most disadvan-
    taged, while trying to find ways to return them to the labour market and
    economic independence.

## REFERENCES

Abrahamson, P. (1994) 'La pauvreté en Scandinavie', in F.-X. Merrien (ed.), *Face
    à la pauvreté. L'Occident et les pauvres hier et aujourd'hui*, Paris: Les Editions
    de l'Atelier, pp. 171–88.
Aron, R. (1969) *Les désillusions du progrès. Essai sur la dialectique du progrès*,
    Paris: Calmann-Lévy.
Aguilar, M. *et al.* (1995) *La caña y el pez. Estudio sobre los Salarios Sociales en
    las Comunidades Autonomas*, Madrid: Fundación Foessa.
Barclay, P. (1995) *Joseph Rowntree Foundation Inquiry into Income and Wealth*,
    York: Joseph Rowntree Foundation.
Castel, R. (1995) *Les métamorphoses de la question sociale. Une chronique du
    salariat*, Paris: Fayard.
European Economic Community (1990) *La perception de la pauvreté en Europe
    en 1989*, Bruxelles, Eurobaromètre.
Commisione di indagine sulla povertà (1994) *La povertà in Italia nel 1993*, Roma,
    documento reso publico il 14 luglio 1994.
Eurostat (1990) *La pauvreté en chiffres: l'Europe au début des années 80*,
    Luxembourg.
Evans, M., Paugam, S. and Prelis, J.A. (1995) *Chunnel Vision: Poverty, Social
    Exclusion and The Debate on Social Security in France and Britain*, London
    School of Economics, STICERD, Welfare State Programme/115.
Gallie, D., Marsh, C. and Vogler, C. (eds.) (1994) *Social Change and the
    Experience of Unemployment*, Oxford: Oxford University Press.
Hauser, R. (1993) *Arme unter uns Teil 1, Ergebnisse und Konsequenzen der
    Caritas-Armutsuntersuchung*, Caritas.
d'Iiribarne, P. (1990) *Le chômage paradoxal*, Paris: Presses Universitaires de
    France.
Jaurez, M. (ed.) (1994) *Informe sociologico sobre la situacion social en España*,
    Madrid: Fundación Foessa (see especially pp. 315–34).
Mendras, H. (1976) *Sociétés paysannes. Eléments pour une théorie de la paysan-
    nerie*, Paris, Armand Colin, revised Folio edition, 1995.
Merrien, F-X. (1994) 'Divergences franco-britanniques', in F-X. Merrien (ed.),
    *Face à la pauvreté. L'Occident et les pauvres hier et aujourd'hui*, Paris: Les
    Editions de l'Atelier, pp. 99–135.
Morris, L. (1995) *Social Divisions, Economic Decline and Social Structural
    Change*, London: UCL Press.
Paugam, S. (1991) *La disqualification sociale. Essai sur la nouvelle pauvreté*,
    Paris: Presses Universitaires de France (3rd revised and augmented edition,
    1994).
Paugam, S. (1993) *La société française et les pauvres*, Paris: Presses Universitaires
    de France (2nd edition, 1995).

Paugam, S. (ed.) (1996) *L'exclusion, l'état des savoirs*, Paris: La Découverte, Coll. 'Textes à l'appui'.
Paugam, S., Prelis, J.A. and Zoyem, J-P. (1994) *Appréhension de la pauvreté sous l'angle de la disqualification sociale*, Rapport du CERC, Eurostat: Commission des Communautés Européennes, 1994.
Paugam, S., Zoygem, J-P. and Charbonnel, J-M. (1993) *Précarité et risque d'exclusion en France*, Paris: La Documentation Française, Coll. 'Documents du CERC', no. 109.
Pugliese, E. (1993) *Sociologia della disoccupazione*, Bologna: Il Mulino (see especially Chapter 5 'Il modello italiano della disoccupazione', pp. 147–89).
Simmel, G. (1908) *Soziologie. Unterschungen öber die Formen der Vergesellschaftung*, Leipizig, Duncker-Humboldt.
Schnapper, D. (1981) *L'épreuve du chômage*, Paris: Gallimard, new revised Folio edition, 1994.
Schnapper, D. (1989) 'Rapport à l'emploi, protection sociale et status sociaux', *Revue française de Sociologie*, XXX, 1, pp. 3–29.
Schultheis, F. (1966) 'L'Etat et la société civile face à la pauvreté en Allemagne', in S. Paugam (ed.), *L'exclusion, l'état des savoirs*, Paris, La Découverte, Coll. 'Textes à l'appui'.
Sgritta, G. and Innocenzi G. (1993) 'La povertà', in M. Paci (ed.), *Le dimensioni della disuguaglianza. Rapporto della Fondazione Cespe sulla disuguaglianza sociale in Italia*, Bologna, Società editrice il Mulino, pp. 261–92.
Wacquant, L. (1992) 'Banlieues françaises et ghetto noir américain: de l'amalgame à la comparaison', *French Politics and Society*, 10, 4.
Xiberras, M. (1994) *Les théories de l'exclusion. Pour une construction de l'imaginaire de la déviance*, Paris: Méridiens Klincksieck (preface by Julien Freund).

# 4 Against Exclusion: The Poor and the Social Sciences[1]

## Giovanna Procacci

## INTRODUCTION

The issue of poverty appears to have been marginalized by the neo-conservative attempt to discredit the problems associated with inequality and by today's more general loss of consensus on welfare policies. The political debate has been reduced to discussing the financial resources compatible with other political objectives, as if poverty would disappear simply because of the amount of money society is prepared to spend on it. With rare exceptions, the scientific debate appears to be increasingly caught between neo-liberal attacks on social policies and the humanitarian aid logic that inspires religious associations and non-governmental organizations. The theme of poverty seems to have become *politically neutral*, reduced to a question of mere figures or humanitarian concerns. The real political choices seem to be only between the market and charity as an undiminished alternative at the basis of all policies directed against poverty.

Despite this theoretical lacuna, poverty continues to grow, as does the anguish of public opinion, tormented by the image of poverty portrayed dramatically by the media, so much so that we even talk of 'media star' poverty (Damon, 1994). Poverty is produced, is made spectacular and even creates its *own* media (journals, reviews, foundations of all kinds). It is talked about and is omni-present. It has never been so spoken of or so visible as in this period of almost obligatory attacks on the policies directed against it. In fact, this suggests that traditional policies are not sufficient and that there is a realization that poverty resists economic development and is a potentially explosive factor on a world scale. Furthermore, the statistical data bode ill: poverty afflicts a quarter of the population of industrialized countries. It has become a non-cyclical constant of the economic system since the 1980s when it began to persist

63

despite a period of strong growth. The World Summit on Development in Copenhagen promoted by the UN in March 1995 felt the need to denounce the neo-liberal hysteria that prevailed there in the light of a disquieting question: is it true that poverty is now simply a moral, humanitarian problem? Or rather has poverty become a political imperative of international security? Whether poverty is moral or political is just one dilemma that the modern analysis of poverty has always had to deal with.

On the one hand, therefore, poverty is seen no longer as a political theme but merely a moral one. On the other, it is seen as growing excessively and fear concerning its destabilizing potential has correspondingly increased. Between these two views, scientific analysis suggests and promotes new concepts which seem to be a response both to the theoretical lacuna and the media outcry. However, no analytical category is neutral, and still less so are the categories that underpin social policies. Here I wish to present a critical analysis of those concepts that largely predominate today in the debate on poverty and social policies – the concept of *underclass* in the USA and that of *social exclusion* in France and Europe. Their similarities can be demonstrated by taking firstly the element that they share: they both break all links between the question of poverty and that of citizenship.

We know that the status of 'the poor' in modern liberal societies only emerged because it posed a constant challenge to the formalization of citizenship in a constitutional framework, and thus to a genuinely consistent view of equality for all. The development of a modern notion of law that made the poor citizens like everyone else coincided with demands for their inclusion as active participants in the economic system. But the 'normality' of the presence of the poor in the socio-economic order came up against the political difficulty of governing conflicts of inequality in a society of 'legal' equals. Hence, the juridical, liberal framework was forced to accommodate social rights which were foreign to its logic, but were a response to the need to counter the risk of dependence in a state of poverty that could prevent the attainment of independent citizenship.

Today, political reasoning has been reversed. Poverty is no longer perceived as an obstacle to citizenship. By contrast, social policies maintain the individual in a state of dependence by virtue of the very fact that they make the individual participate in a system of protection. The result of this strategic reversal is, above all, that we talk once again of 'poverty', an indistinct category that welfare policies have replaced by groups which have rights. Not only does poverty reappear, but it takes an extreme form of growing marginalization, giving rise once again to a doubt that seemed to have been surmounted: are the poor really citizens?

This doubt in turn risks creating a gap in citizenship and thus deepening the process of 'de-citizenship' in which the crisis of work becomes a crisis of political ties and civicness. Thus a reflection on the conditions for a new social contract cannot proceed without taking an opposing view of this trend and subjecting it to critical analysis. The discovery of the political need to *include* the poor was at the origin of modern democracy. Today the debate on social exclusion risks creating a gulf between our societies and the poverty that continues to haunt them. Excluded from the 'polis' and from 'citizenship', poverty would no longer say anything about society, and citizenship would diverge definitively from the strategies that counter poverty most effectively. Analysed as *outsiders* who are the extreme end product of a long social process which generates inequality, poverty risks becoming the target of policies that merely aim to restore the 'human' condition in specific, local instances.

## OUTSIDERS

According to today's analysts of poverty in the USA, outside society and beyond social classes lies the *underclass*. Born as a purely economic concept, the notion of underclass has acquired currency chiefly because of its extraordinary media success. In fact, rarely have sociological categories permeated journalistic language to such a degree (Bagguley and Mann, 1992).

When Gunnar Myrdal used the term in *The Affluent Society* (1962) his concern was to return to a structural analysis of poverty in opposition to the trend towards cultural interpretation. He wished to draw attention to a rarely analysed phenomenon that was rooted in the very structure of the economic modernization process the existence of a poverty that had not been absorbed by growth but seemed to resist it. This persistence of poverty over time, despite the economic growth of the post-war period, led to the fear that underneath the classes involved in the modernizing economy there was the consolidation of a class of unemployed persons who were constantly rejected by it. It was a warning sign which shook our confidence in the attainment of full employment and made us think about necessary reforms to the economy.

By contrast, media reports from the end of the 1970s – such as the famous *Time* magazine cover story in 1977 and Ken Auletta's articles in the *Newyorker* in 1981 – classified under the category of underclass a restricted phenomenon in the heart of cities that were otherwise centres of growth. Journalistic reports described the ways of life in these miserable areas and illustrated the 'behaviour deficiencies' that characterized the city-centre poor and distinguished them from the rest of the poor population. The concept of underclass gradually became remote from the problems of unemployment and instead denoted poverty in its most extreme and persistent form. The logic of the media prefers to describe phenomena using exceptional cases rather than more ordinary cases: the underclass – as an extreme example – became superimposed on the more general notion of poverty and thereby served to obfuscate it.

Its media success in turn, created other dimensions to the concept of underclass, in relation for example, to persistent unemployment. These new dimensions quickly became dominant. Firstly, there was a *behavioural* dimension linked to modes of behaviour likely to be found in these extreme conditions of destitution. Secondly, there was a *racial* dimension and the reports often identified the underclass as composed of blacks or Hispanics. The underclass thus designated referred to groups of the population with a high risk of poverty: adolescent blacks particularly, young unmarried mothers and young unemployed men. Because of this concentration on behavioural aspects, the concept lost its essentially economic character and cultural definitions created a degree of ambiguity which the analysis of poverty in the USA has never completely transcended (Katz, 1989).

At the end of the 1980s, the social sciences resurrected the concept and once again it was in order to convey the structural dimension of poverty rather than to dwell on cultural factors. When Wilson (1987) and Glasgow (1980) used the concept of underclass in their influential works at the beginning of the 1980s, they used a structural analysis of the persistence of poverty centred on 'black male joblessness'. Nevertheless, by virtue of looking for explanations of the persistence of poverty in the ghettos of large towns, their research reinforces the association of underclass with certain parts of the poor black population. To the temporal dimension of a poverty that persists and is undefeated by political action is added a *spatial* dimension that becomes a crucial element in the definition of the underclass (Lynn and McGeary, 1990). The social isolation of poverty in these ghettos plays a decisive role in the immobility of large-scale poverty.

The analysis forms part of a macro-economic framework linking poverty to the transformation of the economy in a phase of deindustrialization and a decrease in employment. The importance attributed to social isolation links the empirical definition of underclass with behavioural analysis. The spatial concentration of the poor in the ghetto can only have a multiplier effect on their behaviour: they resemble each other in attitudes, in relation to work, marriage, school and so on. The result is that instead of measuring the misery that is created by poverty in a wealthy society, the concept of underclass measures sexuality, family models, refusal to work, dependence on welfare and propensity to criminality and drug abuse. Moreover, the analyses it inspires focus not so much on the sources of poverty as on the causes of behaviour which hinders the social mobility of the poor. Instead of analysing the problems that produce the underclass, the underclass itself becomes the real problem.

Thus, in the analysis of the underclass, 'joblessness' is interpreted in terms of 'weak labour-force attachment' encouraged by social isolation. Wilson (1991) specifies that it is a structural concept that refers less to the individual motivation to work than to the marginal position in which certain people find themselves because of structural factors. But he rightly needs to specify this since attachment to work is only analysed insofar as it relates to family structures, marriage, and so on.

In the same way, when Ricketts and Sawhill (1988) tried to measure the underclass for the Joint Center for Political Studies in 1987, they claimed that they wanted to comprehend the convergence of a certain number of 'social ills'. But they adopt a definition of the underclass as 'a subgroup of the American population that engages in behaviours at variance with those of mainstream populations and therefore represents a high social cost. Once they establish that they are measuring the differences in behaviour in zones with a high density of deviance in relation to their 'norm', they use indicators such as 'high school dropouts, prime-age males not regularly attached to the labor force, welfare recipients and female heads'. In their opinion, these indicators allow the profile of the underclass to be sketched since only the behavioural definition can be specified in relation to poverty in general. But as Robert Aponte (1990) shows, this does not work because the 'underclass' ends up coinciding with 'poverty'. Defining its norms and its behaviour is complex and, furthermore, it becomes difficult analytically to distinguish it from similar behaviour outside the ghetto.

Confusing the concept of underclass with poverty deflects attention from the global nature of the problem and centres it on the sub-groups of the poor in an extreme condition of destitution. This 1 per cent of the USA population (2.5 million) which, according to the estimates of Ricketts and Sawhill, belongs to the underclass, ends up representing, as Aponte notes, all of the population living in conditions of poverty. The concept of underclass facilitates a simultaneously dramatic and reassuring account because it minimizes the importance of poverty and reduces it to minorities for which we can propose targeted policies. By so doing, it separates them from the rest of the poor in a stigmatizing way and thus reinforces their political impotence.

As critics have begun to show, the underclass, as a sociological category, remains fairly blurred. Instead of helping explain the apparent 'paradox of poverty' – that is to say, how the risk of poverty continued to grow, particularly among young people, during the 'war on poverty' and the expansion of welfare in the 1970s – in reality, it produced very little new information. Conversely, it came up against empirical contradictions which is surprising, especially given its explicit empirical vocation.

Wilson makes hypotheses on the causal relations between the processes of deindustrialization and social isolation, but he avoids any theoretical precision on the relations between socio-economic structures and poverty. This is what Hughes, quoted by Aponte, called his 'ecological fallacy'. From the aggregated data of census forms, he deduces general implications in relation to the characteristics of individuals which leads him to infer that a high density of crime, unemployment, and so on, in the environment in which they live drives the majority of people to similar behaviour. Thus, the independent and dependent variables become confused. The notion of underclass has always underestimated decisive factors such as institutional barriers, or constant discrimination in the labour market (in relation to blacks as well as women, and even more so black women) or the weight of urban renewal policies.

The theoretical weakness of the concept is not abated by recourse to the terminology of social classes. Wilson himself (1987, p. 7) likens underclass to the concept of *lumpenproletariat*, that Marx used to describe the life of the slums of England in the nineteenth century. However, neither Marx nor, moreover, Weber made the definition of class dependent on behaviour because behaviour is never specific enough for a distinction to be made between classes. How can the existence of the same behaviour outside of a class be explained or indeed, how can different behaviour among members of the same class be explained? No behaviour whose spatial concentration indicates the existence of an underclass is exclusive to the underclass nor even to the poor. Christopher Jencks (1992, p. 144) remarks on the ambiguity of the concept due to the multiplicity of criteria that can be used to classify people. He identifies four criteria – income level, income source, cultural capacity, moral norms – each of which leads to a different definition of underclass and consequently to different evaluations of its numerical size.

Even more serious is the fact that the concept of underclass does not refer to any theory of social division. Nor does it even try to construct one. On the contrary, it designs a class outside the social class structure which is defined by itself, not *vis-à-vis* other classes and is thus bereft of any relational dimension. The underclass does not, therefore, facilitate a conceptualization of social stratification and it does not clarify causal relations that link social structures and their inequalities, primarily poverty. In order to decipher the sources of poverty, the sources of individual behaviour are examined: poverty is born in the individual and there is a class of them. They are less numerous than the poor and the danger that they represent is bigger and more urgent which makes them more interesting as objects of policy.

Although vague from a sociological point of view, the underclass has all the characteristics of a moral category. Here we come up against the weakness of all cultural analyses of poverty in the USA – falling, that is, into the trap of defining a norm according to models of middle-class behaviour to analyse a society which is extraordinarily mixed. In this regard, the determining belief becomes, to use Michael Katz's expression (1993: 470), 'different is worse'. Conscious of this risk, Wilson (1987: 137–8) distances himself from analyses of 'the culture of poverty', where cultural traits assume an autonomous character. By contrast, he tends to link them to socio-institutional mechanisms. The cause of underemployment among young blacks is linked to the labour market, but nevertheless the concept of underclass conveys their aversion to work. Moreover, the very idea of denoting a class below every other class reinforces the idea of passivity and resignation that is linked to a long tradition of moral and subjective interpretations of poverty in the USA. By distinguishing between the deserving poor and those that deserve nothing, a stigmatizing attitude is perpetuated. Thus the underclass can be defined as 'the most modern euphemism for the undeserving poor' (Katz, 1989: 196). Herbert Gans (1990: 273) is still more explicit: 'while (the concept of underclass) seems inoffensively technical on the surface, it hides within it all the moral opprobrium Americans have long felt toward those poor people who have been judged to be undeserving'. He sets out, or as he puts it, deconstructs the dangers of the concept which are all due to its euphemistic, flexible and synthetic character: it ends up assimilating all the poor to one condition which reifies a social division rooted in racial antagonism.

These dangers make the underclass a pseudo-scientific concept that conveys fragments with a common – and, therefore, persuasive – meaning. However, it does not have any analytical advantage. Due to the absence of any theory of social divisions, its theoretical inconsistencies produce an ambivalence due to its dual – structural and behavioural – nature. Moreover, it has quite diverse and even politically incompatible proponents – conservatives stress the behavioural dimension, while liberals stress its structural logic. Greenstone (1991) demonstrates that the cultural and structural approaches share identical problems. In both cases, culture and rationality are treated separately, which obscures the fact that the behaviour attributed to the underclass is, in fact, shared by other social groups.

The underclass represents a reassuring discovery. Since poverty becomes a minority's problem, the analysis can forget more difficult questions, such as the increasing inequality of income among the poor that work, and substitutes research on the causes of behaviour for research on the causes of poverty. As with all analyses that employ a class categorization, the underclass analysis can only lead to strategies of rehabilitation instead of a structural reform of the market or of redistribution. As Laurence Mead (1991: 4) asserts, poverty is no longer a question of inequalities among classes, because 'a politics of conduct is today more salient than a politics of class'. The underclass is a scientific myth that transforms a number of partial truths into a collection of middle-class ideological beliefs. Its result is to renew the conviction that was always at the very heart of the notion of the undeserving poor: goods must be earned through work and/or good behaviour.

Finally, the notion of underclass does not offer real alternatives to the neo-conservative interpretation of policies for the poor. On the contrary, as with 'the culture of poverty', it goes against the intentions of its liberal promoters by reinforcing the moral and subjective structure of the interpretation of poverty which is always subjugated to the middle-class hold over models of behaviour. The reasons for its success have to do with the implications of the financing of political institutions, foundations, research institutes, as well as the support given to it by the media. The advantage of an analysis that avoids the issue of institutional barriers is doubtless an important reason for its success.

Gans (1990: 276) suggests that the real danger in the notion of underclass is that it legitimizes a society that is preparing itself for a future in which a certain number of people will be more or less permanently without work. In this sense, the insistence on the notion of an underclass seems to him to be a sign that a sort of *overclass* is in the making that would dominate this society of classes. Bagguley and Mann (1992) see a similar danger, and read the concept as a collection of ideological beliefs that belong to certain groups of the dominant classes. Although it contains some partial truths, these do not conceal its chaotic nature or the processes that produce the correlations that it takes as given. This is why the concept of underclass ends up producing fairly poor social science as well as inadequate social policies.

The underclass can, therefore, be seen as one of the ideological effects of the dominant classes. After all, it is not unusual to suggest that the dominant classes have an ideology of social inequality. But the concept of underclass goes further: it creates an entity 'outside' society. It isolates the poor, confines them to their ghettos and thus renders unrecognizable the deep ties between their degradation and the processes that are transforming society as a whole. Once all the problems are reduced to one extreme form of poverty, the poor find themselves outside the structure of social classes, separated not only from the other poor, but from society as such. They are, therefore, also 'outside' citizenship.

Barbara Schmitter-Heisler (1991) analyses the concept of underclass *vis-à-vis* the problem of citizenship and asserts that the extremely limited character of the institutions of social citizenship in the USA played a decisive role in the development of the phenomena called 'underclass'. There seems to be a link between a very partial welfare state such as that of the USA and the aggravation of poverty conditions at the lower end of the social ladder. It is this which distinguishes USA society from the European countries. Because of the lack of support institutions, the extension of the legal equality of citizenship to minorities, both ethnic and non-ethnic thanks to the civil rights movements of the 1960s, could not produce an equivalent extension of social rights. By contrast, these social rights were at the origin of the development in Europe of different models of welfare that attained what T.H. Marshall referred to as 'social citizenship'. For this reason it is especially surprising to find that in Europe the debate on poverty has followed quite uncritically the lines of USA research, including the concept of underclass (Herpin, 1993).

## THE EXCLUDED

Despite appearances, there are similarities between the concept of underclass and that of *social exclusion* which recently has come to dominate research on poverty and social policies in France and the rest of Europe, as well as European Community action. Herpin's (1993) article actually deals with the two concepts as if they were synonymous. In effect, for both of them, the analysis of poverty imperceptibly tends to identify all the problems of poverty that afflict our societies with *extreme* poverty.

But they also have different histories and, accordingly, quite different characteristics. When René Lenoir published *Les exclus* in 1974, documenting a huge variety of handicaps, nobody doubted that the notion of exclusion would one day re-emerge from a social sciences' hat that was bereft of ideas. It seemed to contain an application of the theory of global social action, mixing together an assortment of sectoral specific interventions (Chevalier, 1993). It revives an old indistinct image of poverty that haunted conservative thought and seemed to have been taken over by the system of social protection that turned it into a series of identified social risks and targeted policies. Since the climate has changed in the meantime, the concepts cannot but do likewise. But what has produced the current craze for the notion of social exclusion? What drove 'the excluded' onto the media stage?

The success of the concept of exclusion has occurred since it was adopted from the exclusively conservative views that had previously limited its potential. Moreover, the reasons for denouncing such exclusion are certainly not lacking since the effects of the economic crisis were there for everyone to see, as was the increasing gap that it was producing between the rich and the poor. Above all, this increase in inequality increasingly takes the form of social polarization which reinforces the distance of the poor from participation in social life and creates a fear of an ungovernable rupture. The end of the class struggle paradigm and the retreat of Marxist categories that provided both an analysis of social conflict and a vision of a social order without classes, leaves us without the theoretical means to analyse the phenomena that survived the death of the paradigm. Evidence at the end of the 1980s that the employment crisis was not a passing one and that the aim of full employment could no longer be realized, led to 'exclusion from work' being considered an archetype of the relationship between society and the poor today (Messu, 1994).

Unlike underclass, social exclusion does not dwell on the characteristics of class and poverty. It is true that the excluded are a group apart, marginal and separated from the rest of society. But the very nature of the concept makes it a purely negative notion. The excluded do not have any positivity, they are simply outsiders and only signify a disruption. They do not have common interests, they are not the new proletariat; they could even be called a 'non-class' (Rosanvallon, 1995: 203). From this point of view, individual trajectories rather than collective identities, have to be analysed. Classification loses its importance and the statistical approach becomes increasingly inadequate for comprehending the world of the excluded. Because of this bias, as Rosanvallon stresses, the debate on exclusion takes the same individualistic direction as the analysis of the underclass in the US since it focuses on behaviour, individual life courses and on personalized treatment as opposed to impersonal, general measures (Affichard, 1992: 17)

However, the notion of exclusion is as significant from a sociological point of view. It does not represent so much an aggregation or a class, but rather the result of a social decomposition, the indicator of a low degree of integration and the rupture of social ties. 'Exclusion' reflects a holistic conception of society, in which social cohesion is undermined by the polarization of inequalities. Thus, the means of integrating the individual on a professional, family or community basis (Messu, 1994) have to be strengthened. An equally individual trajectory of integration has to correspond to the individual path of marginalization.

The difficulty comes from the transforming effect that the notion of exclusion has *vis-à-vis* the phenomena it analyses. It transforms a process into a condition – the condition of an excluded person – and it is more disposed towards quantifying that condition than understanding it. In fact, exclusion refers to a state of deprivation: it derives from a holistic logic of social cohesion but it nonetheless describes a dual society – one in which those who are within are divided from those outside. In describing the conditions of life on the margins of society, in following the channels of exclusion, it only confirms the existence of rupture, as if there was a possible place 'outside' society, where the suffering of the excluded can be analysed. But as Robert Castel (1992) points out, observing the existence of wants neither allows an understanding of the processes that generate these conditions nor brings out their specific nature. This is so especially if they are analysed as being on the margins of society, since the processes at work in a 'normally' integrated society are not referred to. However, the collection of phenomena that Castel describes as the 'destabilization of the stable' – the precarious nature of work, isolation, the reduction of resources, the weakening of social protection – are not just the conditions prevailing on the margins of society but the processes that are *polarizing* society. The excluded are thus separated not only from society but also from the processes which are responsible for their exclusion.

Many factors have played a role in the success of this notion, which go well beyond the framework of administrative categorization from which it came. Firstly, there was the development of a humanitarian strategy in reaction to an economic analysis of poverty which reduces all differentials to monetary ones (Messu, 1994). With this reaction, the struggle against 'mass poverty' became hugely popular and was promoted by religiously inspired organizations that saw this as a means of reviving private or charitable social assistance. Secondly, the trend of social policies was to equate social with urban, adopting a neat characterization of the urban structure that replaced 'inequality' with 'segregation' (Touraine, 1992). More generally, the reasons for the success of the notion of social exclusion have to do with its capacity for replacing that of inequality, thereby reducing the threat of ungovernability suggested by the latter.

For while exclusion places the problem 'outside society', inequality inevitably raises the problematic issue of the attainment of equality. Etienne Balibar (1992) points to the link between the rise of the concept of exclusion and the disappearance of that of class struggle; exclusion focuses on the identification of typologies at the expense of the dynamic described by the class struggle. This dynamic is essential in social analysis as it shows that inequalities are accentuated, not outside social space, but within it, by its institutions. This is precisely what the notion of exclusion masks. Balibar fears that this will to disregard the phenomena of inequality is only a sign that, fundamentally, we dread less the exclusion of more and more groups of the population than their desire for inclusion and their corresponding claim to change political relationships.

The personalized trajectories of integration that are proposed to the excluded, aim at replacing the demand for participation with a strategy of involvement. This is because participation reflects a power problematic and this 'question of power, in a certain sense, was a screen for action' (Donzelot, 1991: 34). By contrast, 'involving' the excluded and calling on all to collaborate produces a collectivity bound to the realization of each individual's potential, instead of linking them to aims that go *beyond* the individual. This approach also avoids a conflict that questions the distribution of power in society.

Thus the *exclusion-involvement-action* equation is opposed to an *inequality-participation-power* equation. The first expresses a technocratic rationality that does not accommodate conflicts very well, and does not like putting power at stake. The second constitutes a reading of society that made equality the principle as well as the objective of an emancipatory project. The first claims to have integrated the social and the economic by means of an entrepreneurial logic of individual performances, beginning with a local involvement which does not lead to any consideration of central political issues. Meanwhile, the second has been essentially translated into an economic analysis that describes poverty in quantitative terms based on income thresholds.

The return to a localized treatment of problems, which is evident in the current forms of social administration, is a way of trying to reconstruct social exchange on an increasingly individualistic basis (Castel, 1992: 470), implementing a contractual reciprocity on a territorial level, and leaving aside universal rights. However, at work in this localism there is, as Marcel Gauchet (1991: 179) points out, the illusion of decentralization as a palliative which is good for everyone. The individual contract put in place by the French RMI (Minimum Insertion Income) makes an appeal to individual capacities for insertion as educational outcomes of social integration. By contrast, it does not modify the structural conditions which militate against them, nor does it diminish the RMI claimants' distress at being socially non-existent. Returning to a local level means refusing to recognize the collective nature of the problems that affect the poor.

Finally, the notion of social exclusion risks renewing the old vice of liberalism in relation to poverty which was to make poverty visible without promising any subjective rights for the poor. This vice already produced the *impasse* against which the social policies founded on social rights were formulated. The attack on social rights today is justified by their indiscriminate nature – the legacy of a society that 'mistakenly' aspired to equality. In their place, social exclusion presents a very limited target for egalitarian polices, suggesting that, except in extreme cases, inequality is no longer a problem.

Exclusion has the advantage of combining this need for a theory that avoids a consideration of inequality and the humanitarian concern that is increasingly invoked as a way of understanding conflicts. A technocratic concept that has become the password for all financing of research on 'poverty', it allows us to take into account the unjust destiny that we reserve for the poor, excluded from the post-industrial banquet, without questioning the nature of this society or the deep crisis that afflicts it. The success of the notion of exclusion is due precisely to its social neutrality and pseudo-scientific garb.

## CONCLUSION

The underclass refers to a group of the population, identified by a spatial proximity which provides its common characteristics, and places individual behaviour at the centre of analysis. Whereas social exclusion fragments poverty, breaking it down into individual trajectories of rehabilitation, at the same time the emphasis is on the importance of space where these individuals nonetheless live together. In different ways, the two concepts move the emphasis from the social to the urban. Consequently, the policies they inspire are targeted more at the space where poverty is reproduced than at its causes. But the two concepts differ due to the very different contexts from which they have emerged. The strategy of combating exclusion in France today attacks policies that aimed to equalize conditions. The objective here becomes localized social solutions that undermine the potential for political conflicts linked to issues of inequality. By contrast, the context of the underclass is one in which social policies have been dominated by the 'work-ethic', and remains obsessed with putting the members of this underclass back to work.

However, despite their differences, the two concepts have the same strategy for shifting the issue of the poor to the margins, which entails making 'large-scale poverty' the object of analysis. In both cases, a dual society is described, and poverty is reduced to the condition of marginal minorities. If exclusion destroys 'the honour of the citizen' (Balibar, 1992), the notion of the underclass reinforces the barriers that separate the poor ghettos from others in towns. The two concepts thus bi-polarize the poor population: those who are deserving and those who do not deserve to exit from their poverty, the good and the bad poor who have long fought over favours from liberals.

Unquestionably, there is a crisis of social regulation that, as Marcel Gauchet (1993) indicates, now affects all institutional forms of participation. The 'collective actor' is itself in crisis, under the influence of what he calls 'mass individualism'. It is inevitable that this presents a challenge to social cohesion, creating a sort of anomic condition. And even if this 'destructuring' of society and social protection is part of valid reassessment of the needs of the individual against the hegemony of the state over civil society, as Robert Castel (1992) asserts, it nevertheless produces a dangerous gap between those who can derive independence from individualism and those for whom individuality is a burden and the absence of protection the root of insecurity.

Adopting concepts such as underclass and social exclusion which marginalize the poor, runs the risk of merely endorsing the isolation in which they are condemned to live. By tackling the dual risk of the growth of an abandoned population and its perpetuation in a dangerous state of dependence, only citizenship can offer a theoretical means for breaking this isolation and reversing the exclusion-insertion cycle. If a new social contract is to be considered, it cannot take the form of a pure and simple return to the market, excluding those who do not succeed while simply compensating them for their exclusion. Instead, the rules of collective action will have to be reformulated for a highly individualized society. As sociology teaches us, this will require stretching the boundaries of individualism.

## NOTES

1    Translated by Claire M. O'Neill and Martin Rhodes

# REFERENCES

Affichard, J. and de Foucauld, J-B. (eds.) (1992) *Justice sociale et inégalités*, Paris: Editions Esprit.

Aponte, R. (1990) 'Definitions of the Underclass: A Critical Analysis', in H.J. Gans (ed.) *Sociology in America*, Sage Publications, pp. 117–137.

Bagguley, P. and Mann, K. (1992) 'Idle Thieving Bastards? Scholarly Representations of the Underclass', *Work, Employment and Society*, 6, pp. 113–26.

Balibar, E. (1992) 'Inégalités, fractionnement social, exclusion', in J. Affichard, and J-B. de Foucauld (eds.), *Justice sociale et inégalités*, Paris: Editions Esprit, pp. 149–61.

Castel, R. (1992) 'De l'exclusion comme état à la vulnérabilité comme processus', in J. Affichard and J-B. de Foucauld (eds.), *Justice sociale et inégalités*, Paris: Editions Esprit, pp. 135–48.

Chevalier, G. (1993) 'Le social réduit à l'urbain', *Le Monde*, 2 July.

Damon, J. (1994) 'Le Banquet', *Revue du CERAP*, 5.

Donzelot, J. (1991) *Face à l'exclusion: le modèle français*, Paris: Esprit.

Gans, H.J. (1990) 'Deconstructing the Underclass: the Term's Danger as a Planning Concept' *Journal of the American Planning Association*, 56, pp. 271–7.

Gauchet, M. (1991) 'La société d'insécurité', in J. Donzelot (ed.), *Face à l'exclusion: le modèle français*, Paris: Esprit, pp. 169–87.

Gauchet, M. (1993) 'Le mal démocratique', *Esprit*, 195, pp. 67–89.

Glasgow, D.G. (1980) *The Black Underclass*, San Francisco: Jossey-Bass.

Greenstone, J.D. (1991) 'Culture, Rationality and the Underclass' in C. Jencks and P. Peterson (eds.), *The Urban Underclass*, Washington D.C.: Brookings Institution pp. 339–410.

Herpin, N. (1993) 'L'urban underclass chez les sociologues américains: exclusion sociale et pauvreté', *Revue française de sociologie*, XXXIV, pp. 421–39.

Jencks, C. and Peterson, P. (ed.) (1991) *The Urban Underclass*, Washington D.C.: Brookings Institution.

Jencks, C. (1992) *Rethinking Social Policy. Race, Poverty and the Underclass*, New York: Harper Collins.

Katz, M.B. (1989) *The Undeserving Poor*, New York: Pantheon.

Katz, M.B. (1993) *The Underclass Debate*, Princeton: Princeton University Press.

Lenoir, R. (1974) *Les exclus*, Paris: Seuil.

Lynn, L.E. and McGeary, M. (eds.) (1990) *Inner-City Poverty in the United States*, Washington D.C.: National Academy Press.

Mead, L.M. (1991) 'The New Politics of the New Poverty', *Public Interest*, 103 (Spring), pp. 3–20.

Messu, M. (1994) 'Pauvreté et exclusion en France' in F-X. Merrien (ed.) *Face à la pauvreté*, Paris: L'Atelier, pp. 139–69.

Ricketts, E.R. and Sawhill, I.V. (1988) 'Defining and Measuring the Underclass', *Journal of Policy Analysis and Management*, 7, 2, pp. 316–25.

Rosanvallon, P. (1995) *La nouvelle question sociale*, Paris: Seuil.

Schmitter-Heisler, B. (1991) 'A Comparative Perspective on the Underclass', *Theory and Society*, 20, 4, pp. 455–83.

Touraine, A. (1992) 'Inégalités de la société industrielle, exclusion du marché', in J. Affichard and J-B. de Foucauld (eds.), *Justice sociale et inégalités*, Paris: Editions Esprit, pp. 163–174.

Wilson, W.J. (1987) *The Truly Disadvantaged*, Chicago: University of Chicago Press.

Wilson, W.J. (1991) 'Studying Inner-City Social Dislocations', *American Sociological Review*, 56, pp. 1–14.

# II  Welfare Systems Under Stress

# 5 The Four 'Social Europes': Between Universalism and Selectivity[*]

## Maurizio Ferrera

### CONVERGENCE AND PERSISTENCE IN EUROPEAN WELFARE REFORM

In recent years the theme of 'convergence' of the social policies of western countries has gained a pre-eminent position in political and academic debates. It is not difficult to understand the reasons for this new interest. The literature on the crisis of welfare has amply revealed the similarity of the challenges that each country faces. These challenges are of an endogenous nature (like demographic changes or changes in the labour market), as well as of an exogenous nature (the so-called globalization of markets). If the challenges are analogous, it is natural to expect that the policy responses are, to a large extent, the same. Such an expectation should not necessarily depend on functionalist assumptions (common challenges of adaptation produce 'equivalent' responses). For it can also be based on the recognition that – at least within the OECD area – policy innovation occurs on the basis of increasingly swift and intense processes of diffusion and imitation among countries, via learning and lesson-drawing on an international scale (Rose, 1991).

The debate on convergence has been, and still is, particularly lively within the European Union. Under the presidency of Jacques Delors, this concept became a leitmotif even on a prescriptive level. In 1992, for example, a recommendation was approved that officially obliged member states to conform to a series of common objectives in the social protection sector.[1] Over the last few years, the Commission has been actively involved in monitoring the main policies of this sector to measure if, and to what extent, the various national systems are evolving towards analogous goals and formulae.[2] The thesis at the basis of these initiatives (and explicitly formulated in some official documents such as the Green Paper, 'Options for Europe' of 1994) can be synthesized as follows:

- notwithstanding the variety of historical traditions, EU countries share the same 'social model';
- this model is today confronted with analogous challenges and tensions in the face of which it is reasonable to expect similar responses, in a process of more or less spontaneous convergence;
- European institutions must as far as possible go along with this process through the dissemination of information and analyses as well as occasional legislative interventions for the purpose of 'discipline'.[3]

On a descriptive level, this thesis contains without a doubt many (and almost obvious) elements of truth. Remaining at a fairly high level of observation, it is not difficult to recognize the high degree of affinity among European systems of social protection in relation to those of other industrialized areas such as North America, East Asia, Australia/New Zealand, in terms of spending, generosity of services, the extent of insurance cover, mass-level expectations and orientations and so on (CEC, 1995). On the basis of similar macro-affinities it is doubtless reasonable to formulate diagnoses and predictions in terms of convergence. Thus the process of European integration has created common challenges to national welfare arrangements (regarding the free movement of labour, for example) and has promoted the adoption, at a Community level, of constraining measures for all countries (for example, a uniform set of arrangements in relation to maternity leave). Even if European integration has not (yet) explicitly created a 'social dimension', it tends, in other words, to produce a certain degree of almost automatic (and often implicit) 'communitarization' in the area of social policy (Leibfried and Pierson, 1995). Spontaneous convergence can then be plausibly hypothesized in relation to two aspects:

1. The orientation and the general criteria of welfare reform. Due in large part to the work of Community institutions, an 'epistemic community' has been formed on a continental scale in recent years, which is concerned with the analysis of problems and elaboration of solutions as well as being active in mediating processes of institutional diffusion among countries.[4] National debates are thus infiltrated by the same 'buzz words' ('managed care', 'targeting', 'active' policies, etc.) and are encouraged to deal with similar issues according to plans and

concepts that are often elaborated on a supra-national level (for instance the theme of 'social exclusion').

2. Some macro-quantitative measures, such as aggregated levels of social spending are showing signs of alignment, their internal composition is becoming similar, and their growth rates are diminishing.[5] In this case, the observable convergence is the result of the similar dynamics of the financial 'maturation' of insurance schemes, in the presence of analogous socio-demographic pushes, as well as common macro-economic constraints operating within each country, which in turn are partly connected to the developments of economic and monetary integration.

If, however, we move from the general criteria of reform and the macro-quantitative indicators to the institutional framework and specific programmes of the 15 *national* systems of social protection, the convergence thesis becomes much weaker. Closer inspection does show signs of alignment even at this level. Some of the more macroscopic 'regional deviations' for example seem gradually to be attenuating. Southern European welfare states have undertaken the first steps towards establishing plans for a guaranteed minimum income (in line with the 1992 Recommendation), thus bridging one of their more considerable gaps. Scandinavian countries have begun to extend the role of social contributions as an instrument for financing welfare, reducing correspondingly the role of traditional fiscal financing. Certain new ideas, moreover, are materializing in very different institutional contexts, giving place to phenomena of 'qualitative' convergence that are quite surprising. For example, in 1994–95, Sweden and Italy launched two very innovative pension reforms, both of which hinge on the principle of 'defined contributions'.[6] However, much institutional change – the concrete, specific responses to analogous, endogenous and exogenous challenges – continues to follow the patterns of the past. Thus Germany, for example, reconfirmed its loyalty to 'Bismarckian' principles by introducing in 1994 a new insurance plan for long-term sickness assistance (*Pflegeversicherung*), while Britain seems to want to revitalize its own pre-Beveridge tradition of assistance to the poor with the recent introduction of new benefits filtered by the means test.

Seen 'from below', the 'European social model' so dear to Delors thus appears much more heterogeneous than it does 'from above'. This model tends conversely to shatter into a kaleidoscope of historical sediment and national specificity, in which the persistent dynamics tend to overshadow those of convergence. As the abundant literature on the (qualitative) 'types' of welfare has demonstrated,[7] even at this level, it is possible to trace regularities, and configurations of institutional ingredients shared by more or less large groups ('families') of countries. These configurations or 'regimes' have structured (and still structure) the crisis of European welfare in different ways. Even in the presence of common challenges, analogous levels of spending distributions and even normative or epistemic references, the logic of institutional evolution tends to remain different within each family.

The notion that institutional configurations 'matter' in modelling the perception of problems and the attempts to solve crises of public policy is certainly not new in the comparative debate on the welfare state (Heclo, 1974). Recently it has received interesting confirmation. An incisive comparative project on the attitudes of élites in some European countries on the future of social protection has, for example, revealed how beyond generic etiquettes (such as 'explosion of costs', 'social exclusion', and 'privatization'), policy-makers tend to select problems and elaborate solution strategies according to a pattern closely linked to the type of welfare regime in force in their countries (Taylor Gooby, 1995). In his recent work, Esping-Andersen has established some convincing demonstrations of how 'liberal', 'conservative-corporatist' and 'social democratic' regimes (according to his well-know typology) are responding in clearly different ways to the transition from 'fordist' to 'post-fordist' arrangements – sometimes remaining trapped in their own contradictions (Esping-Andersen, 1995).

In the rest of this chapter, we provide a further illustration of this syndrome. Firstly, the profile of the four institutional configurations in which the 'European social model' is articulated today will be dealt with. Then we will illustrate how an idea that today is very much in vogue within the international and supranational epistemic community – *targeting* – finds within each of the four 'families' very distinct interpretations and applications. These reflect in fairly evident fashion the process of 'moulding' operated by the type of institutional configuration in force.

## FOUR SOCIAL EUROPES

In macro-institutional terms, European social protection systems differ principally with respect to the following dimensions:

- the rules of access (eligibility);
- benefit formulae;
- financing regulations;
- organizational-managerial arrangements.[8]

On this basis, four different configurations that distinguish four 'geo-social' European families can be outlined.

The first family is made up of the Scandinavian countries. As is well-known, in this case social protection is a right of citizenship, cover is universal (even in relation to sickness and maternity benefits, which in Sweden and Finland are even provided to those who do not participate in the labour market) and benefits consist of relatively generous fixed amounts that are automatically paid to compensate for various social risks (even if employed workers receive supplementary benefits through compulsory occupational schemes). Public assistance plays a rather circumscribed, residual integrative role.[9] Social protection is primarily financed through fiscal revenues. However, as has been already observed, recent steps have been taken to extend the role of social contributions (for example, in 1994 Denmark introduced them for health and unemployment insurance). Organizationally, the various components of Scandinavian welfare are strongly integrated among themselves and the provision of benefits and services (including a vast range of health and social services) is under the direct responsibility of (central and local) public authorities. The only sector that remains substantially outside this integrated organizational framework is unemployment insurance which is of a voluntary nature and directly managed by trade union organizations.

The second family is the Anglo-Saxon one (the UK and Ireland). Here too, welfare state cover is highly inclusive, but can be considered fully universal only in the health domain. In fact, in the income maintenance sector, inactive citizens and the employed earning less than a certain threshold (£54 weekly in the UK and IR £30 in Ireland in 1995) have no access to National Insurance benefits. These benefits – also flat rate – are, moreover, much more modest than in Scandinavia. The range of social assistance benefits available through means testing is also much more extensive. These two countries have mixed systems of financing: health is entirely tax financed, while cash benefits (especially those of an insurance nature) are largely financed by social contributions. As in Scandinavia, the organizational framework is highly integrated (including unemployment insurance) and entirely managed by the public administration. The social partners play a secondary role.

The third family includes Germany, France, the Benelux countries, Austria and Switzerland. Here the Bismarckian tradition, centred on the linkage between work position (and/or family status) and social entitlements, is still highly visible in the income maintenance sector as well as the health sector. Only Holland and Switzerland made this tradition partially hybrid by introducing plans of a universal nature.[10] Benefit formulae (proportional to income) and financing (through social contributions) largely reflect insurance logics (even if not strictly actuarial), often with diverse disciplines according to the professional groups. This marked occupational approach is reflected also in organization and management. Trade unions and employer organizations participate actively in governing the insurance schemes, preserving a degree of autonomy in relation to the public authorities, especially in health. The majority of the population is covered by social insurance, through their own or derived rights. The insurance obligation comes into effect automatically at the beginning of a job paying income. It should be noted, however, that in Germany and Holland, the highest band of incomes (over about 70 000 DM and around 60 000 HFL annually) are exempted from compulsory insurance health.[11] Those who fall through the insurance net in these countries can receive fairly substantial social assistance benefits, which are, however, less standardized than in Scandinavia or the UK.

Finally, the fourth family is made up of southern European countries: Italy, Spain, Portugal and Greece. These welfare states are distinguished by their lack of homogenous development: the Italian system of protection is quite mature (even if there is a large differentiation between the north and the south of the country), but the Spanish system, and in particular the Greek and Portuguese systems, are still in the process of development. The comparative debate has tended thus far to consider these systems as belonging to the continental family, to the regime of 'conservative-corporatist' welfare.[12] What is the justification for separating them into their own family? We believe that there are two good reasons.

The first is that this area appears to be characterized by a *sui generis* institutional configuration in relation to the four dimensions listed at the beginning of this section. On the one hand, in the southern European countries there is a highly fragmented system – with respect to occupational demarcations – of income guarantees that has a clear 'Bismarckian' stamp. There are also very generous benefits (for example in the pension field). In contrast to the continental European area, in southern Europe there is no articulated net of minimum basic protection. As has already been observed, this abnormality has recently shown some signs of attenuating due to the introduction of guaranteed income schemes at a regional level in Italy and Spain and more recently in Portugal. But the gaps in cover are still considerable. On the other hand, in the course of the last 15 years all four countries have established national health services with a universal vocation, that is to say, based on the rights of citizenship. The universalization of access and the standardization of services can be considered complete only in Italy, where during the 1970s and 1980s the old occupationally fragmented 'mutualistic system' was replaced by a National Health Service.[13] Spain, Portugal and Greece also formally introduced National Health Services. However, the transition from the old category mutualities to the new order is still in course. The aim in these countries is to arrive at a standardized universal health citizenship. Thus, southern European social protection is characterized by a mixed orientation: occupational funds and the social partners play an important role in income maintenance but no longer (or increasingly less) in the health sector. In this last sector, moreover, fiscal revenue is gradually substituting social contributions as a source of finance.

The second justification for placing the four Latin welfare systems in a family of their own is the high 'particularism' that characterizes their functioning in the payment of cash benefits (clientelistic manipulations and fraud) and financing (widespread tax evasion etc.). In southern Europe, not only does welfare have a *sui generis* configuration, but so has the state. This not very 'Weberian' state is largely infiltrated and easily manipulated by organized interests (and in particular political parties). The low degree of 'stateness' of the Latin systems of welfare is a feature that isolates this family of nations from the others in Europe (Ferrera, 1996b).

Because of different genetic preconditions and evolutionary frames, the four institutional configurations of the European social model have witnessed – over the last 15 years – quite distinct welfare 'syndromes', moulding the 'opportunity structure' and thus the strategies of the various actors, constraining and facilitating organized action and programme reform, as well as the cognitive and normative schemes of policy-makers and the policy-takers. Consequently, the four social Europes are facing very different 'solidarity dilemmas'. Within them the 'buzz words' of the international political and academic debate acquire meanings, values and implications that converge very little – as the case of so-called 'targeting' demonstrates.


## DIFFERENT 'UNIVERSALISMS', DIFFERENT 'SELECTIVITIES'

Preoccupation with the costs and efficacy of social policies, has in recent years stimulated a progressive re-evaluation of the notion of selectivity. This refers to the limitation of access to services on the basis of specific conditions of need or income,[14] in order to avoid the dispersion of resources, reach those who are genuinely not self-sufficient and contain aggregate spending. For some countries, the new emphasis on selectivity implies the institutionalization or consolidation of guaranteed minimum income schemes, or, to be more precise, nets of protection aimed at the support of those who have no access to social insurance benefits. Targeting has become an important ingredient of the policy recommendations formulated by authoritative international organizations such as the OECD and the World Bank, and its virtues are increasingly praised by the various international and supranational exponents of the policy communities dealing with social issues, not only in reference to advanced countries but also developing countries (Gough, 1995). In other words, we are confronted by a guiding idea which has a strong potential for orientating the process of social learning.

Analysts of the 'Labour'[15] school are perplexed by this revival of selectivity from which, according to them, some dangerous threats to the efficacy and stability of welfare could emerge, including a progressive and stigmatizing 'ghettoization' of the beneficiaries of means-tested services, a qualitative decline of services ('welfare for the poor becomes poor welfare') and an erosion of middle-class support, with consequent risks of a welfare backlash.[16]

In the arguments of both the supporters and the opponents of selectivity, the scant attention paid to what above we called institutional configurations, is striking. The merits and demerits of targeting are presented and discussed with a tacit clause of *ceteris paribus*, as if its practical viability and its organizational, distributive and policy implications were the same for every country or family of countries, independent of pre-existing arrangements.[17] As has been suggested, it is in fact these arrangements that structure the opportunities and the direction of welfare reform. Thus, it is natural to expect that grafting (or attempts at grafting) selectivity onto these systems tends to lead to quite different policy syndromes in the four social Europes outlined above.

The Anglo-Saxon institutional configuration is tacitly taken as a point of reference in the debate. In the UK and to a lesser extent in Ireland, targeting has been widespread and intense. As the literature has revealed, the British welfare state has recorded a remarkable growth in means-tested services in the course of the last 15 years. The beneficiaries of these services represented 15.9 per cent of the population in 1992, with an increase of 6.7 percentage points with respect to 1980, while in 1992, spending in this area absorbed about a third of the total social security budget – by far the highest percentage in Europe (Gough, 1995).

This marked 'residualization' of British welfare is generally seen in the context of the politico-ideological climate of the 1980s and the long Conservative hegemony. The prevalent interpretation, put briefly, is in terms of class relations. Nevertheless, the explicit discretionary measures of the

Thatcher and Major governments on this terrain were certainly not explosive: some restriction of the criteria and requisites for eligibility in relation to insurance benefits, the introduction of two new means-tested plans (Housing Benefit and Family Credit) and the revision of unemployment benefits from April 1996 (CEC, 1995). The residualization of social protection has been much more a 'creeping' phenomenon, and in a certain sense 'automatic'. On the one hand it appears connected to the lack of a re-evaluation of insurance benefits (in particular National Insurance old age pensions). On the other, it is also linked to the growth, in the last 15 years, of precarious and part-time jobs often bereft of insurance cover because of the above mentioned barriers to access. Both of these dynamics pushed a growing number of beneficiaries to ask for supplementary assistance from Income Support. Without removing any responsibility from the Conservatives, it can be said that their actions were not politically and organizationally 'heroic'. They simply put a stop to 'universalistic maintenance' in the absence of which the system built by Beveridge tends inexorably to decline towards selectivity – particularly in periods of economic crisis, and social and labour market transformations.

It should be noted that the 'selective' logic adopted by Conservative governments found important reinforcements in other elements of the British institutional configuration. The highly unitary nature of the system of social insurance precluded the emergence of horizontal distributive tensions among occupational categories. The high centralization and the modest involvement of the social partners (in particular trade unions) in the policy process kept government decisions (or non-decisions) at a low level of visibility. The policy legacy, already heavily marked by the principle of selectivity (from the time of the Poor Laws), sustained the dynamics of residualization with cognitive and normative predispositions congruent with, or at least not opposed to it.

Moreover, it is precisely the Anglo-Saxon institutional configuration which-in the absence of 'universalistic maintenance'-tends to produce the negative results associated with selectivity in the political debate: a means-test objectively experienced as stigmatizing, the formation of dependency traps and high levels of non-take-up etc.

While in Anglo-Saxon countries the adoption of selectivity through the means-test represents an 'easy' option in politico-institutional terms, in Scandinavian countries this situation is turned on its head. Far from 'naturally' moving towards targeting, the configuration of their welfare systems renders them virtually immune to it, at least on the benefit side.[18] Several factors sustain the particular strength of Scandinavian universalism with respect to Anglo-Saxon universalism: the absence of minimum earnings requisites for access to social insurance, the highly standardized procedures for the definition and the adjustment of the 'basic amount' of cash benefits and the presence of semi-universalist, earnings-related supplementary benefits. Furthermore, there is the deep-rooted culture of *folkhemmet* (i.e. the welfare state as a common house for all and not only for the poor). The introduction of means-testing in such a context would be a veritable 'injury' to the institutional and symbolic fabric of Scandinavian welfare. Thus, not even 'bourgeois' governments (including the one that ruled Sweden at the beginning of the 1990s in a moment of serious economic and financial crisis) ever seriously considered this option.[19]

To say that Scandinavian (in particular Swedish) universalism does not have an aptitude for targeting does not mean that it is impermeable to 'cuts'. During the course of the last 5 years in Sweden, restrictive measures that would be difficult even to propose in many European countries have been introduced. For example, the introduction of a waiting period for the first day of illness and the first five days of unemployment, the reduction of replacement rates for short-term benefits, the increase in pensionable age and the shift to a contributory formula for pensions (with a much less generous formula than the one recently introduced in Italy). Although incisive (and probably regressive in distributive terms), such cuts do not however make inroads into the universalistic framework of the system. They merely render it a little less solid. In other words, the Scandinavian institutional configuration makes it easier to impose sacrifices *erga omnes* rather than modify protection on the basis of the actual conditions of need. In the spring of 1995, the Social-Democratic government of Stockholm gave a further example of this, preferring to cut the amount of universal family allowances (for the first time since they were established in 1948) to the option of grading them on the basis of income.

In the third 'social Europe', coupling selectivity with the institutional configuration brings about very different challenges to those of Anglo-Scandinavian Europe. As mentioned above, in continental countries the majority of the population is included in occupational schemes that are still largely based on the insurance logic which dictates that distributed benefits are linked to contributions and/or earnings. Even if the insurance logic has in large part become a façade,[20] nonetheless it is a façade that considerably constrains selectivity. In the first place, the only kind of selectivity that is viable is *exclusive* and not *inclusive*: since everyone is already covered by generous programmes, the only option is to try and exclude the better off from certain benefits. As mentioned earlier, this has been foreseen for a long time by the German and Dutch health systems. Given that the universal ethos is less rooted in these countries than in Scandinavia, targeting 'out' theoretically encounters less obstacles 'of principle' but still requires discretionary measures that withdraw consolidated entitlements. The road is thus politically more uneven than in the UK. Paradoxically, this is the case notwithstanding the fact that selectivity of an exclusive type is largely immune to several of the perverse effects of inclusive selectivity. In fact, the 'affluence test' does not have the stigmatizing effect associated with the 'poverty test', and does not operate as a disincentive to the take-up of benefits to which citizens are already accustomed. In the second place, the presence of a multiplicity of category schemes raises serious dilemmas for horizontal solidarity: that which is fair (and acceptable) for one category may not be for another. Finally, the high level of involvement of the social partners complicates the framework. In particular, unions in these countries tend to defend welfare 'separatism' and to oppose the regulatory intrusion of public powers (even for equitable ends) so as not to lose important resources of legitimacy. In France, for example, unions oppose every attempt to reform social security in the direction of 'conditional' universalism that is supported by the Socialist party (Bonoli and Palier, 1995). The only benefits in which targeting has some chance of success are family allowances which in many countries of this area are universal as opposed to category (work-related) benefits.

Finally we come to the fourth 'social Europe', the Latin one. The institutional configuration of this area makes grafting selectivity easier in principle, but in fact more difficult and risky than in continental Europe, notwithstanding the common 'Bismarckian' heritage of the two 'families'. Firstly, as mentioned above, they are mixed systems of social protection – universalist in health and occupational in social security. The first sector offers a terrain that is potentially more hospitable to selectivity, at least in the 'targeting out' version (exclusion of benefits or higher co-payments for the more well-to-do classes). The Italian *Servizio Sanitario Nazionale* has already taken many steps in this direction and has become the most targeted among all European national health services (Ferrera, 1995a). In the Iberian countries and Greece, Italian ways have not yet caught on but may do so in the future, as soon as the process of organizational transition from the old to the new system is complete. It must be noted, however, that health targeting in southern Europe is particularly susceptible to two types of perverse effect, given the persisting contributory nature of financing (and the high rates of evasion, as explained below). The first perverse effect is of a distributive type, in which the same 'exclusive' thresholds of income are applied to categories of contributors that are subject to different rates. The second perverse effect is of a socio-political type: the persistence of contributory finance continues to feed the perception that health services are a 'return' on contributions paid. Thus, exclusive selectivity risks producing perceptions of iniquity and resentment on the part of the excluded classes that can be mobilized in an anti-universal direction, especially when standards of services are declining, at least on a non-clinical level (Ferrera, 1995; 1996a).

In the corporatist, work-related sector of income maintenance, selectivity tends to encounter analogous obstacles to those in the third continental Europe, for example the insurance ethos, the dilemmas of horizontal solidarity and the hostility of unions. However, the framework becomes complicated by the high 'polarized' character of protection levels. On the one hand, the generosity of many benefits (especially pensions) which are obviously disproportionate to individual and category contributions has brought about pressures for both a restrictive reduction of formulae (see the recent reforms in Portugal, Greece and Italy) (CEC 1995), and a selective revision of many situations of privilege. In Italy, thresholds of income were introduced for minimum, invalid and recently, survivors pensions. In both Italy and Greece, a limit to benefit accumulation (such as multiple pensions) was introduced. In short, the 'over-protection' enjoyed by certain categories within the social security system, legitimizes policies that prune back benefits, and smooths the way for selectivity, despite the insurance legacy.

A second 'window of opportunity' for the introduction of targeting is created by the considerable gaps in the income support net. They have brought about pressures for the modernization of public means-tested assistance through the establishment of minimum income guarantee schemes. There has also been strong encouragement in this direction from Community institutions. Furthermore, insofar as it represents a completion of welfare state development, the introduction of 'inclusive' selectivity is judged in positive terms, as a step towards alignment with the more progressive European welfare states. It should be noted, however, that the 'institutional windows' for selectivity in southern Europe are difficult to open (notwithstanding their promises in equity terms) because of the still highly 'maximalist' culture of welfare that permeates the unions, which are still important actors in social policy formation.

The most marked challenge that the southern European configuration poses for the adoption of selectivity, however, is linked to what we called earlier its low degree of 'stateness': a low administrative capacity and a state apparatus easily manipulated by particular groups. Latin welfare states lack one of the essential prerequisites of every targeting policy, that is, the possibility of verifying, through standardized and impartial procedures, the effective needs of claimants/ beneficiaries. Of particular relevance in this respect are the deficiencies of southern European tax systems which are inefficient in controlling evasion and verifying incomes. Because of these deficiencies, targeting risks causing perverse outcomes, favouring contributors that are not needy but fraudulent in their tax declarations, and penalizing contributors that are needy and honest. Beyond certain thresholds (which have already been overtaken in the Italian case), such perverse policy outcomes tend to provoke resentment in large areas of public opinion. In tandem with the phenomenon of 'clientelistic use' of many benefits (for example invalidity pensions in Italy, subsidies for agricultural employment in Spain), the iniquities of the various systems of exemption on the basis of (verified) income, erode the overall legitimacy of the welfare state and can lead to real syndromes of welfare backlash. In short (and in conclusion), however relatively viable on a politico-institutional level, in Southern Europe selectivity risks bringing about more problems and contradictions than it promises to resolve in terms of social equity and the overall legitimacy of the welfare state.

## CONCLUSION

Pushed forward by the dynamics of European integration, not to mention a complex web of endogenous and exogenous challenges, European social protection systems have started a process of gradual institutional transformation inspired by largely similar principles and criteria. This process could potentially lead to a gradual qualitative convergence among the various systems. The existence of a large and active international epistemic community, as well as the activism of European Community institutions, are two factors that favour this tendency. However, convergence is confronted by strong checks in the different institutional configurations of the 'European social model'. These configurations 'filter' common socioeconomic challenges. They model perceptions, interests and thus the strategies of actors. They define the constraints and opportunities of institutional change. Ignoring the role of these configurations can lead to misleading generalizations not only on a descriptive level, but also on a prescriptive level. As we have tried to reveal in relation to targeting, the four social Europes react differently to the stimuli coming from the same 'idea'. Policy diagnoses and recommendations characterized by institutional blindness risk producing misleading interpretations and undesired perverse effects.

Is European welfare thus destined to remain fractured into different models of solidarity, the prisoners of their past and their various institutional logics? To a certain degree, the answer is yes, at least for some time to come. Among the many European policy spaces, 'social Europe' is still strongly under-institutionalized and the rhetoric of subsidiarity militates in favour of national social specificities. As mentioned above, the process of integration has begun slowly to erode the status quo. But the definition of a new social contract on a continental scale, of a true welfare state on a community level, is a slow and uneven process. As was already the case in historical processes of state-building at the national level, within the European Union too, social solidarity will be difficult to institutionalize – and much more difficult than achieving the single market or even a single currency.

## NOTES

* Translated by Claire M. O'Neill
1 Council Recommendation 92/442/EEC of 27.7.92.
2 To this end, a series of 'Observatories' were established on family policy, policies for the old, policies against social exclusion and occupational pensions policies. For an illustration of the work done by the various Observatories, see Commaille and Thozet-Teirlinck (1995).
3 A debate is in progress on the opportunity for and the substance of these interventions See CEC (1994).
4 An 'epistemic community' is a network of experts that shares the same nucleus of knowledge, similar normative orientations and that is actively involved in the promotion of certain solutions to certain problems in the conviction that they contribute to increased collective welfare. See Haas (1992).
5 For a discussion of the dynamics of convergence of social spending in European countries, see CEC (1993; 1995) and Kosonen (1994).
6 According to this criterion, benefits are linked to past contributions on the basis of pre-determined coefficients instead of pensionable earnings (Cf. CEC, 1995).
7 For a review, see Ferrera (1993).
8 Naturally, there are other relevent dimensions of variation among European welfare states. However the four indicated seem to the more significant for our discussion.
9 On this point, see Gough (1995).
10 On the Dutch case and its mixed character, see Ferrera (1993). For a more in-depth discussion of the Swiss case, see Rossi and Sartoris (1995).
11 In Germany and Austria, there is also a minimum threshold of earnings for compulsory insurance providing income maintenance benefits.

12    On this point, see the discussion in Ferrera (1996b).
13    For a reconstruction of this process, see again Ferrera (1993 and 1995).
14    For a discussion of the various meanings of selectivity and targeting, see Gough (1995).
15    We use this expression in Baldwin's sense (1992), to indicate those authors that have explored the characteristics of the 'social-democratic model' of social policy, explaining its genesis primarily in terms of class struggle and social-democratic hegemony, and consider the Scandinavian model, resting on institutionalized universalism, as the highest stage of the welfare state's evolution.
16    For a review of the debate on the implications of targeting, see Mitchell *et al.* (1994).
17    The objection does not hold for Gough (1995), who emphasizes the historical and institutional sequences that led to different 'regimes' of public assistance.
18    Scandinavian fiscal systems subject all cash benefits to income taxes. Thus, they selectively claw back a part of what they distribute in the form of benefits.
19    Another factor that impedes selectivity in Scandinavian countries is the high public sensitivity to risks of 'gender' discrimination. Targeting tends, in fact, to penalize female workers in particular.
20    In the sense that benefit formulae have little actuarial substance and tend to be more generous than they would under a stringent application of insurance criteria.

## REFERENCES

Baldwin, P. (1992) *The Politics of Social Solidarity*, Cambridge: CUP.
Bonoli, G. and B. Palier (1995) 'Entre Bismarck et Beveridge', *Revue Française de Science Politique*, 45, 4, pp. 669–99.
Commaille, J. and Thozet-Teirlink, M. (1995) *The European Community and the Social Sphere. The State of Knowledge and its Application*, Brussels: Commission of the European Communities (CEC).
CEC (1993) *Social Protection in Europe*, Brussels.
CEC (1994) *Options for Europe, Green Paper on Social Policy*, Brussels.
CEC (1995) *Social Protection in Europe*, Brussels.
Esping-Andersen, G. (1995) 'Welfare States Without Work', paper presented to the conference on *Comparative Research on Welfare State Reforms*, ISA RC19, University of Pavia, 14–17 September, 1995.
Ferrera, M. (1993) *Modelli di solidarietà, Politica e riforme sociali nelle democrazie*, Bologna: Il Mulino.
Ferrera, M. (1995) 'The Rise and Fall of Democratic Universalism', *Journal of Health Politics, Policy and Law*, 2, pp. 275–302.
Ferrera, M. (1996a) 'The Partitocracy of Healthcare: Towards a New Welfare Politics in Italy?', *Res Publica*, 38, 2, pp. 447–60.
Ferrera, M. (1996b) 'The "Southern Model" of Welfare in Social Europe', *Journal of European Social Policy*, 6, 1, pp. 17–37.

Gough, I. (1995) 'Diverse Systems, Common Destination? Social Assistance in Comparative Perspective', paper presented at the conference on *Comparative Research on Welfare State Reforms*, ISA RC19, University of Pavia, 14–17 September.

Haas, P. (ed.) (1992) 'Special Issue on Epistemic Communities', *International Organization*, 46, Winter.

Heclo, H. (1974) *Modern Social Politics in Britain and Sweden*, Yale: YUP.

Kosonen, P. (1994) *European Integration: A Welfare State Perspective*, Helsinki: University of Helsinki Sociology of Law Series no. 8.

Leibfried, S. and P. Pierson (eds.) (1995) *European Social Policy: Between Fragmentation and Integration*, Washington, The Brookings Institute.

Mitchell, D., Harding A. and Gruen, F. (1994) 'Targeting: A Survey', paper presented to the conference on *Social Security: A Time For Redefinition?*, ISSA, Vienna, 9–11 November.

Rose, R. (1991) 'What is Lesson-Drawing?', *Journal of Public Policy*, 11, 1, pp. 3–30.

Rossi, M. and Sartoris, E. (1995) *Ripensare la solidarietà*, Locarno: Dadò.

Taylor Gooby, P. (1995) 'Squaring the Welfare Circle', paper presented at the conference on *Comparative Research on Welfare State Reforms*, ISA RC19, University of Pavia, 14–17 September.

# 6 The Evolution of Financial Poverty in Western Europe
## Karel Van Den Bosch

## INTRODUCTION[1]

In many countries in Europe there has been talk of 'new poverty'. As the brief review by Room (1990) makes clear, the concept of 'new poverty' is somewhat confused, and is used in rather different ways in various countries. However, one of the constant elements appears to be that it is claimed (or the impression is created) that poverty is on the increase. As causes or indicators of the supposed rise in poverty, reference is often made to high and/or increasing levels of unemployment, growing numbers of people who are dependent on social assistance, and more homeless people on city streets.

However, these indicators of increasing poverty may be misleading. For example, in Belgium unemployment has increased strongly since the end of the 1970s, the number of people who are dependent on social assistance has grown more than five-fold between 1976 and 1992, and the number of persons who are taken care of in centres for the homeless has risen substantially during the last ten years (Vranken and Geldof, 1993, p. 167, p. 188f). Yet, research has shown that financial poverty in Belgium has not increased between 1985 and 1992, and that it has clearly come down in the region of Flanders between 1976 and 1992 (Cantillon *et al.*, 1993).

The reasons for these at first sight counterintuitive trends in poverty rates are diverse and complex. They are related to developments that are less visible, such as a secular improvement in pension benefits and growing labour market participation by married women. Another important reason is that throughout the reforms and cutbacks in social security during the 1980s, it has been a consistent policy of the Belgian government to protect those with the lowest incomes.

In any case, the Belgian example shows that there is no simple relationship between trends in unemployment levels and numbers of persons on social assistance on the one hand, and the poverty rate on the other. The impact of, for example, growing unemployment on poverty levels may be dampened or compensated by other, less visible developments. In order to determine trends in financial poverty there is no alternative to looking at direct evidence, derived from micro-data on the incomes or expenditures of households or families.

The aim of this chapter is to investigate trends in financial poverty in a number of European countries. The questions that will be addressed are:

- Have overall levels of poverty increased, decreased or remained stable?
- Has the incidence of poverty shifted from certain demographic groups to others?
- How has the social income transfer system coped in its task of protecting people from poverty?

The analysis is inevitably somewhat superficial; it is not possible to analyse the underlying causes of developments, or to discuss changes in social policy in particular countries. The chapter merely sets the stage for possible further research.

Answers to the questions asked will be sought by analysing the Luxembourg Income Study (LIS) database. LIS brings together data from a large number of household income surveys, which can be analysed through remote access (cf. Smeeding *et al.*, 1990). In addition, I will use published results, in particular from De Vos and Zaidi (1993a–c, 1994a–d), and from a number of national studies.

In concentrating upon financial poverty, I do not want to imply that it exhausts the concept of social exclusion. Financial poverty is only one aspect of the much wider concept of social exclusion. Nevertheless, in highly monetarized, free-market societies such as those of Western Europe, having sufficient income is an important condition for social participation. The consequences of not having enough money are diverse and often subtle, but they make themselves felt throughout life. They include less contacts with friends and relatives because of lack of transport, health problems due to food of lesser quality or substandard housing, and also the constant mental stress of not being able to make ends meet.

Also, ensuring a minimum level of income for everyone is certainly not the only goal of social policy in general, or even of social security income transfers in particular. But it is of sufficient importance to merit an investigation of its own.

Another important characteristic of the approach taken in this chapter is that the focus is on trends in poverty rates within individual countries, and not on the level of the EU as a whole. Because of the very different social and economic conditions pertaining in the countries of the EU, estimates of Union-wide poverty rates have little meaning and relevance, in my opinion. But the main reason for the approach taken here is that public policy concerning poverty and income distribution is still overwhelmingly a national responsibility. Although developments in the world economy, as well as continuing European integration, have forced a certain degree of convergence on national policies, it is still surely true that the social security systems of Western European countries differ greatly, as regards basic principles as well as on the level of the rules that govern actual transfers. Also, while a number of parallel tendencies can perhaps be identified (for example, a greater reliance on means-tested benefits), the policies followed by the various governments during the last two decades have differed in important ways (cf. Mishra, 1990, p. 96, who concludes that 'significant policy differences exist' between different countries and Mangen, 1991). In the context of this paper, it is impossible to do justice to this subject, which merits a (large) study in its own right. To give only one example: while the level of the minimum income guarantee has been reduced in the UK and The Netherlands during the 1980s, France introduced a minimum income scheme in 1988, and in Belgium the real value of minimum social assistance benefits was increased during a time when other benefits and wages were frozen. Therefore, the nation-state seems the appropriate level on which to study trends in financial poverty.

## PREVIOUS STUDIES

Previous research on the evolution of poverty in Europe is relatively scarce, and, unfortunately, inconclusive and even somewhat confusing in its results. The first such study was by O'Higgins and Jenkins (1990). They defined poverty as having an equivalent income below 50 per cent of the country's average. They concluded that the number of poor in the 12 EC-nations of that time rose slightly from about 39 million around 1975 to about 40 million around 1980, but then jumped to around 44 million in 1985. Between 1980 and 1985, poverty appeared to have risen in five countries: Denmark, Germany, Ireland, Italy and the UK. In the other seven countries the poverty rate seemed to have remained stable.

The Eurostat (1990) study, 'Poverty in Figures', however, reports that, using relative country-specific poverty lines, the total number of poor in the same group of countries (excepting Luxembourg) increased only marginally from 49 million in 1985 to 50 million in 1985 (p. 63). The poverty rates had risen in Ireland, Italy, the Netherlands and the UK, but had dropped in Belgium, Greece, Spain and France, while remaining at about the same level in Denmark, Germany and Portugal.

The main reason for these apparent discrepancies seems to be that in order to obtain their 1985 figures, O'Higgins and Jenkins (1990) relied for six countries on extrapolations from earlier years, made on the basis of reports by national consultants. Several of these extrapolations resulted in stable poverty rates for countries where Eurostat reports a decrease. The Eurostat study itself uses extrapolations for four countries. Furthermore, in some countries (Belgium and The Netherlands) different databases were used, or different methods: while Eurostat used expenditure as the measure of economic resources for all countries, O'Higgins and Jenkins used income wherever possible. However, even where there are no apparent differences in data or methods used, results from different studies often diverge substantially from each other. One reason for this may be that the figures published by O'Higgins and Jenkins as well as those reported by Eurostat were not directly derived from micro-data. O'Higgins and Jenkins relied on national consultants, who used a variety of methods, but in many cases seem to have worked on the basis of published tables. All Eurostat results were derived from an analysis of secondary data provided by national statistical institutes. In view of these problems, only results derived directly from micro-data will be presented in this study.

## METHODS

Poverty measurement involves choices on a number of more or less technical issues. Here I do not want to attempt a full discussion of these matters. (The interested reader is referred to Ruggles, 1990 or Gustafsson, 1995, for an extensive discussion.) I will merely indicate the choices made, and the main reasons for making them.

In this study, disposable household income will be used as the preferred measure of economic resources to assess poverty status. This choice may seem fairly obvious as income is a good index of a household's command over market goods and services. Nevertheless, Eurostat (1990) and a number of other studies, including De Vos and Zaidi (1993a–c, 1994a–d), whose results will be used extensively below, have opted for household expenditure. The main reason is a practical one: in the Household Budget Surveys which these studies use, income does not seem to be measured well and is seriously underreported in number of countries (Hagenaars *et al.*, 1992, p. 5).

Poverty is assumed to be a household phenomenon; the assumption is that the members of a household share resources in such a way that either all, or none are poor. While there is clear evidence of unequal divisions of power and income within some households and families (Jenkins, 1991), it is extremely difficult to measure within-household distributions. However, even though the household is the preferred level of poverty analysis, not all data sources allow this. In a number of surveys, families or tax-units are the unit of measurement. Moreover, definitions of what constitutes a family differ. For example in Sweden, persons of 18 years or older living with their parents are regarded as separate families. In these cases, there is no choice but to use the unit imposed by the database. For the determination of trends in poverty it is obviously important that the unit of measurement remains the same over the years. This will usually be the case when the same kind of survey is used for all years in any single country. Even though poverty status assessment is carried out on the level of the household or the family, the number of poor will be counted in terms of persons.

A range of methods to identify poverty lines can be found in the literature (see Callan and Nolan, 1991, and Van den Bosch, 1993a, for reviews.) However, in the present context, only one approach is feasible: the relative one, where the poverty line is set at a certain percentage of mean or median equivalent income. The particular percentage is largely arbitrary, but 50 per cent (of the mean) appears to be a popular one, and will also be used here.

The choice of an equivalence scale is, in effect, almost equally arbitrary. As shown by the reviews of Whiteford (1985) and Buhmann *et al.* (1988), *inter alia*, the range of scales used or presented in the literature is very large. In O'Higgins and Jenkins (1990) and Eurostat (1990), the scale recommended by the OECD (1982) has been used, which assigns a factor of 1.0 to the first adult in a household, 0.7 to each additional adult, and 0.5 to each child. (The equivalence scale value for the household is found by summing the individual factors. The equivalent income of a household is calculated by dividing disposable income by the equivalence scale value.) Compared with almost all other equivalence scales, the OECD-scale is very steep (Buhmann *et al.*, 1988), that is the assumed needs of households increase very strongly with the number of household members. Several authors have questioned its appropriateness for opulent western countries (Haveman, 1990, Deleeck *et al.*, 1992, Van den Bosch, 1993b). Consequently, following Hagenaars *et al.* (1992) and De Vos and Zaidi (1994), I will use a 'modified' OECD-scale with factors 1.0 for the first adult, 0.5 for each additional adult, and 0.3 for each person aged less than 18. This scale is situated at about the middle between flat and steep scales.

The use of country-specific poverty lines implies that poverty is regarded as a country-specific phenomenon. This choice seems defensible in a study where the focus is on trends in poverty rates within individual countries. If the aim was to compare poverty rates across countries, or to determine the evolution of poverty in the EU as a whole, a good argument could be made that a Union-wide poverty line should be used, as was done in Eurostat (1990). In the present study, such a Union-wide approach would make little sense: it produces country-wide poverty rates of up to 70 per cent (in Portugal, Eurostat, 1990), which are of no relevance within a national context.

A consequence of using relative poverty lines is that a nation-wide improvement in incomes which leaves the relative positions of households unchanged, has no effect on the poverty rate. As Gustafsson (1995, p. 370) writes, such a procedure, which introduces a 'moving target' is not without its problems. For this reason, I will also present poverty rates based on 'absolute' poverty lines, which are kept at the same real level across years.

A practical problem with the use of the number of people below the poverty line (the so-called head-count) as a measure of the extent of poverty is that it can be rather sensitive to the precise level of the poverty line. In addition to the results from the 50 per cent threshold, I will also present poverty rates derived from poverty lines set at 40 per cent and 60 per cent of average equivalent income. Furthermore, I will use the poverty gap, which is less sensitive to the level of the poverty line, as a measure of the extent of poverty. The poverty gap is defined as the aggregate income shortfall of all poor households with respect to the poverty line.

## COMPARABILITY OF THE LIS DATA SETS

In order to be able to give a reliable picture of trends in poverty, great care is needed to ensure comparability across years. It is not sufficient just to use the same poverty line. It is also necessary to make sure that the surveys from which the data are taken are comparable.

There are 11 Western European countries for which the LIS database contains data for two or more years. They are listed in Table 1 in the Appendix to this chapter. Three conditions were looked at in order to evaluate the comparability of the surveys across years within each country. In the first place, the surveys should be all of the same kind (for instance all budget surveys, or all tax surveys). Secondly, the unit of measurement should remain the same across years. Thirdly, the trend in average household income per head of the population as calculated from LIS data should be roughly equal to the same trend as calculated from national account statistics. The national account statistics, as published by the OECD, do not provide a measure that coincides perfectly with household disposable income, and that is available for all countries. It was judged that the sum of Final Consumption Expenditure and Net Saving probably comes closest. The results of this comparison are presented in Table 6.1 in the Appendix to this chapter.

As a result of this comparison, the Austrian and the Italian data sets in LIS are judged not to be comparable across years, and no results for these countries will be presented below. Germany is represented in LIS by five data sets, derived from three kinds of surveys, which do not seem to be comparable to each other. Since LIS staff recommended not to use the 1989 data sets, only results from the 1978 and 1983 Income and Consumer Survey data sets will be shown here. The Dutch 1991 survey is probably not comparable to the other Dutch surveys. In the following tables, this will be indicated by a space between the Netherlands 1987 and 1991 rows. The same remark applies to the UK 1974 data sets. Within the other countries, all data sets shown in Table 1 are regarded as comparable.

De Vos and Zaidi (1993b, 1994c–d) estimated trends in poverty, using Household Budget Survey data, for three countries which are not (yet) represented in LIS, viz. Greece, Portugal and Spain. These will be presented, where possible, along with the other results. Because income is underreported in several of the Household Budget Surveys, De Vos and Zaidi (1994a, pp. 2–8) prefer expenditure to income as the measure of economic resources to assess poverty status. A comparison of the trends in average expenditure per capita according to the surveys with those according to national account statistics shows that there are no apparent problems of comparability across years, except possibly for Spain.


## TRENDS IN THE OVERALL EXTENT OF POVERTY, AND ITS DISTRIBUTION ACROSS DEMOGRAPHIC GROUPS

In this section, I will discuss trends in the overall poverty rates and poverty gaps in the several countries (Table 6.2 in the Appendix). I will look at relative as well as 'absolute' poverty. In the first case, the poverty line is set at the same percentage of average equivalent income in each year. The trend in 'absolute' poverty is measured by translating the relative poverty line in a reference year to the other years, using the consumer price index, thus keeping the poverty line constant in terms of purchasing power. Poverty rates are given in terms of individuals. In addition to poverty rates, the aggregate poverty gap as a percentage of aggregate disposable income (as estimated from survey data) is shown, where available.

At the same time, I will discuss the extent of poverty for three demographic groups: children (that is persons below 18 years), elderly persons (that is adults aged 65 or over) and non-elderly adults, as shown in Table 6.3 in the Appendix. Unfortunately, in some LIS data sets it was not possible to distinguish between elderly and non-elderly persons on the individual level. In these cases, the elderly are defined as individuals living in a household where the head is 65 or over. In order to retain comparability of results across years, this definition was also used for all other surveys for the same country. This change of the definition of elderly persons only had a minor effect on measured poverty rates and poverty gaps.

In Belgium, the extent of relative poverty appears to have remained stable – at a comparatively low level – in the period 1985 to 1992 (cf. Cantillon *et al.*, 1993). Furthermore, no important changes in the distribution of poverty across broad demographic groups appear to have occurred. When the poverty line is kept at its 1985 level in terms of purchasing power, the extent of poverty falls by about one third.

In Denmark, important changes appear to have occurred. Poverty rates fell considerably at the 50 per cent and 60 per cent thresholds, but much less at the 40 per cent line. It appears that poverty has fallen in particular (by about three-quarters) for the elderly. Further analysis has shown that this is a result of a large number of elderly persons being just below the poverty line in 1987, and being just above it in 1992. Since, in real terms, average equivalent income hardly changed between 1987 and 1992, the 'absolute' poverty rates behave in much the same way as the relative ones.

In Finland, relative poverty has increased somewhat between 1987 and 1991. Poverty has gone up particularly among the elderly. This finding contrasts with that of Ritakallio (1994) who reports that relative poverty has gone down in Finland in the period 1985 to 1990. Finland experienced a sharp economic downturn in 1991, which may explain the difference. If my findings are correct, they would constitute a break in the trend of decreasing relative poverty in Finland between 1966 and 1985 (Gustafsson and Uusitalo, 1990). When the poverty line is kept at its 1987 level, the extent of poverty diminishes in Finland in the period studied.

In France, the results from tax surveys indicate a decline in relative poverty between 1979 and 1984. The decrease is even larger when the poverty line is kept at the same real level. The decline in the overall poverty rate is mainly due to a large reduction in the incidence of poverty among the elderly; among non-elderly persons the poverty rate remains stable. For the subsequent period 1984/85 to 1989, De Vos and Zaidi (1994b) report an increase in relative poverty rates. Poverty has increased in particular among children, and also among non-elderly adults. When a constant poverty line is used, overall poverty rates remain virtually stable. For reasons given above, the LIS results are not comparable with those of De Vos and Zaidi.

For Germany during the period 1978 to 1983, the LIS data sets produce stable relative poverty rates. The poverty rate has increased somewhat among children, and fallen for other persons, though the changes are modest. When the poverty line is kept at the same real value, German poverty rates would appear to have fallen during the period 1978 to 1983. By contrast, Becker (1995), using data from the same surveys but a slightly different income concept, reports a clear increase in the number of persons below half of average equivalent income: from 6.4 per cent to 8.7 per cent. After 1983, however, the number of persons below half of average equivalent income appears to have stabilized.

For Greece, De Vos and Zaidi (1994c) report that relative poverty has increased slightly between 1982 and 1988. This rise is located solely among the elderly. 'Absolute' poverty has gone up a little more.

In Ireland, the number of persons in relative poverty has increased considerably, both in the period 1973 to 1980, as well as between 1980 and 1987 (Callan *et al.*, 1989). Table 3 reveals that there has been a dramatic change in the demographic composition of the poor: poverty among the elderly has fallen by more than two-thirds, while poverty among children has almost doubled.

The findings for the Netherlands are somewhat confusing. Between 1983 and 1987, poverty appears to have declined somewhat. (This statement is equally true for relative and 'absolute' poverty.) This result is mainly due to the apparent virtual eradication of poverty among the elderly in 1987 – consider the poverty gap in particular. There is no evident reason why such a large decline should have occurred, and it may well be a data artefact. The 1991 survey may well be more representative for the population than the 1983 and 1987 surveys, but it is almost certainly not comparable with the latter. The SCP (1994, p. 205) reports that the number of poor households doubled between 1979 and 1983, from 4 per cent to 8 per cent. After 1983, it stabilized to 7 per cent, as measured in 1987 and 1991. The SCP uses a political poverty line, which is equal to the level of the minimum guaranteed income in social assistance. In the period of 1983 to 1991, this level has declined in real terms in some years, and it certainly has fallen behind the so-called modal income.

In Norway, the extent of relative poverty appears to have been fairly stable in the period 1979 to 1991. At the 50 per cent line, there is a peculiar jump in the poverty rate in 1986. As this jump is not replicated at the other lines, nor is reflected in the poverty gaps, it is probably due to a data quirk. The same quirk (if it is one) appears in the poverty rate for the elderly in 1986; the trend in the poverty gap among the elderly is always downward. No changes in relative poverty of any importance are measured for children and non-elderly adults. Since Norwegians appear to have enjoyed a considerable general improvement in living standards, 'absolute' poverty has been more than halved in the period from 1979 to 1991.

For Portugal, De Vos and Zaidi (1994d) report a modest decline in relative poverty rates between 1980 and 1989. The decline appears to be greatest among children. When the poverty line is kept at a constant real value, poverty rates have come down by more than a third. De Vos and Zaidi's (1993b) results also indicate a small decline in relative as well as 'absolute' poverty in Spain between 1980 and 1988. Table 6.3 in the Appendix shows that poverty seems to have come down considerably among the elderly, but to have remained stable among the non-elderly. The 1988 survey is, however, probably not quite comparable to the 1980 one.

In Sweden, the general picture that emerges is that the extent of relative poverty was more or less stable between 1975 and 1981, then increased in the period up to 1987 (though from a rather low level) and stabilized again between 1987 and 1991. The small decline in measured poverty in the first period is due to an apparently virtual elimination of poverty among the elderly in 1981, and it is unclear whether this is realistic. Over the period 1975–1991 as a whole, it seems nevertheless that relative poverty has declined among the elderly, while it has increased for non-elderly adults, and perhaps also for children. When the poverty line is kept at the same real value across years, there is an almost continual decrease in poverty rates, though the pace of decline was somewhat slower between 1987 and 1991 than in the other periods. Gustafsson and Uusitalo (1990, p. 258), using a 'political administrative' poverty line, which is based on guidelines for the level of social assistance, report a somewhat different trend in poverty rates in Sweden between 1967 and 1985. 'Poverty declined very rapidly until 1975, and continued to decline although with a somewhat slower pace until 1980, when it was at its lowest level. [...] In the beginning of the 1980s, poverty rates increased, except for 1985, when there was a decrease.'

For the UK, I present figures about trends in poverty from three sources: LIS, De Vos and Zaidi (1993c) and Goodman and Webb (1994). All of them use Family Expenditure Survey data. Fortunately, the three sources are in broad agreement with each other. During the 1970s, there was a modest decline in poverty. In the early 1980s, there was an increase in poverty rates, which accelerated in the second half of the decade. As a result, in 1991 the poverty rate was more than three times what it was in 1978. An important reason for this steep rise in relative poverty was that those at the very top experienced 'meteoric rises' in income, while the incomes of those at the very bottom were rising only slowly (Goodman and Webb, 1994, p. 25). When the poverty line is kept at the same level in terms of purchasing power, we indeed observe downward, rather than upward, trends in poverty rates. However, by 1991 even the absolute poverty rate seems to have increased; in that year 20 per cent more persons were below half of 1979 average income than in 1979 itself (Hills, 1995, p. 32). The trends in relative poverty have not been the same for all demographic groups. During the 1970s, and even in the beginning of the 1980s, there was a strong decline in the poverty rate among the elderly (in 1982 it was only a third of what it was in 1973), while poverty remained stable, or even rose a little, among children and non-elderly adults. In 1988, however, the poverty rate for the elderly rose quickly back to its 1973 level, and it has continued to rise after that year. At the same time, poverty among the non-elderly has nearly tripled.

Overall, then, there are two countries where relative poverty rates have sharply increased: Ireland 1973–1987, and the UK, 1982–1991. In a number of countries, modest increases in poverty were measured: Finland 1987–1991, France 1984/85–1989 (after a decline in poverty between 1979 and 1984), Greece 1982–1988 and Sweden 1981–1992. In Denmark 1987–1992, Portugal 1980–1989 and perhaps in Spain, 1986–1988, poverty appears to have declined, though not by very much. Stable poverty rates were found for Belgium. Results for Germany and The Netherlands were inconclusive.

When an 'absolute' approach is taken, where the poverty line is set at a constant level in terms of purchasing power, the results are rather different. Poverty rates increase in only one country, Greece 1982–1988. Sharp falls in 'absolute' poverty are found in a number of countries: Belgium 1985–1992, France 1979–1984, Norway 1979–1986, Portugal 1980–1989 and Sweden 1975–1992.

The trends were not the same for all demographic groups. In some countries, relative poverty among the elderly fell sharply. This was the case in Denmark 1987–1992, France 1979–1984 and Ireland 1973–1987. Smaller declines in poverty were measured in Germany 1978–1983, Norway 1979–1991, Sweden 1975–1992 and perhaps in Spain 1980–1988. Poverty among the elderly also fell in the UK during the 1970s and the early 1980s, but these gains were reversed in the last half of the decade and the early 1990s. Apart from the UK, increases in poverty among the elderly were measured only in Greece 1982–1988 and Finland 1987–1991.

By contrast, relative poverty among children appears to have declined in only one country, viz. Portugal 1980–1989. Increases in the proportion of children in poverty were found in several countries: France 1979–1989, Ireland 1973–1987, the UK 1979–1991, and perhaps in Germany 1978–1988. The upturn in the poverty rate for children was particularly sharp in the UK. In the other countries, the extent of relative poverty among children appeared to be stable, or the results were inconclusive.

For non-elderly adults, there is only one country where there is a clear and strong trend in the poverty rate: the UK, where it has steadily increased since the end of the seventies. Smaller rises are measured in France 1984/85–1989, Ireland 1973–1987 and Sweden 1975–1992. In the other countries, only insignificant changes were measured.


## THE IMPACT OF SOCIAL SECURITY TRANSFERS ON THE EXTENT OF POVERTY

In this section, I will look at the impact of social security transfers (including social assistance) on income poverty. Specifically, I will consider whether social security transfers have succeeded in dampening possible poverty enhancing effects of increasing unemployment and other economic and social developments, or whether, conversely, rising poverty rates are the result of a reduction in the effectiveness of social security transfers as regards minimum income protection. For this analysis, only results from LIS are available.

The impact of social security transfers on the extent of poverty is measured by comparing poverty rates and poverty gaps before and after transfers are granted. That is, every household's poverty status is evaluated on the basis of disposable income (after transfers) and on the basis of disposable income minus income transfers (before transfers). This method has been applied earlier by Deleeck *et al.* (1992) and Hausman (1993). It differs from the most common procedure of measuring the impact of income transfers on income inequality and poverty, where the distribution of gross income (market income plus transfers before taxes and social security contributions are paid) is compared with the distribution of net disposable income (Mitchell, 1991). One reason for not adopting the latter method is that gross income is an administrative concept rather than an economic one. The level of gross income depends to a considerable degree on the division of social security contributions between employees and employers. Employees' contributions are part of gross income, while those of employers are not, but a good argument can be made that in an economic sense both are in fact borne by employees. Consequently, cross-country comparisons of the redistributional impact of social security transfers where gross income is used as the baseline may be quite misleading. The same can be true for comparisons across time within a single country if contribution rules have changed. A practical advantage of the method used here is that it can also be applied when the variable gross income is not available, as is the case in a number of LIS surveys. A possible disadvantage of this method is that it may overestimate the impact of transfers on poverty when the latter are measured gross of taxes and social security contributions. An implication of the approach is, obviously, that we look only at the impact of social security benefits, not at that of social security contributions or taxes.

The results are shown in Table 6.4 in the Appendix. Overall, the conclusion must be that for the countries and the periods studied, there is no evidence that the impact of social security on the extent of poverty has diminished. On the contrary, in all countries, except Finland, the trend in the proportion of the pre-transfer poverty gap that is filled by social security transfers is upward, rather than downward. In some countries, viz. Denmark 1987–1992, France 1979–1984 and the UK 1974–1986, large reductions in the poverty rate among the elderly can be attributed to an improved performance by social transfers. (The reverse trend occurs in Finland.) In a number of countries (Denmark 1987–1992, France 1979–1984, Norway 1979–1991, Sweden 1975–1992 and even the UK 1974–1986) increases in pre-transfer poverty among children and/or non-elderly adults have been compensated or considerably dampened by social security transfers. There is no country where the proportional reduction in the poverty gap among children due to social transfers has become smaller, and only one (Finland) where the impact of social transfers on the poverty gap among non-elderly adults has declined. Social security transfers appear to be as important in fighting or preventing poverty as ever. In this context, it is worth pointing out that the figures also show that without social security transfers, the extent of poverty, even among the non-elderly, would be much larger than it actually is.

## CONCLUSION

In this paper I have investigated trends in financial poverty and the impact of social security transfers in a number of European countries. Data were used from the Luxembourg Income Study (LIS) database, as well as a number of published results, in particular from De Vos and Zaidi (1993a–c, 1994a–d), and from some national studies. A relative poverty definition has been used, where persons in households with incomes below half of average equivalent income are regarded as poor, although I have also looked at trends in 'absolute' poverty. The main findings are as follows.

Sharply rising trends in poverty were found in two countries (Ireland and the UK), while modest increases in poverty were measured in a number of other countries, including Germany, France and Sweden. In several countries, poverty has remained stable, or has declined. When an 'absolute' approach is taken, where the poverty line is set at a constant level in terms of purchasing power, poverty rates increase in only one country (Greece), while sharp falls in 'absolute' poverty are found in several countries. This conclusion is in accord with a recent OECD study, which found that trends in income inequality differ strongly across countries. Some countries (notably the UK) experienced a large increase in income inequality in the 1980s, while others showed only a modest rise or little change (Atkinson *et al.*, 1995, p. 80).

There is evidence of a shift of poverty from the elderly to families with children. In several countries, poverty among the elderly fell considerably, while a decrease in poverty among children was found in only country (Portugal). By contrast, in some countries, poverty among children rose sharply, in particular in the UK.

The study found no evidence that the impact of social security transfers on the extent of poverty has diminished. In some countries large reductions in the poverty rate among the elderly can be attributed to an improved performance by social transfers. Also, in several countries increases in pre-transfer poverty among children and/or non-elderly adults have been compensated or considerably dampened by social security transfers. Social security transfers appear to be as important in fighting or preventing poverty as ever. Thus, in spite of a number of problematic economic, social and demographic developments, the 'old social contract' still appears able to stand its ground in terms of income protection in most western European countries. Whether it will continue to be able to do so in the future, in the face of growing polarization and exclusion in the labour market, is an open question (cf. Rosanvallon, 1995).

NOTES

1    I thank the participants in the conference 'A New Social Contract?' as well as Michael Förster, Richard Hauser, Ive Marx, Veli-Matti Ritakallio and Koen Vleminckx for useful comments on the first version of this paper.

REFERENCES

Atkinson, A., Rainwater, L. and Smeeding, T. (1995) *Income Distribution in OECD Countries, Evidence from the Luxembourg Income Study*, Social Policy Studies 18, Paris: OECD.
Becker, I. (1994) 'Stabilität in die Einkommensverteilung – Ergebnisse für die Bundesrepublik Deutchland bis zur Wiedervereinigung', *Arbeitspapier 6, EVS-Projekt*, Frankfurt a. M.: Johann Wolfgang Goethe-Universität.
Bhumann, B., Rainwater, L., Schmaus, G. and Smeeding, T. (1988) 'Equivalence Scales, Well-Being, Inequality, and Poverty: Sensitivity Estimates across Ten Countries using the Luxembourg Income Study (LIS) Database', *The Review of Income and Wealth*, 34, 2, pp. 115–42.
Callan, T. and Nolan, B. (1991) 'Concepts of Poverty and the Poverty Line', *Journal of Economic Surveys*, 5, 3, pp. 243–61.
Callan, T. *et al.* (1989) *Poverty, Income and Welfare in Ireland*, General Research Series Paper no. 146, Dublin: The Economic and Social Research Institute.
Deleeck, H., Van den Bosch, K. and De Lathouwer, L. (1992) *Poverty and the Adequacy of Social Security in the EC: A Comparative Analysis*, Aldershot: Avebury.
De Vos, K. and Zaidi, M. (1993a) *Research on Poverty Statistics Based on Micro-data: Results for Germany*, Rotterdam and Tilburg: Erasmus University and Economics Institute.
De Vos, K. and Zaidi, M. (1993b) *Trend Analysis of Poverty in Spain (1980–1988)*, Rotterdam and Tilburg: Erasmus University and Economic Institute.
De Vos, K. and Zaidi, M. (1993c) *Trend Analysis of Poverty in Spain (1980–1988)*, Rotterdam and Tilburg: Erasmus University and Economics Institute.
De Vos, K. and Zaidi, M. (1994a) *Objective Monetary Poverty, Study on Trends in the 1980s*, Rotterdam and Tilburg: Erasmus University and Economics Institute.
De Vos, K. and Zaidi, M. (1994b) *Trend Analysis of Poverty in France (1984/85–1989)*, Rotterdam and Tilburg: Erasmus University and Economics Institute.
De Vos, K. and Zaidi, M. (1994c) *Trend Analysis of Poverty in Greece (1982–1988)*, Rotterdam and Tilburg: Erasmus University and Economics Institute.
De Vos, K. and Zaidi, M. (1994d) *Trend Analysis of Poverty in Portugal (1980–1989)*, Rotterdam and Tilburg: Erasmus University and Economics Institute.
Eurostat (1990) *Poverty in Figures. Europe in the Early 1980s*, Luxembourg: Office for Official Publications of the European Communities.

Goodman, A. and Webb, S. (1994) *For Richer, For Poorer: The Changing Distribution of Income in the United Kingdom, 1961–91*, Commentary no. 42, London: The Institute for Fiscal Studies.

Gustafsson, B. (1995) Assessing Poverty. Some Reflections on the Literature, *Journal of Population Economics*, 8, 4, pp. 361–81.

Gustafsson, B. and Uusitalo, H. (1990) 'The Welfare State and Poverty in Finland and Sweden from the Mid-1960s to the Mid-1980s', *The Review of Income and Wealth*, 36, 3, pp. 249–66.

Hagernaars, A., De Vos, K. and Zaidi, M. (1992) *Statistiques relatives à la pauvreté, basées sur des microdonnées, Resultats pour neuf Etats Membres des Communautés Européennes*, Rotterdam: Erasmus University.

Hauser, R. and Semrau, P. (1989) *Trends in Poverty and Low Income in the Federal Republic of Germany*, Working Paper No. 306.

Hausman, P. (1993) 'The Impact of Social Security in the European Community', in J. Berghman and B. Cantillon (eds) *The European Face of Social Security, Essays in Honour of Herman Deleeck*, Aldershot: Avebury, pp. 109–22.

Haveman, R. (1990) 'Poverty Statistics in the European Community: Assessment and Recommendations', in R. Teekens and B. van Praag (eds.), *Analysing Poverty in the European Community*, Eurostat News Special Edition. Luxembourg: Office for Official Publications of the European Communities, pp. 459–67.

Hills, J. (1995) *Inquiry into Income and Wealth, Volume 2: a summary of the evidence*, York: Joseph Rowntree Foundation.

Jenkins, S. (1991) 'Poverty Measurement and the Within-Household Distribution: Agenda for Action', *The Journal of Social Policy*, 20, 4, pp. 457–83.

Ruggles, P. (1990) *Drawing the Line: Alternative Poverty Measures and their Implications for Public Policy*, Washington D.C.: The Urban Institute Press.

Smeeding, T., Rainwater, L. and O'Higgins, M. (1990) *Poverty, Inequality and the Distribution of Income in an International Context: Initial Research from the Luxembourg Income Study (LIS)*, London: Wheatsheaf.

Sociaal en Cultureel Planbureau (SCP) (1994) *Sociaal en Cultureel Rapport 1994*, Rijswijk: Sociaal en Cultureel Planbureau.

Van den Bosch, K. (1993a) 'Poverty Measures in Comparative Research', in J. Berghman and B. Cantillon (eds.), *The European Face of Social Security, Essays in Honour of Herman Deleeck*, Aldershot: Avebury, pp. 3–23.

Van den Bosch, K., Callan, T., Estivill, J., Hausman, P., Jeandidier, B., Muffels, R. and Yfantopoulos, J. (1993b) 'A Comparison of Poverty in Seven European Countries and Regions using Subjective and Relative Measures', *Journal of Population Economics*, 6, pp. 235–59.

Vranken, J. and Geldof, D. (1993) *Armoede en Sociale Uitsluiting, Jaarboek 1992–1993*, Leuven and Amersfoort: Acco.

Mangen, S. (1991) 'Political Change and the Objectives of the Continental Welfare State', in Th. Wilson and D. Wilson (eds.), *The State and Social Welfare: The Objectives of Policy*, London and New York: Longman, pp. 165–90.

Mishra, R. (1990) *The Welfare State in Capitalist Society: Policies of Retrenchment and Maintenance in Europe, North America and Australia*, New York: Harvester Wheatsheaf.

Mitchell, D. (1991) *Income Transfers in Ten Welfare States*, Aldershot: Avebury.

O'Higgins, M. and Jenkins, S. (1990) 'Poverty in Europe: Estimates for the Numbers in Poverty in 1975, 1980, 1985', in R. Teekens and B. van Praag (eds.), *Analysing Poverty in the European Community*, Erostat News Special Edition. Luxembourg: Office for Official Publications of the European Communities, pp. 187–212.

OECD (1982) *The OECD List of Social Indicators*, Paris: OECD.

Ritakallio, V.-M. (1994) *Finnish Poverty: A Cross-National Comparison*, Working Paper 119, Luxembourg: Luxembourg Income Study.

Room, G. (1990) 'New Poverty' in the European Community, Basingstoke: Macmillan.

Rosanvallon, P. (1995) *La Nouvelle Question Sociale, Repenser l'Etat-providence*, Paris: Editions du Seuil.

Whiteford, P. (1985) *A family's needs: Equivalence Scales, Poverty and Social Security*, Research Paper No. 27, Development Division, Department of Social Security (Australia).

# Appendix A

*Table 6.1* Comparability of the LIS surveys across years within countries

| *Country/Year* | *Name of LIS Survey* | *Unit of Measurement* | *Trend in income per capita* *Nat. accounts* | *LIS* | *Price Index* |
|---|---|---|---|---|---|
| Austria 87 | Austrian Microcensus | Family | 100.0 | 100.0 | 100.0 |
| Austria 91 | Austrian Microcensus | Household | 124.3 | 89.1 | 111.5 |
| Belgium 85 | Panel Survey of the Centre for Social Policy | Household | 100.0 | 100.0 | 100.0 |
| Belgium 88 | Panel Survey of the Centre for Social Policy | Household | 114.6 | 109.5 | 104.1 |
| Belgium 92 | Panel Survey of the Centre for Social Policy | Household | 152.6 | 133.2 | 117.3 |
| Denmark 87 | Income Tax Survey | Household | 100.0 | 100.0 | 100.0 |
| Denmark 92 | Income Tax Survey | Household | 129.1 | 116.1 | 118.1 |
| Finland 87 | Income Distribution Survey | Household | 100.0 | 100.0 | 100.0 |
| Finland 91 | Income Distribution Survey | Household | 131.8 | 142.8 | 124.0 |
| France 79 | Survey of Individual Income Tax Returns | Tax Unit | 58.8 | 54.8 | 59.0 |
| France 84 | Survey of Individual Income Tax Returns | Tax Unit | 100.0 | 100.0 | 100.0 |
| Germany 78 | Income and Consumer Survey | Household | 73.1 | 91.9 | 76.9 |
| Germany 81 | Transfer Income Survey | Household | 89.7 | 91.7 | 89.8 |
| Germany 83 | Income and Consumer Survey | Household | 94.8 | 120.0 | 97.6 |

*Table 6.1*   Continued

| Country/Year | Name of LIS Survey | Unit of Measurement | Nat. accounts | LIS | Price Index |
|---|---|---|---|---|---|
| | | | *Trend in income per capita* | | |
| Germany 84 | German Socio-Economic Panel Study | Household | 100.0 | 100.0 | 100.0 |
| Germany 89 | German Socio-Economic Panel Study | Household | 121.5 | 113.6 | 106.5 |
| Italy 86 | Bank of Italy Income Survey | Household | 100.0 | 100.0 | 100.0 |
| Italy 91 | Bank of Italy Income Survey | Econ. Family | 162.0 | 218.7 | 132.3 |
| Netherlds 83 | Additional Enquiry on the Use of Public Services | Household | – | 100.0 | 100.0 |
| Netherlds 87 | Additional Enquiry on the Use of Public Services | Household | 100.0 | 100.0 | 100.0 |
| Netherlds 91 | Socio-Economic Panel of the Central Bureau of Statistics | Household | 116.9 | 147.2 | 107.9 |
| Norway 79 | Survey of Norwegian Tax Files | Tax Unit | 48.9 | 41.0 | 54.5 |
| Norway 86 | Income and Property Distribution Survey | Household | 100.0 | 100.0 | 100.0 |
| Norway 91 | Income and Property Distribution Survey | Household | 133.5 | 139.3 | 130.6 |
| Sweden 75 | Income Distribution Survey | Unknown | 32.3 | 32.8 | 38.0 |
| Sweden 81 | Income Distribution Survey | Tax Unit | 62.0 | 63.4 | 76.2 |
| Sweden 87 | Income Distribution Survey | Tax Unit | 100.0 | 100.0 | 100.0 |
| Sweden 92 | Income Distribution Survey | Tax Unit | 154.8 | 167.3 | 133.1 |

*Table 6.1*   Continued

| Country/Year | Name of LIS Survey | Unit of Measurement | Trend in income per capita | | Price Index |
| | | | Nat. accounts | LIS | |
| --- | --- | --- | --- | --- | --- |
| UK 74 | Family Expenditure Survey | Unknown | 22.7 | 49.5 | 28.0 |
| UK 79 | Family Expenditure Survey | Family | 52.4 | 53.2 | 57.8 |
| UK 86 | Family Expenditure Survey | Family | 100.0 | 100.0 | 100.0 |

Notes
Nat. accounts: trend in Final Consumption Expenditure plus Net Saving of
Households per head of the population according to National Accounts
LIS: trend in disposable income per head of the population according to LIS
survey
Price Index: Price index of private household consumption
All figures are expressed as a percentage of corresponding amount for the year
which is nearest 1985
Sources: Nat. accounts: Calculated using aggregate amounts from OECD National
Accounts, Table 8, various editions, and population figures from UN
Demographic Yearbook, various editions
DPI (LIS): Calculated from results out of Luxembourg Income Study database
Price Index: OECD Main Economic Indicators, various editions

*Table 6.2*  Trend in poverty in a number of European countries, using relative and 'absolute' poverty lines

| Country/Year | Persons below line at: 40% | 50% of average equivalent income in given year | 60% | Poverty gap (1) | Index line (2) | Persons below line at: 40% | 50% of average equivalent income in reference year* | 60% | Measure of Resources | Source |
|---|---|---|---|---|---|---|---|---|---|---|
| Belgium 85 | 2.2% | 5.8% | 13.8% | 0.7% | 100 | 2.2% | 5.8% | 13.8% | Income | LIS |
| Belgium 88 | 2.3% | 6.2% | 14.4% | 0.7% | 111 | 1.8% | 5.2% | 12.4% | Income | LIS |
| Belgium 92 | 2.1% | 5.5% | 11.8% | 0.6% | 118 | 1.6% | 3.3% | 8.3% | Income | LIS |
| Denmark 87 | 3.8% | 8.9% | 15.9% | 1.5% | 100 | 3.8% | 8.9% | 15.9% | Income | LIS |
| Denmark 92 | 3.3% | 5.5% | 12.0% | 1.1% | 97 | 3.5% | 6.3% | 13.5% | Income | LIS |
| Finland 87 | 2.6% | 5.5% | 11.6% | 0.8% | 100 | 2.6% | 5.5% | 11.6% | Income | LIS |
| Finland 91 | 2.8% | 6.4% | 12.1% | 0.9% | 114 | 1.7% | 3.8% | 7.5% | Income | LIS |
| France 79 | 6.6% | 13.2% | 23.2% | 1.8% | 95 | 7.9% | 16.1% | 26.9% | Income | LIS |
| France 84 | 5.7% | 11.9% | 22.9% | 1.6% | 100 | 5.7% | 11.9% | 22.9% | Income | LIS |
| France 89 | 6.9% | 14.7% | 25.0% | | 109 | 6.0% | 12.7% | 22.5% | Expend. | DV94b |
| Germany 78 | 3.7% | 8.2% | 15.5% | 1.1% | 98 | 2.1% | 4.5% | 8.7% | Income | LIS |
| Germany 83 | 3.1% | 8.0% | 16.2% | 0.9% | 100 | 3.1% | 8.0% | 16.2% | Income | LIS |
| Germany 78 | | 6.4% | | | | | | | Income | Becker |
| Germany 83 | | 8.7% | | | | | | | Income | Becker |
| Germany 88 | | 8.9% | | | | | | | Income | Becker |
| Germany 83 (3) | | 8.3% | | | | | | | Income | Hauser |
| Germany 87 (3) | | 7.7% | | | | | | | Income | Hauser |
| Germany 90 (3) | | 8.8% | | | | | | | Income | Hauser |
| Greece 82 | 9.5% | 17.4% | 27.6% | | 100 | 9.5% | 17.4% | 27.6% | Expend. | DV94c |
| Greece 88 | 10.7% | 17.9% | 26.9% | | 97 | 11.9% | 19.2% | 28.9% | Expend. | DV94c |

Table 6.2 Continued

| Country/Year | Persons below line at: 40% | 50% (of average equivalent income in given year) | 60% | Poverty gap (1) | Index line (2) | Persons below line at: 40% | 50% (of average equivalent income in reference year*) | 60% | Measure of Resources | Source |
|---|---|---|---|---|---|---|---|---|---|---|
| Ireland 73 (4) | 7.5% | 15.9% | 26.4% | | | | | | Income | Callan |
| Ireland 80 (4) | 9.3% | 17.4% | 27.6% | | | | | | Income | Callan |
| Ireland 87 (4) | 10.5% | 21.2% | 32.2% | | | | | | Income | Callan |
| Netherlands 83 | 6.5% | 9.3% | 17.4% | 2.7% | 100 | 6.5% | 9.3% | 17.4% | Income | LIS |
| Netherlands 87 | 4.4% | 8.3% | 15.6% | 1.9% | 100 | 4.5% | 8.4% | 15.8% | Income | LIS |
| Netherlands 91 | 3.7% | 7.7% | 18.1% | 1.5% | 134 | 2.2% | 3.4% | 5.1% | Income | LIS |
| Norway 79 | 2.7% | 4.8% | 13.3% | 0.9% | 81 | 4.7% | 14.8% | 25.8% | Income | LIS |
| Norway 86 | 2.1% | 6.4% | 11.8% | 0.8% | 100 | 2.1% | 6.4% | 11.8% | Income | LIS |
| Norway 91 | 2.1% | 5.3% | 11.2% | 0.8% | 105 | 1.9% | 4.1% | 9.4% | Income | LIS |
| Portugal 80 | 16.1% | 26.4% | 35.8% | | 100 | 16.1% | 26.4% | 35.8% | Expend. | DV94d |
| Portugal 89 | 15.5% | 24.5% | 33.3% | | 123 | 9.2% | 16.0% | 23.5% | Expend. | DV94d |
| Spain 80 | 9.7% | 17.5% | 26.7% | | 100 | 9.7% | 17.5% | 26.7% | Expend. | DV93b |
| Spain 88 | 8.2% | 15.7% | 25.4% | | 97 | 5.6% | 11.8% | 19.8% | Expend. | DV93b |
| Sweden 75 | 2.5% | 5.2% | 11.5% | 0.9% | 90 | 3.5% | 8.6% | 17.0% | Income | LIS |
| Sweden 81 | 2.9% | 4.6% | 8.3% | 0.8% | 86 | 3.9% | 7.7% | 15.4% | Income | LIS |
| Sweden 87 | 3.8% | 6.3% | 10.5% | 1.3% | 100 | 3.8% | 6.3% | 10.5% | Income | LIS |
| Sweden 92 | 3.8% | 6.0% | 10.5% | 1.3% | 126 | 2.7% | 3.7% | 5.4% | Income | LIS |
| UK 74 | 4.5% | 11.4% | 19.6% | 1.2% | 185 | 0.4% | 0.6% | 1.4% | Income | LIS |
| UK 79 | 4.1% | 10.8% | 19.5% | 1.2% | 93 | 5.5% | 13.9% | 22.8% | Income | LIS |
| UK 86 | 5.9% | 13.0% | 23.2% | 2.3% | 100 | 5.9% | 13.0% | 23.2% | Income | LIS |

Table 6.2 Continued

| Country/Year | Persons below line at: 40% 50% 60% of average equivalent income in given year | | | Poverty gap (1) | Index line (2) | Persons below line at: 40% 50% 60% of average equivalent income in reference year* | | | Measure of Resources | Source |
|---|---|---|---|---|---|---|---|---|---|---|
| | 40% | 50% | 60% | | | 40% | 50% | 60% | | |
| UK 85 | 3.7% | 13.2% | 24.7% | | 100 | 3.7% | 13.2% | 24.7% | Income | DV93c |
| UK 88 | 8.8% | 19.0% | 28.1% | | 120 | 3.5% | 10.1% | 18.7% | Income | DV93c |
| UK 78 (5) | 1.8% | 6.8% | 16.4% | | | | | | Income | Goodman |
| UK 82 (5) | 2.5% | 7.8% | 18.2% | | | | | | Income | Goodman |
| UK 85 (5) | 2.7% | 10.7% | 22.9% | | | | | | Income | Goodman |
| UK 88 (5) | 7.4% | 18.3% | 28.1% | | | | | | Income | Goodman |
| UK 91 (5) | 10.6% | 20.4% | 29.7% | | | | | | Income | Goodman |

Notes

*Reference year is year where index line is 100

(1) Aggregate poverty gap using 50% poverty line, as a percentage of aggregate disposable income

(2) Real value of line as a percentage of poverty line in year closest to 1985

(3) These poverty rates for Germany are based on equivalence scale with factors 1.0 for the first adult, 0.8 for other adults and varying from 0.45 for young children to 0.9 for children aged 16 to 21

(4) Results for Ireland are based on equivalence scale with factors 1.0, 0.6, 0.4

(5) These poverty rates for the UK are based on equivalence scale with factors 0.61 for the first adult, around 0.4 for other adults and varying from 0.09 for young children to 0.36 for children aged 16 or over; income is income before housing costs

Sources: LIS: Luxembourg Income Study, Becker (1994), Callan, Nolan et al. (1989), De Vos and Zaidi (1993a, 1993b, 1993c, 1994 b, 1994c, 1994d), Goodman and Webb (1994), Hauser and Semrau (1989)

Table 6.3  Poverty rates and poverty gaps by age, using 50 per cent relative poverty line

| Country/Year | Poverty rates | | | | Poverty gaps | | | | Source |
|---|---|---|---|---|---|---|---|---|---|
| | All persons | Children | Elderly 65+ | Adults –65 | All persons | Children | Elderly 65+ | Adults –65 | |
| Belgium 85 | 5.8% | 4.7% | 11.3% | 5.2% | 0.7% | 0.5% | 1.4% | 0.6% | LIS |
| Belgium 88 | 6.2% | 4.9% | 10.6% | 5.8% | 0.7% | 0.4% | 1.5% | 0.6% | LIS |
| Belgium 92 | 5.5% | 4.9% | 10.6% | 4.7% | 0.6% | 0.4% | 1.4% | 0.5% | LIS |
| Denmark 87 | 8.9% | 4.0% | 25.9% | 6.5% | 1.5% | 0.4% | 2.6% | 1.6% | LIS |
| Denmark 92 | 5.5% | 3.6% | 6.3% | 5.9% | 1.1% | 0.4% | 1.6% | 1.3% | LIS |
| Finland 87 | 5.5% | 3.4% | 10.1% | 5.4% | 0.8% | 0.3% | 1.0% | 0.9% | LIS |
| Finland 91 | 6.4% | 3.1% | 14.4% | 6.0% | 0.9% | 0.3% | 1.4% | 1.1% | LIS |
| France 79* | 13.2% | 12.8% | 16.0% | 12.7% | 1.8% | 1.3% | 2.0% | 2.0% | LIS |
| France 84* | 11.9% | 13.1% | 7.3% | 12.4% | 1.6% | 1.3% | 0.8% | 1.9% | LIS |
| France 84/85 | 12.4% | 12.9% | 24.8% | 10.0% | | | | | DV94 |
| France 89 | 14.7% | 16.6% | 24.3% | 11.9% | | | | | DV94 |
| Germany 78 | 8.2% | 4.9% | 20.9% | 7.2% | 1.1% | 0.4% | 3.3% | 1.1% | LIS |
| Germany 83 | 8.0% | 6.5% | 18.8% | 5.8% | 0.9% | 0.5% | 2.5% | 0.6% | LIS |
| Germany 88 | 10.6% | 11.0% | 19.4% | 7.8% | | | | | DV93a |
| Greece 82 | 17.4% | 15.9% | 33.7% | 14.5% | | | | | DV94 |
| Greece 88 | 17.9% | 15.0% | 37.8% | 14.4% | | | | | DV94 |
| Ireland 73 (1) | 14.8% | 15.7% | 33.8% | 14.4% | | | | | Callan |
| Ireland 80 (1) | 16.2% | 18.5% | 24.4% | 15.2% | | | | | Callan |
| Ireland 87 (1) | 19.8% | 26.0% | 9.7% | 17.3% | | | | | Callan |
| Netherlds 83* | 9.3% | 7.0% | 6.4% | 10.8% | 2.7% | 1.5% | 1.5% | 3.5% | LIS |
| Netherlds 87* | 8.3% | 8.9% | 2.7% | 9.2% | 1.9% | 1.1% | 0.1% | 2.5% | LIS |

Table 6.3  Continued

| Country/Year | Poverty rates | | | | Poverty gaps | | | | Source |
|---|---|---|---|---|---|---|---|---|---|
| | All persons | Children | Elderly 65+ | Adults –65 | All persons | Children | Elderly 65+ | Adults –65 | |
| Netherlds 91* | 7.7% | 9.2% | 7.2% | 7.3% | 1.5% | 1.5% | 1.0% | 1.6% | LIS |
| Norway 79* | 4.8% | 4.4% | 6.7% | 4.6% | 0.9% | 0.5% | 1.7% | 0.9% | LIS |
| Norway 86* | 6.4% | 3.9% | 16.4% | 4.4% | 0.8% | 0.5% | 1.1% | 0.8% | LIS |
| Norway 91* | 5.3% | 3.9% | 9.5% | 4.5% | 0.8% | 0.4% | 0.6% | 1.0% | LIS |
| Portugal 80 | 26.4% | 27.9% | 42.3% | 22.1% | | | | | DV94 |
| Portugal 88 | 24.5% | 22.9% | 42.9% | 20.7% | | | | | DV94 |
| Spain 80 | 17.5% | 16.9% | 32.3% | 15.0% | | | | | DV94 |
| Spain 88 | 15.7% | 16.5% | 24.7% | 13.6% | | | | | DV94 |
| Sweden 75* | 5.2% | 2.1% | 8.6% | 5.5% | 0.9% | 0.2% | 0.6% | 1.3% | LIS |
| Sweden 81* | 4.6% | 4.5% | 0.9% | 5.9% | 0.8% | 0.4% | 0.0% | 1.2% | LIS |
| Sweden 87* | 6.3% | 3.1% | 4.3% | 8.1% | 1.3% | 0.3% | 0.3% | 2.0% | LIS |
| Sweden 92* | 6.0% | 2.6% | 4.9% | 7.6% | 1.3% | 0.3% | 0.5% | 2.0% | LIS |
| UK 74 | 11.4% | 10.8% | 34.4% | 6.8% | 1.2% | 0.9% | 4.2% | 0.8% | LIS |
| UK 79 | 10.8% | 10.7% | 25.9% | 7.2% | 1.2% | 1.1% | 2.0% | 1.1% | LIS |
| UK 86 | 13.0% | 17.4% | 13.3% | 11.0% | 2.3% | 2.4% | 1.2% | 2.5% | LIS |
| UK 85 | 13.2% | 19.2% | 16.7% | 9.9% | | | | | DV93b |
| UK 88 | 19.0% | 22.3% | 36.7% | 13.4% | | | | | DV93b |
| UK 73 (2) | 9.7% | 7.2% | 29.6% | 4.8% | | | | | Goodman |
| UK 78 (2) | 6.8% | 7.6% | 10.6% | 3.9% | | | | | Goodman |
| UK 82 (2) | 7.8% | 9.0% | 8.7% | 5.8% | | | | | Goodman |
| UK 85 (2) | 10.7% | 13.1% | 12.7% | 7.0% | | | | | Goodman |

*Table 6.3* Continued

| Country/Year | Poverty rates | | | | Poverty gaps | | | | Source |
|---|---|---|---|---|---|---|---|---|---|
| | All persons | Children | Elderly 65+ | Adults –65 | All persons | Children | Elderly 65+ | Adults –65 | |
| UK 88 (2) | 18.3% | 19.3% | 31.2% | 11.6% | | | | | Goodman |
| UK 91 (2) | 24.0% | 26.9% | 37.0% | 15.1% | | | | | Goodman |

Notes

*Elderly are defined as persons in households where the head is 65 or over; adults –65 are similarly defined as persons over 16 in households where the head is younger than 65

(1) Results for Ireland are derived using an equivalence scale with factors 1.0, 0.66 and 0.33
   Figures shown for the elderly are poverty percentages for households headed by an elderly person
   Figures shown for adults are for ALL adults, regardless of age

(2) These poverty rates for the UK are based on an equivalence scale with factors 0.61 for the first adult, around 0.4 for other adults and varying from 0.09 for young children to 0.36 for children aged 16 or over; income is income before housing costs
   Figures shown for children are poverty percentages for persons living in households with children
   Figures shown for the elderly are for pensioners; figures shown for adults are for non-pensioners living in households without children

Sources: See Table 6.2

Table 6.4  Impact of social security transfers on poverty rates and poverty gaps, by age of persons, using 50 per cent relative poverty lines

| Country/Year | Poverty rates before and after social transfers | | | | | | | | Reduction in poverty gap due to social transfers | | | |
| | All persons | | Children | | Elderly 65+ | | Adults –65 | | All persons | Children | Elderly 65+ | Adults –65 |
| | before | after | before | after | before | after | before | after | | | | |
|---|---|---|---|---|---|---|---|---|---|---|---|---|
| Belgium 85 | 33.6% | 5.8% | 24.0% | 4.7% | 88.9% | 11.3% | 27.6% | 5.2% | 95.0% | 90.5% | 97.4% | 93.5% |
| Belgium 88 | 35.1% | 6.2% | 24.1% | 4.9% | 86.8% | 10.6% | 28.7% | 5.8% | 95.0% | 91.0% | 97.1% | 93.4% |
| Belgium 92 | 34.5% | 5.5% | 24.4% | 4.9% | 92.0% | 10.6% | 26.7% | 4.7% | 96.4% | 92.6% | 97.9% | 95.3% |
| Denmark 87 | 32.0% | 8.9% | 20.1% | 4.0% | 84.5% | 25.9% | 23.7% | 6.5% | 88.9% | 90.1% | 94.3% | 82.5% |
| Denmark 92 | 36.6% | 5.5% | 27.1% | 3.6% | 83.3% | 6.3% | 28.3% | 5.9% | 93.0% | 94.4% | 96.6% | 89.6% |
| Finland 87 | 21.8% | 5.5% | 17.6% | 3.4% | 56.6% | 10.1% | 16.9% | 5.4% | 85.9% | 86.5% | 95.2% | 77.0% |
| Finland 91 | 23.0% | 6.4% | 20.7% | 3.1% | 50.9% | 14.4% | 18.3% | 6.0% | 84.1% | 90.0% | 92.2% | 76.4% |
| France 79* | 35.9% | 13.2% | 33.3% | 12.8% | 80.8% | 16.0% | 25.1% | 12.7% | 85.0% | 73.4% | 95.8% | 67.4% |
| France 84* | 38.4% | 11.9% | 34.9% | 13.1% | 88.1% | 7.3% | 28.8% | 12.4% | 88.1% | 78.1% | 98.5% | 76.1% |
| Germany 78 | 24.5% | 8.2% | 12.3% | 4.9% | 73.8% | 20.9% | 20.3% | 7.2% | 87.6% | 79.8% | 90.6% | 85.8% |
| Germany 83 | 26.2% | 8.0% | 15.9% | 6.5% | 72.2% | 18.8% | 18.5% | 5.8% | 90.4% | 80.6% | 92.4% | 89.0% |
| Netherlds 83* | 33.5% | 9.3% | 24.0% | 7.0% | 77.3% | 6.4% | 28.8% | 10.8% | 85.2% | 83.7% | 96.9% | 78.8% |
| Netherlds 87* | 34.3% | 8.3% | 26.9% | 8.9% | 77.7% | 2.7% | 28.4% | 9.2% | 90.0% | 87.5% | 99.7% | 85.7% |
| Netherlds 91* | 30.2% | 7.7% | 22.9% | 9.2% | 75.8% | 7.2% | 23.1% | 7.3% | 89.4% | 78.3% | 97.5% | 85.8% |
| Norway 79* | 23.2% | 4.8% | 14.1% | 4.4% | 78.5% | 6.7% | 12.8% | 4.6% | 91.4% | 84.1% | 96.1% | 80.7% |
| Norway 86* | 22.3% | 6.4% | 10.5% | 3.9% | 75.0% | 16.4% | 11.4% | 4.4% | 91.7% | 72.2% | 97.2% | 78.0% |
| Norway 91* | 25.6% | 5.3% | 16.0% | 3.9% | 73.6% | 9.5% | 15.1% | 4.5% | 91.8% | 87.7% | 98.2% | 80.9% |
| Sweden 75* | 30.4% | 5.2% | 15.3% | 2.1% | 93.9% | 8.6% | 18.1% | 5.5% | 93.5% | 91.0% | 99.0% | 80.2% |
| Sweden 81* | 38.6% | 4.6% | 23.8% | 4.5% | 98.2% | 0.9% | 25.3% | 5.9% | 95.7% | 88.9% | 99.9% | 87.5% |
| Sweden 87* | 40.0% | 6.3% | 22.7% | 3.1% | 98.2% | 4.3% | 26.7% | 8.1% | 94.1% | 93.2% | 99.7% | 81.0% |

124

*Table 6.4*  Continued

| Country/Year | Poverty rates before and after social transfers | | | | | | | | Reduction in poverty gap due to social transfers | | | |
| | All persons | | Children | | Elderly 65+ | | Adults –65 | | All persons | Children | Elderly 65+ | Adults –65 |
| | before | after | before | after | before | after | before | after | | | | |
|---|---|---|---|---|---|---|---|---|---|---|---|---|
| Sweden 92* | 43.3% | 6.0% | 29.6% | 2.6% | 97.1% | 4.9% | 31.3% | 7.6% | 94.1% | 95.6% | 99.3% | 85.3% |
| UK 74 | 20.1% | 11.4% | 15.2% | 10.8% | 72.0% | 34.4% | 11.7% | 6.8% | 81.0% | 55.4% | 87.3% | 75.4% |
| UK 79 | 27.5% | 10.8% | 23.4% | 10.7% | 78.5% | 25.9% | 17.4% | 7.2% | 87.8% | 76.8% | 95.0% | 79.9% |
| UK 86 | 37.2% | 13.0% | 37.7% | 17.4% | 76.7% | 13.3% | 27.6% | 11.0% | 83.9% | 77.6% | 96.9% | 75.2% |

Notes
*Elderly are defined as persons in households where the head is 65 or over; adults –65 are similarly defined as persons over 16 in households where the head is younger than 65
Source: LIS, and own calculations

# 7 In Defence Of Welfare: Social Protection and Social Reform in Eastern Europe[1]
## Ulrike Götting

## INTRODUCTION

The people of Central and Eastern Europe have experienced a sizeable deterioration in social welfare since the beginning of the transition. From 1989, open unemployment rapidly increased, poverty spread, and the problem of homelessness became more acute. Other social indicators, such as morbidity levels or mortality rates, generally worsened as well. Everywhere, the social costs of transition turned out to be considerable and much higher than expected. The picture looks rather better in the more advanced transition countries of Central Europe where the decline in employment and income has recently come to a halt. In South Eastern Europe and the Commonwealth of Independent States (CIS), however, social conditions have continued to deteriorate. Unemployment and poverty are still on the rise, and the public service infrastructure is weakening further.

These changes in social conditions have fostered an image of post-communist welfare states coming under the knife of reformers. However, this is not what has happened in Central and Eastern Europe. An examination of actual policy developments suggests that the welfare state is an area of public policy where only few changes of note have occurred in recent years. While almost all political and economic institutions of the communist regime were fundamentally challenged during the first five years of transition, social protection systems were largely maintained and consolidated. Despite strong reformist ambitions at the beginning, post-communist governments did not bring about major shifts in social policy. Neither has the old welfare state been radically dismantled, as announced and repeatedly demanded by prominent economic liberals in the wake of the peaceful revolutions. Nor have post-communist social reformers succeeded in transforming it into some variant of 'the strong' West European welfare state, as initially intended. Compared with other areas of reform (for example, liberalization of markets, external economic policy, industrial relations, constitution-making, change of government), welfare state institutions, on the whole, have remained notably stable.

This chapter aims to contribute to our understanding of what is actually happening in the post-communist welfare state. It goes on to explore the dynamics of welfare state rebuilding in six Central and East European (CEE) countries over the period 1989 to mid-1995, namely Bulgaria, the Czech Republic, Hungary, Poland, Romania, and Slovakia.[2] Section two begins by investigating institutional continuities and changes in the realm of social policy. On the whole, the policy review does not suggest that the old social protection systems have been substantially contracted or reformed. Section three turns to the politics of social policy to understand why, except perhaps for the Czech Republic, no comprehensive reform of the system of social guarantees has occurred to date. The analysis points to the unpopularity of welfare state retrenchment and to the lack of political consolidation in post-communist societies. Section four goes on to examine the inadequacies of the social protection systems in place. The worsening of many welfare indicators, this chapter argues, cannot be attributed to a 'retreat of the state' in welfare provision, but should be related mainly to changes in the labour market. The final section briefly summarizes the evidence.

## THE WELFARE STATE'S DURABILITY: A REVIEW OF REFORM POLICIES

In all CEE countries, social policy transformation has turned out to be a protracted process. The first five years of the post-communist era provide only few indications that pre-existing welfare state institutions have undergone significant changes. This outcome is remarkable because all governments had strong reformist ambitions at the beginning and made considerable efforts to develop comprehensive plans for social reform.

### Reform Ambitions

After the demise of communism, a profound reform of existing social protection systems was considered an indispensable element of societal transformation. At that time, hardly anyone advocated maintaining the old welfare state institutions. The majority of the political forces envisaged major departures from the status quo. The economic liberals' reform programme was to radically reduce state social protection and give emphasis to private security-enhancing arrangements instead. They argued that the old social protection systems imposed too heavy a financial burden on the economy in general and the state budget in particular. Moreover, they viewed radical social reforms as a necessary step to break the 'culture of dependency' cultivated over the long period of communist rule. They wanted to introduce, as Vaclav Klaus used to say, a 'market economy without an adjective': an economic regime that would not be encumbered with much social policy and would not smack of state *dirigisme* and paternalism. Therefore, economic liberals demanded that overall social expenditures should be curtailed, major welfare responsibilities be shifted to the private sector, and government support be strongly 'targeted'.

The main alternative approach that became increasingly popular in the region – in particular among social policy experts working in the respective administrative branches or involved in social policy research and advising the government – was a radical 'Europeanization' of the social protection systems. Rather than giving up the idea of a strong welfare state, the ambitious plan was to introduce West European institutional arrangements and social security standards as soon as possible. The German-Austrian 'social insurance model' or 'social market economy' approach enjoyed great popularity and was regarded as the best model to meet concerns for both 'economic efficiency' and 'social justice'.[3] Reform proposals that have been worked out in accordance with this approach included the following structural shifts in the welfare state in the medium run:

- a new public-private mix in benefit provision. Contrary to the old regime, social insurance was thought to be only one, though still the main source of income support. Public programmes should be supplemented by private welfare arrangements. Yet social insurance should continue to play the dominant role for virtually everyone, with benefits satisfying the criterion of 'social adequacy';
- a reduction in the redistributive effects of state intervention. As in Germany, social insurance should help people to preserve their social status in case of lost earnings and not aim at reducing income inequalities which were (increasingly) generated in the market. Hence, the preference for strongly earnings-related benefit formulas;
- as in West European political economies, there should be a clear distinction between insurance benefits and non-insurance-type schemes.

Social insurance was seen as cushioning those 'standard risks' individuals were regularly exposed to in market economies; citizens could, therefore, be obliged to adequately provide for these in advance (such as sickness, invalidity, old age, unemployment). Other state support schemes (family benefits, housing subsidies, aid for the chronically handicapped, social assistance, and so on) were seen as instruments of inter-personal redistribution designed to meet particular needs and, thus, should be targeted;

- the introduction of off-budget financing of social security and cost sharing between employers and employees. This was to regain transparency and strengthen cost awareness and accountability among policy makers, programme administrators, and beneficiaries. More generally, the driving force of reforms was to limit the heavy burden which social policies imposed on the economy in general and the state budget in particular;

- a reduction in enterprises' social policy functions. It was intended to largely insulate the welfare state from the sphere of production. Key social benefits should no longer be channelled through the enterprise. In particular, the bulk of social assets and facilities owned by state enterprises should be transferred to local agents. This was to reduce the enterprises' non-wage labour costs and make the benefits available to all citizens.

- and finally, the old command mode of social policy-making was supposed to change. To account for a plurality of interests, post-communist élites wished to introduce intermediate bodies of interest co-ordination and associational self-regulation. Only the general issues of benefit regulation should remain in the realm of the government and/or parliament, while newly emerging collective actors were supposed to take responsibility for routine scheme management.

These plans were demanding and implied a major overhaul of existing institutions. But to what extent have these ambitious plans been implemented? Which social reform strategies have post-communist governments actually pursued in the countries under study? Which major departures from the status quo have been accomplished so far?

**Coping with Unemployment and Poverty**

One clear example of institutional reform was the introduction of *unemployment insurance* right at the outset of transition. All CEE countries strove to set up insurance-type schemes: benefits should replace wages, payments should not be subject to a means-test and the scheme should be funded by earmarked contributions deducted from wages. Political actors strongly rejected the idea of introducing just a flat-rate scheme, as proposed by experts from the International Monetary Fund (IMF) and the World Bank who were concerned with the fiscal strains and the characteristics of unemployment in the transformation period. A flat-rate benefit at or above the minimum wage, some advisors argued, would be more targeted on the poorer strata than an earnings-graded scheme, as equal benefits replace a larger percentage of lower than higher incomes. If coupled with earnings-related contributions, the flat-rate scheme would have a distinct redistributive effect. It would also be much easier to implement and operate than an insurance programme.

For East European social policy makers, however, an insurance-type scheme appeared a much more attractive model. First, the concept of unemployment insurance was widespread in the West and such arrangements were apparently working quite well. Considering that there was no time for experimentation, political actors were inclined to copy the 'well-tried' institutions of the West European welfare states. Second, the new risk of unemployment was put into the same category as sickness and old-age to be cushioned by income replacement benefits. Flat-rate payments were considered a deviation from the 'philosophy' of social insurance and had the flavour of a statist emergency measure. Third, it was especially the high-wage sectors (heavy industry, mining) where massive labour shedding was expected to occur immediately. Yet workers with higher salaries were to receive less under a flat-rate scheme compared to an earnings-graded system. Governments were reluctant to demand additional sacrifices from these groups and feared the unions' resistance. Finally, long-term unemployment was not the primary concern and the difficulties in administering an insurance-type scheme in the transition economies were underestimated.

Consequently, the initial programmes have been frequently revised. All countries set up rather generous income support schemes at the beginning. Yet governments soon started to tighten eligibility criteria, to reduce the replacement rate and the duration of payments, to define upper limits to benefit levels, and the like. Today, all schemes provide only modest income support for the unemployed and operate *de facto* as flat-rate systems.[4] Average unemployment benefits are close to or even below minimum wages and subsistence minima. Moreover, only the minimum benefit is indexed for inflation. The result is that with the increasing duration of unemployment the 'real' replacement rates have turned out to be much lower than the initial ratios stipulated by law.[5] In addition, due to both changes in benefit regulation and the incidence of long-term unemployment, the coverage of the schemes has sharply declined. There is a growing number of persons who have exceeded the maximum duration of payments, but who have only slim chances to build up entitlements again through participation in the labour market. Retrenchment measures affecting access to benefits and the duration of payments have added to the decline in the share of the unemployed receiving benefits.[6]

Unemployment benefits have been supplemented by a diversified set of *active labour market policies*. All CEE countries established a network of public employment services and introduced a series of measures intended to foster the reintegration of displaced workers into the labour market, among them training and retraining programmes, job creation schemes, self-employment subsidies, public works, and – somewhat later – programmes targeted to sub-groups of the unemployed (for example, the youth, women, long-term unemployed, Gypsies). Initially, financial and administrative constraints abounded, seriously limiting the actual implementation of these policies. Nevertheless, many of the active measures have been significantly improved and extended since. In 1992, a remarkable three to four per cent of the labour force was, on a yearly average, involved in some kind of labour market programme in Poland and Czechoslovakia. The figure for Hungary was somewhat lower, whereas in Bulgaria and Romania active measures were only beginning to take effect (Scarped and Reutersward, 1994: 284).

However, labour shedding only partly translated into unemployment. A significant decline in employment has been accomplished by squeezing workers out of the labour force, notably women[7] and the elderly. Over the period 1990 to 1992, a great many older workers agreed to end their employment contract and make use of *early retirement* offers or disability pensions. Among the countries investigated, early retirement has been used most extensively in Poland and the Czech Republic to cut back on the employment of older workers (Boeri, 1994a: 21, 42f.). Roughly estimated, unemployment rates would have been about two percentage points higher in both countries by the end of 1993, if all early retirees had been registered unemployed instead. The impact of early retirement programmes in Hungary, Bulgaria, and Slovakia has been much more limited.[8] Both the rising number of unemployed persons and the growing number of pension recipients put strong upward pressure on social outlays. The most impressive (and often cited) figure is the development of pension entitlements in Poland. From 1989 to 1993, the number of Polish pensioners increased by 28 per cent, compared to the annual growth rates of between two and three per cent in previous years (Barbone and Marchetti, 1995: 67; Sachs, 1995: 3).

Apart from unemployment insurance, *social assistance* now provides a safety net for the unemployed in transition countries, just as it does for other population groups. Hitherto, social assistance in cash or in kind had been provided mainly for the destitute handicapped and frail elderly. These programmes were not designed to support people solely lacking an adequate income. Nor did the population under communist rule have an actionable right to government support. All CEE countries have reshaped and extended these patchy schemes since.

Poland reformed its social assistance scheme as early as late 1990 and has enacted several minor amendments since. The programme now provides various benefits in cash or in kind for sub-groups of the population demonstrating financial need. The Federal Parliament of Czechoslovakia passed a bill in 1991 which determines a living minimum income to be guaranteed by the state. Social assistance in cash and/or in kind is provided up to this nation-wide benchmark defined (other social transfers deducted), if the claimants pass a tight means-test. Likewise, Bulgaria adopted a new scheme in March 1991 to flank economic reforms, which grants social aid according to age and household size. Romania also reformed its welfare scheme and enacted a special support allowance for those who had exhausted their entitlement to unemployment benefit in mid-1992. The Social Welfare Bill finally adopted in Hungary in late 1992 was to systematize eligibility criteria and to introduce new kinds of benefits in order to protect large families, pensioners, and the long-term unemployed from marginalization. In sum, everywhere throughout the region, efforts made to protect the poor are noteworthy, although another striking similarity is that none of the countries has so far decided on an unconditional minimum income to protect the poorest strata effectively.

## Social Security Reform

The review of reform efforts in other social policy sub-fields provides a more mixed picture. There is more national variation both in the overall state of reform and in the priorities set. In all six countries, hundreds of bills, decrees, and regulations have been devised to compensate for the failures of the existing welfare systems. However, most of those measures adopted were emergency solutions, aiming to ensure the basic functioning of the existing arrangements rather than to radically alter the programmes in place. Contrary to initial proclamations, post-communist governments decided not to basically challenge the institutions inherited, but to largely adhere to pre-1989 programmes and try to consolidate them over the long term. Reform goals have became much less ambitious and, compared with other policy areas, the pace of reform has been decidedly slow. As the following outline aims to indicate, in fact, only a few long-term structural modifications in financing and benefit provision have been enacted. Altogether, the Czech reformers' record seems the most successful so far, though even in this case the reform process is proceeding only slowly and is being carried out in a very pragmatic way.

One of the instances of institutional reform deserving mention is the shift towards the *off-budget financing* of social security which has been realized in Hungary and Slovakia to date. The Hungarian Social Insurance Fund was established as an independent body to finance the core programmes of the welfare state as early as in 1989. In March 1990, a reform of financial responsibilities was adopted. The Social Insurance Fund was assigned the task of covering expenditures on health care, pensions, and sick pay, while family allowances were to be paid from the central budget from then on. The institutional autonomy of this body was achieved in May 1993, when the general elections to the pension and health care insurance boards were held.[9] These two bodies now have a major say in pension and health care reform, yet final budget decisions have remained the responsibility of the parliament. In contrast, the Hungarian government has been less successful in limiting the payroll tax burden. Contribution rates which were traditionally divided into employees' and employers' parts in that country have been repeatedly increased and reached an extraordinarily high level[10] in 1993 (see Table 7.1). Nevertheless, the funds have to be regularly supported by transfers from the central budget.

In the wake of the tax reform which took effect in both successor states of Czechoslovakia in 1993, social security financing was divided between the employer and the individual worker. The reform reduced the financial burden on companies and shifted a large part of the financial responsibilities on to the employees (see Table 7.1). In Slovakia, the shift towards contribution-based financing was supplemented by efforts to set up an autonomous National Insurance Company in charge of the pension, health care, and sickness funds. The institution is governed by a tripartite board of representatives nominated by the Slovak parliament. However, the initial problems of off-budget financing were tremendous, in particular as the state started to cut down regular transfers to the funds. Today, the funds continue to record huge deficits, and transparency in financing has not yet increased.

In contrast, the Czech government has retained state control over the social insurance funds. The reason is quite obvious. In the past years, contribution revenues repeatedly exceeded expenditures, especially in the case

*Table 7.1*  Social insurance contributions as a percentage of wages (1993)

| Country | Social Insurance Funds[a] | | Employment Funds | |
|---|---|---|---|---|
| | Employer[b] | Employee | Employer[b] | Employee |
| Bulgaria | 35[c] | 0 | 7 | 0 |
| Czech Republic | 35 | 135 | 3 | 1 |
| Hungary | 44[d] | 10 | 7 | 2 |
| Poland | 45 | 0 | 3 | 0 |
| Romania | 27.5[c] | 1 | 5 | 1 |
| Slovakia | 35 | 13.5 | 3 | 1 |

[a] including health care
[b] computation base differs a little from conventional methods used in OECD countries
[c] average payroll burden
[d] lower rates for the agricultural sector
Source:  Data provided by national authorities

of the Employment Fund. Thus the state could use the surplus for other (social policy) purposes without consulting anyone else.[11] In the other transition countries, too, governments have not been inclined to give up control over payroll tax revenues, given the growing financial imbalances in their own budgets. Therefore, they have repeatedly postponed the project to separate the funds from the general budget and to grant these institutions any financial and organizational autonomy.

Nor is the outcome of reform efforts very impressive, if we examine changes to entitlements. *Pension reform*, in particular, has proceeded very slowly. Everywhere, major reform bills were still pending or not yet fully drafted in the period considered.[12] There were only very few institutional changes in this core area of the welfare state up to now, and that in Poland, Hungary, and the Czech Republic. In Poland, a series of proposals for comprehensive pension reform have been worked out since the beginning of transition. Yet the only major reform adopted up to now was a modification of the pension formula in October 1991. The change in the formula was to strengthen the link between individual contributions and benefit levels, that is the insurance element of the scheme.[13]

The Hungarian parliament passed a bill on private pension and health care funds in November 1993. The law offers tax privileges to companies and employees that launch so-called 'voluntary mutual benefit funds' to provide pensions, medical services, or short-term cash benefits. Efforts to reform the existing pension system have failed, however. Certainly, the level of benefits has been repeatedly adjusted to the rising cost of living. Yet basic features of the Hungarian pension system, such as the pension formula or the standard retirement age, have not been altered.[14]

Only the Czech government has engineered more far-reaching reforms in pensions provision. As in Hungary, it took the government a long time to work out the principles of the pension system's future design. Again, the first reform realized was the bill on complementary pensions passed in early 1994. The Klaus government rejected the idea of introducing an occupational pension regime, as Hungary did, and opted for an individual approach instead, encouraging citizens to contribute to private pension funds. The law roughly regulates the statutes of the funds and stipulates that the state will subsidize each participant's contributions directly (rather than granting tax allowances).[15] The second initiative which aimed to reform the existing basic pension programme was pending until very recently. In particular, the new design of the pension formula (a strong reduction of the replacement rate in line with the neo-liberal reform agenda) and an envisaged increase in the standard retirement age over a period of 12 years met strong parliamentary resistance. As it happened, the bill passed through parliament with a bare majority in mid-1995. In short, the Czech government actually managed to scale back one of the core social programmes inherited from the past regime.

On the whole, CEE countries' *health care systems* have undergone more dramatic changes than the pension schemes. Here, it is the Czech Republic, Hungary, and Slovakia that took the first steps towards establishing a new public-private mix in health service provision and introducing a contributory health insurance arrangement. In the other three cases, the adjustments made have not basically challenged the existing 'public service model' to date.[16] Everywhere, physicians and medical personnel are now allowed to set up private practices, and patients are granted the right to consult doctors of their own choice. Beyond that, the reform outcome appears more mixed. The privatization of health care services has generally been limited to pharmacies, except for the Czech Republic where the government has vigorously pursued the privatization of medical facilities since 1992.

Both in Hungary and Slovakia, one statutory, semi-autonomous health insurance body has been created. Only the Czech government abolished the state monopoly in the health insurance market in the course of 1993, yet enrolment has remained mandatory. There are presently 27 health insurance companies in the Czech Republic which serve different population groups, but operate under the same legislative framework. These companies heavily compete for 'attractive' members (young people, high wage earners), despite a system of revenue redistribution introduced to avoid adverse selection. However, many of the newly founded companies have strongly miscalculated their premiums; some are even said to be on the brink of insolvency. In view of this situation, a number of hospitals no longer accept their insurance cards and refuse to treat policy holders who cannot pay cash in advance.

In all three cases, a very delicate issue of health care reform has been the design of performance-based reimbursement regimes for medical providers under contract with the health insurances. Policy makers had great difficulties in assessing the incentive effects of payment systems on providers' behaviour and, thus, the financial implications of the reform.[17] Both the Czech and Slovak health care reforms provide ample indication of the adverse effects of hasty policy-borrowing. Both countries introduced, one after another, the German fee-for-service method of reimbursing medical suppliers. It turned out that the German list of medical procedures – and the point values attached to them on which reimbursement was based – did not really suit the national conditions. Moreover, fee-for-service payments were introduced without a sufficient regulatory mechanism of price fixing or budget limiting. These 'technical mistakes' have exacerbated the problem of cost containment. The laws had to be revised frequently, and further revisions are on the agenda. Unsurprisingly, policy makers began to view the introduction of market forces into the health sector as an expensive enterprise and one to be pursued more cautiously.

Changes in other programme areas have been rare, even in the Czech case. Although constituting a significant expenditure item, *sick pay provisions* are still generous and the financial burden is still carried by the social security funds in most CEE countries. These schemes offer manifold opportunities for 'abuse': employers can temporarily reduce their wage bill at the public expense, 'sick' employees may go moonlighting, and doctors can increase their salaries by prescribing long periods of home rest. Only Hungary and Poland – which already had special regulations under the old regime – amended these programmes prior to mid-1995. Already under communist rule, Hungarian employers had to pay for the first three days of sick leave; from the beginning of 1992, they had to bear the financial burden for the first ten days of sick leave. In Poland prior to the regime change, sickness benefits were paid out of the enterprise wage funds in the state sector, whereas private sector employees on sick leave were paid out of the Social Insurance Fund. Only recently, after years of debate, new legislation has been adopted. Since March 1995, the rules for financing are harmonized and employers have to bear the costs for the first 35 days of sick leave per year. In the other four countries, reforms are still pending.

Likewise, post-communist governments have refrained from scaling back existing *family benefit schemes.* Hungary, for instance, had a quite generous family benefit system under the old regime, and there were serious debates concerning the design of the scheme after 1989. However, the Antall government, with the Ministry of Social Welfare headed by a Christian Democrat, resisted pressure from external advisors to give up universalism in order to contain costs. But the thrust of policy has changed since the socialist-liberal cabinet headed by Gyula Horn took over in mid-1994. Facing severe budgetary pressures, the government has made the family benefit scheme a target of reform, so as to limit social expenditures. The government's austerity package of March 1995 included substantial cuts in family benefits. Unsurprisingly, the plan was highly unpopular and led to the resignation of both the Minister of Social Welfare and the Minister of Health. In July 1995, the Hungarian Constitutional Court quashed the bill. The judges argued that the cutback was not reasonable without giving young couples the opportunity to reconsider their family planning. To date, it is uncertain whether the reform will be actually implemented.

The issue of targeting family allowances has been a major issue in the other countries as well. As in Hungary, the Polish Ministry of Labour remained reluctant to impose sizeable restrictions on family benefits in the early years of transition, but continued to use the programme as an instrument for supplementing low household incomes and reducing poverty among children. In view of the budgetary situation, the government has recently decided for some streamlining of the programme. In early 1995, the family allowance was turned into a universal scheme, but targeted towards low-income households.

In the Czech Republic and Slovakia, too, family allowances (and related compensations for price increases) became means-tested, but cuts have not been substantial. For the time being, the income limit is set at a fairly high level which excludes only a small segment of the population from benefit provision. Moreover in the Czech case, the cutback was more than offset by an extension of the period of paid child-care leave from three to four years.[18] Thus in the case of family benefits, the Czech government did not pursue a strategy of residualization. However, it has succeeded in installing a mechanism for trimming benefits in the future: the income-test.[19]

**Comparative Assessment**

The general pattern we can observe is that political actors in CEE countries have been reluctant to pursue comprehensive social reforms. Table 7.2 offers a brief summary of policy development in the post-communist era. As argued above, the most important changes have occurred in the area of unemployment compensation, labour market policies, and social assistance. Despite strong reformist ambitions at the outset of transition, a great many of the other programmes in place have seen only minor adjustments (cf. also Cichon, 1995a; ILO-CEET, 1994). However, reform outcomes have varied both across countries and policy areas. The health care sector has experienced more dramatic changes in all countries than pension provisions. Housing programmes, one of the areas not considered above, quickly came under attack in some countries, while other programmes, such as sick leave provisions, have been left untouched. In the Czech Republic, the existing social programmes have undergone more radical reform than in the other cases. Hungary, Slovakia, and recently also Poland have implemented important changes, too. Nevertheless, even in those cases, social reforms have not been pursued vigorously. While at the outset of transition an overhaul of the welfare state structure was considered an indispensable element of the transformation agenda, the perception and goals of policy makers seem to have changed in the meantime. As Rys (1995: 6) notes, the critical question is no longer *how* to reform the welfare state in place, but *whether* social reform is necessary at all: 'how far can the existing patched up system continue to perform its basic social protection functions before breaking down?'

## THE POLITICS OF SOCIAL REFORM: THE PROBLEM OF AGENCY

What accounts for the welfare state's remarkable degree of stability? Why did post-communist governments not embark on sweeping social reforms right after the fall of communism as they did in other areas of societal transformation? And how can we explain the national variations sketched above? This section addresses these questions by briefly examining the political context of social policy-making in CEE countries.

The reasons for the slow pace of social reforms are manifold. First of all, it doubtless took reformers some time to study foreign models and develop distinct reform plans. They had to acquaint themselves with social policy techniques and modes of social protection governance applied in the West before they could formulate reform plans for their own

*Table 7.2*    Social reform outcomes (as of mid-1995)

| Policy area | Country | | | | | |
|---|---|---|---|---|---|---|
| | Bulgaria | Czech Rep. | Hungary | Poland | Romania | Slovakia |
| Labour market policies | x | x | x | x | x | x |
| Social assistance | x | x | x | x | x | x |
| Pensions | – | x | (x) | (x) | – | – |
| Health care | – | x | x | – | – | x |
| Sick pay | – | – | (x) | x | – | – |
| Family support | – | x | – | x | – | (x) |
| Financing | – | (x) | x | – | – | x |

x   important structural shifts
(x) few changes
–   practically no change

countries. However, this is not peculiar to the welfare state; it holds true for many other areas of public policy as well. Competence may explain the delay of reforms in, say, the first two years, yet it does not provide a sufficient explanation. The reason for the present inactivity is certainly not that policy makers lack insight into the problems or possible solutions.

Initially, the idea of sequencing may also have played a role. Except for the area of unemployment compensation, a significant reform of social security was clearly not the first priority of post-communist governments when taking power. Major social reforms could be launched, so the initial schedule went, after the most pressing tasks of stabilization and restructuring had been accomplished. Skilful sequencing, however, cannot account for the fact that there has been no increase in parliamentary activity in the field of social policy over the last two years, nor for the fact that major reform projects have not been passed by parliament. Even in the more advanced transition countries, such as Hungary and Poland, it has become highly unlikely that major reforms will be brought about in the near future.

Political explanations seem to be more important. Given the fiscal strains post-communist governments are facing, welfare state reform is a highly unpopular and politically risky undertaking. In mature welfare states, in the East as in the West, changes in core programmes affect entitlements of large segments of the population. None of the transition countries has the financial resources to cure the failures of the old welfare regime by merely topping up what is already in place. Rather, social policy transformation will impose losses on various groups: to make some income groups, occupations, or cohorts worse-off in relative or absolute terms compared with the situation under the old regime. In short, there is a zero-sum game in which governments have to pursue reforms very cautiously, if they want to be re-elected.

Up to this point, the story must sound very familiar to students of Western welfare states. To implement structural changes in the social protection systems in place, in essence, turns out to be a case of welfare state retrenchment.[20] This does not only apply to the neo-liberal reform scenario, but also to the strategy of 'welfare state Europeanization' sketched in the previous section, though to a minor extent. As we know from Western countries, welfare state retrenchment is politically difficult to pursue; so we should not be surprised by the sluggishness of social security reform in the Eastern part of Europe. Jeffrey Sachs (1995) has recently argued this point, referring particularly to the politics of pension reform in Poland. He claims that social reforms have not yet progressed far because of the electoral considerations of populist politicians. He maintains that the welfare state enjoys strong support throughout the region. Left-wing parties have succeeded in winning the recent elections almost everywhere precisely because they promised the electorate the maintenance of an extensive system of social guarantees.

However, this is much too simple a story. To understand why post-communist governments have been reluctant to embark on sweeping social reforms, we have to fully acknowledge the particularities of the political context in transition countries. Three factors – which Sachs fails to mention – should be stressed:

• The *social costs of transition*: by maintaining the status quo, political actors are responding to actual needs arising from the process of economic restructuring. To curtail social benefits and diminish expenditures, means to impose losses on those who have little and may be on the brink of poverty. Inflationary waves brought average benefit levels in real terms down close to the poverty line, thus giving political actors little room to manoeuvre. The defence of the welfare state is not simply a case of populist politics. Ultimately, it reflects the attempt of post-communist governments to prevent poverty and to cope with rising unemployment, while trading-off other policy goals for the time being.[21]

- The *weakness of the post-communist state*: one must recall that, to launch reforms, political actors have to be 'strong' enough to carry out their policy intentions. 'Strength' means, first of all, that post-communist coalition governments must have the ability to reconcile conflicting interests and actually come to a decision. On the contrary, political instability invites political actors to adopt short-term, 'trial-and-error' policies. Unfortunately, it is the latter scenario that has become the reality in most post-communist societies. Frequent changes of government and unstable parliamentary majorities, most notably in Bulgaria, Poland, and Slovakia, have rendered major social reforms very unlikely. Adding to political instability, post-communist governments do not usually possess sufficient financial and administrative resources to implement policies.[22]

- The *lack of intermediary powers*: the problem is not only that the state itself is generally rather weak. In addition, social reformers generally work independently in bringing about reforms. Neither business, nor the majority of the trade unions support radical changes. Almost everywhere, the employers' side is still very weakly organized[23] and has hardly any impact on political decision-making; thus, they have not exerted pressure for a dismantling of the welfare state. In contrast, the trade unions have regained considerable power in many CEE countries and do their best to prevent a sizeable deterioration in social conditions. This situation also impedes the process of decentralization of welfare state functions. Governments still lack strong, reliable societal partners, organized interests outside the realm of the parliamentary system, which could be used to overcome resistance, launch reforms, and assume welfare responsibilities.

Together, these variables may help to explain the cross-country variations outlined in the previous section. Compared with its neighbouring countries, the Czech Republic clearly has the strongest government in the region, providing political stability for the country's transformation process. The parliamentary opposition is fragmented and cannot hope to come to power after the next elections, despite growing dissatisfaction among the population with the policies of the ruling coalition. The unions substitute to some extent for the weak parliamentary opposition. Despite his strong anti-union opinion, Prime Minister Klaus has so far accepted the unions as 'social partners' and has chosen a very pragmatic course towards capitalism to ensure social peace.[24] Moreover, due to the smoothness of economic reforms, far fewer people have become dependent on the social safety net and the revenue base of the state has not shrunk as dramatically as in the other cases. With sufficient financial and administrative resources and backed by parliament, political actors were able to implement a number of far-reaching and probably irreversible changes in the welfare state. This is why social policy transformation has proceeded further in the Czech Republic than elsewhere.

## THE CREEPING EROSION OF SOCIAL PROTECTION: A GLANCE AT OUTCOMES

To recognize the welfare state's durability, however, does not mean that everything is fine with the social protection systems in place. The case for institutional continuity should not be mistaken for a proposition about the social adequacy and financial viability of the existing programmes. This qualification is extremely important for societies in transition, though basically it holds true for Western welfare states as well (cf. Pierson, 1994). Three points have to be considered:

First of all, the *status quo ante* already had many deficiencies and was widely regarded as 'inadequate'. Formerly, the social protection systems were broad and universal, but guaranteed only a relatively low standard of living. The quality of services was often very poor and the health sector, in particular, was heavily under-financed in many CEE countries in the 1980s. Poverty, too, did exist, though it had been a taboo subject for most of the time. Institutional inertia merely perpetuates these deficiencies.

What is more, the welfare state institutions that survived the regime change largely unchallenged have to perform their tasks in a fundamentally new socioeconomic environment. Formerly, the social protection systems operated under the conditions of a full employment economy, that is a labour market regime which minimized citizens' dependence on the welfare state, while providing a broad revenue base. Moreover, social insurance benefits were supplemented by extensive subsidies on staple consumer items (such as foodstuff, housing, energy, transport, and drugs) and by a developed system of fringe benefits, mostly benefits in kind. As economic reform proceeds, these other components of the state socialist approach to social policy are gradually becoming much less important. Unemployment has increased markedly, most prices have been liberalized, and enterprises are reducing, albeit slowly, their social benefit provision.[25]

The remaining institutions, the social protection systems, are heavily over-burdened. They were not designed to meet these tremendous demands and challenges. Thus, preserving them as they are does not suffice. Rather, if the protection systems in place were to prevent a sizeable deterioration in social welfare during the period of transition, governments would have to significantly expand and improve them. In contrast, the non-adjustment of institutions – the politics of merely defending the status quo – is likely to create serious problems, especially when the economic conditions are changing as profoundly as they are in post-communist societies.

Thirdly, in stressing the welfare state's overall durability we should not trivialize the importance of minor changes. Small cuts and slight tax increases, a gradual tightening of eligibility criteria and the phasing out of support may well have significant redistributional effects overall. The cumulative outcome of minor changes may hit some segments of the population particularly hard, and the long-term consequences of small alterations are often difficult to assess.

Indeed, there is a strong indication that many welfare indicators have worsened in the region since 1989. To begin with, both registration data and survey-based measures of joblessness indicate the incidence of *mass unemployment* (Boeri, 1994b: 16f.). The unemployment rate remained low in 1990 in all CEE countries, but far exceeded the threshold of ten per cent in the following years, except for the Czech Republic where the total number of registered unemployed in the labour force has remained strikingly low (see Table 7.3). Large-scale unemployment means a sharp break with the state commitment to full employment to which people had become accustomed in the previous 40 years. From the very beginning, when the problem was still insignificant in quantitative terms, the populations of these countries reacted with anxiety and nervousness to the looming threat. Their fear of unemployment was exacerbated by the risk of losing access to the extensive system of fringe benefits.

High levels of unemployment may well become a persistent feature of labour markets in transition countries. As Boeri (1994a; 1994b) has revealed, 'transitional unemployment' appears to take the form of a *stagnant pool*. Exit rates from unemployment to jobs have so far been extremely low in CEE countries (except for the Czech Republic), while job-to-job mobility has been higher than labour market experts initially expected. Most workers directly moved from the state to the private sector without an intervening spell of unemployment or left the labour force altogether. As the private sector hardly recruited from the unemployment pool, it has been very difficult for the unemployed to find a new job. The result has been a rapid increase in the average duration of unemployment,

*Table 7.3*  Registered unemployment as a percentage of the labour force
1990–94, (end of year)

| Country | 1990 | 1991 | 1992 | 1993 | 1994[a] |
|---|---|---|---|---|---|
| Bulgaria | 1.5 | 11.1 | 15.3 | 16.4 | 12.8 |
| Czech Republic | 0.8 | 4.1 | 2.6 | 3.5 | 3.2 |
| Hungary | 2.5 | 8.0 | 12.3 | 12.1 | 10.4 |
| Slovakia | 1.5 | 11.8 | 10.4 | 14.4 | 14.8 |
| Poland | 6.1 | 11.8 | 13.6 | 15.7 | 16.0 |
| Romania | n.a. | 3 | 8.4 | 10.2 | 10.9 |

[a] OECD Estimates
Source: EBRD, 1995: App. 11.1

which apparently perpetuates itself (due to the disqualification, stigmatization, and discouragement effects of long-term unemployment). Hence, there are only slim chances to reduce the large stock of unemployment built up in the near future.

In all of the countries, except for Hungary, more women were registered as unemployed than men in the period considered. A further marked feature of unemployment throughout the region is the rapid growth of youth unemployment. The jobless rate among the young was much higher than the average rate for the work force as a whole. The risk of becoming jobless was also higher for unskilled than for skilled workers. Minority groups, especially the less skilled Gypsy population living in rural areas far from the capital, were suffering disproportionately from employment adjustment (CEC, 1993: 5–8). Finally, there were marked regional disparities in the incidence of unemployment. Apart from the importance of on-the-job search mentioned above, it is the increasing mismatch between the regional distribution of unemployment and vacancies that accounts for the low outflow from unemployment in transition countries (Boeri, 1994b: 9–11).

Rising unemployment has sustained high *social spending* even as the real value of many social benefits has declined. As Table 7.4 indicates, social outlays as a percentage of GDP substantially increased in most CEE countries in the first years of transition. In Poland and Hungary social spending sharply increased from 1989 through 1993, followed by Slovakia and Bulgaria which also experienced high increases, by contrast with only modest changes in the Czech Republic. In Romania, social security expenditures slightly decreased over the period, but price controls remained in force for many food products and other staple consumer items which may explain the growing share of explicit subsidies in the government budget. Hence, soaring expenditures not only mirror the emergence of open unemployment but also reflect the state's assumption of responsibilities for health services and many other welfare facilities previously provided by enterprises.[26]

On the whole, the picture that emerges is of declining *benefit levels* in real terms. However, there seems to be considerable variation across countries and programmes.[27] Unemployment compensation has been cut down close to the subsistence level everywhere (see above). Yet as the average wage level is still rather low throughout the region, average benefits come very close to the wages that job-seekers, in particular the unskilled, are facing in the market. For many unskilled workers unemployment benefits presently turn out to be too low to avoid deprivation, but too high to accept job offers (Scarped and Reutersward, 1994: 270). Family allowances also usually figure among those social benefits which have lost a considerable part of their purchasing power since 1989, and this decline has only partly been offset by price compensations attached to wages (UNICEF, 1993: 64). By contrast, most CEE countries have made sizeable efforts to preserve the living standards of pensioners. In Hungary, for instance, the average pension-average wage ratio remained fairly

*Table 7.4*  Government outlays and social expenditures as a percentage of GDP (1989/1993)

| Country | Total expenditure[a] | | Social outlays[b] | | Subsidies[c] | |
|---------|------|------|------|------|------|------|
| | 1989 | 1993 | 1989 | 1993 | 1989 | 1993 |
| Bulgaria | 61.4 | 45.7 | 10.4 | 12.9 | 15.5 | 3.9 |
| Czech Rep.[d] | 64.5 | 48.5 | 13.2 | 14.6 | 16.6 | – |
| Hungary | 49.3 | 54.5 | 15.8 | 22.5 | 10.7 | 3.1 |
| Poland | 48.8 | 50.7[e] | 10.0 | 21.0 | 12.9 | 3.3 |
| Romania | 42.7 | 31.0 | 9.5 | 8.9 | 0.4 | 5.5 |
| Slovakiad | 64.5 | 55.5 | 13.2 | 17.0 | 16.6 | 4.8 |

[a] including extra-budgetary funds
[b] social security and social service expenditures
[c] explicit subsidies on energy, housing, food, etc.
[d] 1989 figures are for Czechoslovakia
[e] figure is for 1992
Sources: EBRD, 1994: 87; Sachs, 1995: 2

unchanged over the period 1989 through 1992. In Poland, the ratio between pensions and wages became much more favourable (increasing by more than 30 per cent), whereas it fell by roughly 14 per cent in Bulgaria throughout this period (UNICEF, 1993: 79).

Minimum wage policy has been an important mechanism for reducing benefit levels. Minimum wages have only been adjusted infrequently to inflation in CEE countries and have declined much more than average wages over the period 1990 to 1993. While minimum wages represented up to 70 per cent of national average wages at the outset of transition, the ratio declined to between 30 and 40 per cent before the end of 1993. This pattern of minimum wage erosion emerged regardless of whether inflation was high or not. In fact, as Vaughan-Whitehead (1993) indicates, post-communist governments have used the minimum wage as an instrument for controlling labour costs and limiting public expenditure. Because the minimum wage served as an anchor of the social protection system[28] and public sector wages were tied to the minimum wage as well, any increase had enormous financial implications. Governments tried their best to keep that benchmark at a constant level, the price of this policy being a creeping erosion of social protection standards during the early years of transition.[29]

Poverty data provide a good indication of social welfare systems failing to meet need. There is ample evidence that standards of living have deteriorated and that poverty has spread enormously since the beginning of transition. This holds true for all countries studied, but most of all for Bulgaria and Romania. In 1992, approximately a quarter of all Bulgarian households were living in poverty, if the poverty line is taken as only 35 per cent of the 1989 average wage – the lowest officially calculated poverty threshold. The poverty rate rises to more than 60 per cent if a wider poverty definition is used.[30] In Romania, anti-poverty measures, such as food subsidies, reduced the proportion of the poor in 1990. Yet that policy could not be sustained, leading to a rapid rise in the number of the poor in the subsequent period. A high level of poverty is also recorded in Poland, while the incidence of poverty has so far been contained at much more tolerable levels in the other three cases (see Table 7.5). This development is mainly related to a sharp contraction in real average earnings. Price liberalization supported by strict wage controls led to a steep decline in real wages in CEE countries over recent years. On average, people earned less in real terms in 1993 than in 1989 and a considerable number of them lost their jobs in the regular economy. While poverty was highest among pensioners in the past, it spread particularly among large and single-parent families between 1989 and 1992 as well as among the long-term unemployed and the 'working poor' (UNICEF, 1993: 5–14).

*Table 7.5*  Estimates of the percentage of people living in poverty (1989–92)

| Country | Poverty line[a] | Percentages | | | |
|---|---|---|---|---|---|
| | | 1989 | 1990 | 1991 | 1992 |
| Bulgaria[b] | 35 | – | – | – | 23.3 |
| | 50 | – | – | – | 62.7 |
| Czech Republic | 28 | 1.5 | 2.2 | 10.4 | 6.9 |
| | 35 | 4.8 | 6.5 | 24.1 | 17.6 |
| Hungary[c] | 30 | 3.4 | – | 6.1 | – |
| | 45 | 14.7 | – | 25.2 | – |
| Poland[c] | 34 | 7.8 | 19.1 | 17.7 | 20.4 |
| | 45 | 18.1 | 38.9 | 38.0 | 40.2 |
| Romania[b] | 35 | 19.9 | 7.5 | 14.1 | 29.5 |
| | 50 | 45.2 | 25.3 | 34.4 | 58.7 |
| Slovakia[b] | 30 | 1.1 | 1.2 | 4.4 | 29.5 |
| | 40 | 4.7 | 4.8 | 28.5 | 58.7 |

[a]  expressed as a percentage of the 1989 average wage
[b]  data are for households
[c]  data are for individuals
Source: Cornia, 1994: 298, based on Unicef survey data

An analysis of non-income-based welfare indicators also points to a significant deterioration in social conditions. For instance, life expectancy for men has significantly diminished in most countries since the beginning of transition and mortality rates also increased, in particular among the adult elderly. However, infant mortality rates mostly reveal a downward trend between 1989 and 1992, with the exception of Bulgaria and Romania where the negative trend can be mainly attributed to a weakening of health systems. As investments in the health sector have been negligible for two decades or more, health facilities, especially hospital buildings, are generally in a derelict state. Revenue shortfalls and the spread of corruption have exacerbated the crisis of the health care sector. In addition, the proportion of children attending kindergarten has steeply declined since 1989. Only in Hungary has the pre-school enrolment rate remained unchanged. Bulgaria and, even more markedly, Romania both also saw a sharp drop in secondary enrolment rates over the period 1989 to 1992 (UNICEF, 1993: 15–31).

Nevertheless, the structure of poverty in CEE countries still differs crucially from the situation in Latin America, as Milanovic (1994: 4) has stressed. Up to now, the poor have not represented a distinct underclass in post-communist societies. The gap between the poverty threshold and the income of the average poor is still quite narrow. Moreover, the educational and skill levels of the majority of the poor are quite high, and most of them have access to durable goods and dwellings. This suggests, as Milanovic goes on to argue, that if economic recovery is soon resumed and trickles down, a large number of the poor may escape poverty relatively easily. If income growth comes too late and/or only higher income groups enjoy the benefits of economic revival, the picture of poverty in Central and Eastern Europe may worsen dramatically.

## CONCLUSION

Post-communist welfare states have shown a remarkable degree of durability so far. Most changes of note in the old regime occurred in the field of labour market policies and social assistance, while other core social programmes did not experience significant reform. Policy makers' hesitation in committing themselves to comprehensive welfare state reform was mainly due to the particularities of the societal context. Action on poverty relief had to take precedence over any structural reform of the social security system. Moreover, political instability combined with limited financial and administrative capacities generally created a considerable barrier to institutional reform. As in the industrialized West, the dominant picture is one of a 'frozen landscape' (cf. Esping-Andersen, 1996): in contrast to other more central arenas of transformation politics, on the whole, welfare state institutions have remained relatively stable. The existing structure of social protection, however, is hopelessly overburdened with the demands and challenges of transition. The public welfare system, semi-reformed as it is, still has many structural deficiencies in the allocation of scarce resources and presently safeguards only a barely minimum standard of living.

The defence of the welfare state has been a key instrument for ensuring social peace and securing economic reforms against a political backlash. However, difficult discussions on the future financial liabilities and the structure of benefit provision are to be expected. In this situation, national consensus-building is a *sine qua non*. Already at the beginning of transition, most CEE countries have created national tripartite bodies of consultation and interest reconciliation to alleviate social tensions and ease the implementation of economic reforms. These institutions may now play an important role in reaching a social consensus on the future shape of the post-communist welfare state.

The interpretation suggested by the development of welfare states in Central and Eastern Europe diverges from the standard questions raised in 'transitology'. Usually, students of transition countries are concerned with the difficulties of transplanting Western-type institutions to a different societal context. The sociological research question is: how do the new institutions of capitalism and modern democracy work on the basis of pre-existing organizational structures and social ties? How much of 'the old' can we still discover in the new social order (for example, Stark, 1995; Offe, 1994)? Regarding the welfare state, this chapter suggests a different research agenda. In this area of societal transformation, the critical issue rather appears to be the persistence of inadequate institutional arrangements. Hence, we should ask: to what extent, if at all, do the old welfare state institutions accomplish their tasks, given the new socio-economic environment of the post-communist era?

## NOTES

1   The author wishes to thank Frank Bönker, Bob Deacon, Johan De Deken, Miriam Kotrusova, Erika Kvapilova, Martin Rhodes, Helmut Wiesenthal, and Maciej Zukowski for helpful comments and suggestions on an earlier draft. Despite this long list, the usual disclaimers apply.

2   If not indicated otherwise, the empirical findings and assessments presented are based upon a study of legislative material, press items, and interviews carried out with policy makers and consultants in four of the countries (Bulgaria, Hungary, and the Czech and Slovak Republics) during 1994. However, as the national social protection systems have been constantly under revision in the period considered, this outline cannot claim to be complete or up-to-date in every respect.

3   Note that all CEE countries have historical affinities to this model. It is not only the 'golden West', but also their own 'golden past' which has served as a point of reference (Offe, 1993). Remarkably, the Scandinavian model only played a minor role in post-communist social policy discourse. It was taken into consideration mainly in the Baltic States. In Hungary, the Scandinavian approach was entered into the policy debate by academics, such as Zsuzsa Ferge and Júlia Szalai.

4   Only in Poland did the government give up its initial commitment to the insurance principle and opt for a flat-rate approach in early 1992. However, the reintroduction of an insurance-type scheme is presently under discussion.

5   See Scarped and Reutersward (1994: 271f., 290) who have estimated real replacement rates. If wage inflation is taken into account, replacement rates are generally below those in OECD countries.

6    According to data provided by the Labour Ministries, the proportion of registered unemployed receiving unemployment benefits has fallen from 70–80 per cent to 40–50 per cent (in Poland, Hungary, the Czech Republic, and Romania) or even less than that (in Slovakia and Bulgaria) over the period 1990/91 to 1994.

7    This issue is explored in greater detail below.

8    Own calculation based on data provided by the Labour Ministries.

9    The General Assembly of the Pension Insurance has 60 members, two-thirds of whom represent the interests of the insured and one-third employers' interests; in the case of the National Health Insurance, the insured and employers are represented by 30 persons each.

10   Note that, for the time being, low wages partly offset the high payroll tax burden. Notwithstanding the high social insurance contributions, total labour costs are still much lower in CEE countries than in the Western part of Europe, and even lower than in the low wage countries of the European Union, such as Portugal, or in East Asia (Salowsky, 1993). Adequate measures of cost competitiveness, however, are still difficult to construct for Eastern Europe, given the problems of assessing labour productivity. For an intra-regional comparison see OECD, 1993.

11   This has been a very controversial point among the coalition partners. Recently, Prime Minister Klaus and his Civic Democratic Party have been forced to comply with the establishment of a special pension fund, albeit as part of the state budget and not as a separate body (Rys, 1995: 11).

12   Experts from the World Bank and the IMF express growing concern about the sluggishness of pension reform in CEE countries. A way out of the impasse, they argue, is suggested by the Chilean model of pension reform. That is, to shift, at least partly, from a pay-as-you-go to a funded financing system, while changing the basic features of the pension system. Resistance against reform would become smaller, it is argued, and the capital accumulated would promote economic recovery in the transition countries (cf., with different emphasis, Holzmann, 1994; Barr, 1994: 208–20; Sachs, 1995; de Fougerolles, 1995).

13   On Polish pension reform, see for example, Inglot, 1995 and Zukowski, 1995.

14   In February 1993, the Hungarian parliament decided to raise slowly the retirement age for women, beginning in 1995, while a decision affecting the retirement age of men was postponed. Shortly before the 1994 general elections, the Antall government suspended the project on the grounds that it should be made more tolerable for the elder cohorts affected.

15   The scheme has become an important instrument of capital formation. The Czech Republic's 41 private pension funds have one million participants and expect assets of US$ 100 million by the end of 1995. Hungary's 39 funds have less than 200,000 participants and expect assets of US$ 30 million by that time (de Fougerolles, 1995: 7).

16   On health care reform in CEE countries, see for example, the special issue of RFE/RL Research Report, 1993 and Schoukens, 1994 as well as the country reports of Orosz, 1994, Filer *et al.*, 1995, and Krizan *et al.*, 1995.

17    Especially given that there is no ideal Western model to follow in Eastern Europe. For many Western countries also have problems in building an appropriate incentive environment for the health care sector.

18    Everywhere in the region, child-care leave has provided an important cushion for redundant female workers, though the statistical data available are insufficient to assess precisely its impact on employment patterns. Survey-based measures of labour force trends at least provide indication that the activity rate of women has declined more strongly in most CEE countries from 1989 to 1992 than the activity rate of men (CEC, 1993: 16). This pattern was most pronounced in Czechoslovakia which can be attributed partly to the fact that, in mid-1990, the government had extended the period of paid child-care leave from two to three years to reduce the female labour supply.

19    Noticeably, the Labour Ministry stressed the 'political' rather than the financial implications of the reform during the parliamentary debate. Even if we cannot expect to save much money by this step, means-testing is necessary, Czech reformers argued, to 'change the people's mind' and cure them of their 'claim-attitudes' acquired over the long period of communist rule.

20    See, in particular, Pierson (1994; 1995) who has outlined the distinctive qualities of retrenchment politics in Western welfare states.

21    See the replies by Cichon (1995b) and by Kabaj and Kowalik (1995) to Sachs's article. This issue is treated more thoroughly in the next section of this paper.

22    One major constraint is large-scale tax evasion. In Bulgaria, for instance, where the deficiencies of the contribution collection system are said to be particularly bad, the Ministry of Finance estimated that about 75–80 per cent of the self-employed and 25–30 per cent of enterprises did not pay social insurance contributions in 1993.

23    The state sector, which is still quite large in most CEE countries due to the slow pace of privatization, is represented by the government. Business associations, newly founded to represent the growing private sector, still suffer from a low degree of organizational density and from being highly fragmented into competing organizations (cf., for example, Wiesenthal and Stykow, 1994).

24    On 'Czech-style Thatcherism' and the unions' impact, see Rutland, 1992/93; Orenstein, 1994.

25    On the latter issue, see the collection of articles in Schaffer *et al.* (1995).

26    A third reason why social expenditure-GDP ratios are an inadequate indicator for what is happening in the welfare state in Central and Eastern Europe is that (measured) GDP has sharply declined – by up to 30 per cent since 1989. The state has not only more tasks to fulfil; there is also much less to be distributed. If GDP declines strongly, an increasing share of social expenditure in GDP may well go along with a reduction of social spending in absolute terms.

27    Unfortunately, comprehensive cross-national data on this point have not been available.

28    Minimum wages serve as a reference wage for calculating social benefits, in particular for defining the lower and upper bounds of benefit provision. If

the minimum wage was regularly adjusted, it was thought, transfer levels would be kept in line with wage growth.

29 The Polish story reads slightly differently. In contrast to the other countries, Poland improved the purchasing power of the minimum wage (from 19 per cent in 1989 to roughly 40 per cent of the average wage in 1993). This was possible because unemployment benefits were disconnected from the minimum wage (Vaughan-Whitehead, 1993: 7f.)

30 Under the old regime, 'subsistence minima' and 'social minima' were regularly calculated for various prototypical families, but were not used as a base for setting minimum wages and social benefits. The 'subsistence minimum' typically oscillated between 25 and 35 per cent and the 'social minimum' between 35 and 50 per cent of the national average wage (Cornia, 1994: 297).

# REFERENCES

Barbone, L. and Marchetti, D. (1995) 'Transition and the Fiscal Crisis in Central Europe', *Economics of Transition* 3, pp. 59–74.

Barr, N. (1994) 'Income Transfers: Social Insurance', in Barr, N. (ed.), *Labour Markets and Social Policy in Central and Eastern Europe: the Transition and Beyond*, London: Oxford University Press, pp. 192–225.

Boeri, T. (1994a) 'Labour Market Flows and the Persistence of Unemployment in Central and Eastern Europe', in T. Boeri (ed.), *Unemployment in Transition Countries: Transient or Persistent?*, Paris: OECD, pp. 13–56.

Boeri, T. (1994b) '"Transitional" Unemployment', *Economics of Transition*, 2, pp. 1–25.

CEC (Commission of the European Communities) (ed.) (1993) *Employment Observatory. Central & Eastern Europe*, 5 December 1993, Brussels.

Cichon, M. (ed.) (1995a) *Social Protection in the Visegrád Countries: Four Country Profiles* (ILO-CEET Report No. 13), Budapest.

Cichon, M. (1995b) 'Social Expenditure in Central and Eastern Europe Under Challenge: Financing A Decent Society Or Cutting Corners?', *ILO-CEET Newsletter* 1, pp. 8–10.

Cornia, G.A. (1994) 'Poverty, Food Consumption, and Nutrition During the Transition to the Market Economy in Eastern Europe', *American Economic Review*, 84, 2, pp. 297–302.

EBRD (1994) *Transition Report. Economic Transition in Eastern Europe and the Former Soviet Union*, London.

EBRD (1995) *Transition Report. Investment and Enterprise Development*, London.

Esping-Andersen, G. (1996) 'After the Golden Age? Welfare State Dilemmas in a Global Economy', in G. Esping-Andersen, *Welfare States in Transition: National Adaptations in Global Economies*, London: Sage, pp. 1–31.

Filer, R.K., Veprek, J., Vyborná, O., Papes, Z. and Veprek, P. (1995) 'Health Care Reform in the Czech Republic', in J. Svejnar (ed.), *The Czech Republic and Economic Transition in Eastern Europe*, San Diego: Academic Press, pp. 395–411.

de Fougerolles, J. (1995) 'The Latin American Experience with Private Pension Funds: Lessons for Eastern Europe', *Transition* (newsletter issued by the Transition Economics Division of the World Bank) 6, 7–8, pp. 4–7.

Holzmann, R. (1994) 'Kapitalgedeckte und private Renten für Osteuropa?', unpublished manuscript, Saarbrücken.

ILO-CEET (International Labour Organization-Central and Eastern Europe Team) (1994) *The Bulgarian Challenge: Reforming Labour Market and Social Policy*, Budapest: ILO-CEET.

Inglot, T. (1995) 'The Politics of Social Policy Reform in Post-Communist Poland. Government Responses to the Social Insurance Crisis During 1989–1993', *Communist and Post-Communist Studies*, 28, pp. 361–73.

Kabaj, M. and Kowalik, T. (1995) 'Letter to the Editor: Who Is Responsible for Postcommunist Successes in Eastern Europe?', *Transition* 6, 7–8, pp. 7–8.

Krizan, P., Durian, J. and Krnác, P. (1995) 'The Reform of the Structure, Management and Financing of the Slovak Health Service 1989 to 1993', *Sociologia* 27, pp. 101–6.

Milanovic, B. (1994) 'A Cost of Transition: 50 Million New Poor and Growing Inequality', *Transition*, 5, 8, pp. 1–4.

OECD (1993) 'Competitiveness in Central and Eastern European Countries', *Economic Outlook*, 53 (June).

Offe, C. (1993) 'The Politics of Social Policy in East European Transitions: Antecedents, Agents, and Agenda of Reform', *Social Research* 60, pp. 649–84.

Offe, C. (1994) 'Designing Institutions for East European Transitions', unpublished manuscript, Bremen.

Orenstein, M. (1994) 'The Czech Tripartite Council and its Contribution to Social Peace', unpublished manuscript, New Haven/Prague.

Orosz, E. (1994) 'Health and Health Care under Socio-Economic Transition in Hungary', unpublished manuscript, Budapest.

Pierson, P. (1994) *Dismantling the Welfare State? Reagan, Thatcher, and the Politics of Retrenchment*, Cambridge: Cambridge University Press.

Pierson, P. (1995) 'The New Politics of the Welfare State', *ZeS-Arbeitspapier* 3/95, Bremen: Zentrum für Sozialpolitik.

RFE/RL Research Report (1993) *Special Series: Health Care Crisis*, 2, 40, 8 October 1993.

Rutland, P. (1992/93) 'Thatcherism, Czech-style: Transition to Capitalism in the Czech Republic', *Telos* 94, pp. 103–29.

Rys, V. (1995) 'Social Security Developments in Central Europe: Return to Reality', unpublished manuscript, Geneva.

Sachs, J. (1995) 'Postcommunist Parties and the Politics of Entitlements', *Transition*, 6, 3, pp. 1–4.

Salowsky, H. (1993) 'Soziale Sicherheit, Lohnfindung und Arbeitskosten in den Reformländern Mittel- und Osteuropas', *IW-Trends* 20, pp. 89–100.

Scarped, S. and Reutersward, A. (1994) 'Unemployment Benefit Systems and Active Labour Market Policies in Central and Eastern Europe: An Overview', in Boeri, T. (ed.), *Unemployment in Transition Countries: Transient or Persistent?*, Paris: OECD, pp. 255–307.

Schaffer, M.E., Jackman, R., Fajth, G., Lakatos, J., Rein, M., Tratch, I. and Woergoetter, A. (1995) 'Round table on "Divestiture of Social Services from State-Owned Enterprises"', *Economics of Transition* 3, pp. 247–66.

Schoukens, P. (1994) 'Die Entwicklung der Gesundheitssysteme in acht Ländern Mittel- und Osteuropas', in Internationale Vereinigung für Soziale Sicherheit (ed.), *Umstrukturierung der Sozialen Sicherheit in Mittel- und Osteuropa. Trends – Politiken – Optionen*, Geneva: ISSA, pp. 125–41.

Stark, D. (1995) 'Das Alte im Neuen. Institutionenwandel in Osteuropa', *Transit*, 9, pp. 65–77.

UNICEF (1993) Central and Eastern Europe in Transition: Public Policy and Social Conditions, *Regional Monitoring Report* 1, Florence: UNICEF-ICDC.

Vaughan-Whitehead, D. (1993) Minimum Wage in Central and Eastern Europe: Slippage of the Anchor, *ILO-CEET Report* 1, Budapest.

Wiesenthal, H. and Stykow, P. (1994) 'Unternehmerverbände im Systemwechsel. Entwicklung und Status organisierter Wirtschaftsinteressen in den Transformationsprozessen Ostmitteleuropas und Russlands', *Arbeitspapiere AG TRAP 94/5*, Berlin.

Zukowski, M. (1995) 'Das Alterssicherungssystem in Polen – Geschichte, gegenwärtige Lage, Umgestaltung', *ZeS-Arbeitspapier* 8/95, Bremen: Centre for Social Policy Research.

# III Welfare and the Global Arena

# 8 Negative and Positive Integration in the Political Economy of European Welfare States*

Fritz Scharpf

## INTRODUCTION

The process of European integration is characterized by a fundamental asymmetry, described accurately by Joseph Weiler (1981) as a dualism between supranational European law and intergovernmental European policy making. As Weiler (1994) points out, political scientists have for too long focused only on aspects of intergovernmental negotiations while largely ignoring the establishment, by judge-made law, of a European legal order with precedence over national law. This omission has kept us from recognizing the politically significant parallel between Weiler's dualism and the more familiar contrast between 'negative' and 'positive integration' (Tinbergen, 1965; Rehbinder and Stewart, 1984), that is, between measures increasing market integration (by eliminating restraints on trade and distortions of competition) and common European policies to shape the conditions under which markets operate.

The main beneficiary of supranational European law has been negative integration. Its basic rules were already contained in the 'primary law' of the Treaties of Rome. From this foundation, liberalization could be extended, without much political attention, through the interventions of the European Commission against infringements of Treaty obligations, and through the decisions and preliminary rulings of the European Court of Justice (ECJ). By contrast, positive integration depends on the agreement of governments in the Council of Ministers and is subject to all the problems of intergovernmental policy making. This explains the frequently deplored asymmetry between negative and positive integration (Kapteyn, 1991; Merkel, 1993). The most likely result is a competency gap, in which national problem-solving capacity is severely constrained while European policy is restricted by the lack of intergovernmental agreement. As a consequence, the political economy of European democracies is being fundamentally changed.


## NEGATIVE INTEGRATION: THE LOSS OF BOUNDARY CONTROL

After World War II, the boundaries of the state became coextensive with the boundaries of markets for capital, services, goods and labour. Initially a response to the Great Depression – which ended an earlier era of open capital markets and free world trade – these boundaries were certainly not impermeable. But transactions across them were effectively controlled by national governments: investment opportunities were generally restricted to national economies and firms were mainly challenged by domestic competitors. International trade grew slowly, and since governments controlled imports and exchange rates, international competitiveness was not much of a problem. While these conditions lasted, government interest rate policy controlled the rate of return on financial investments. If interest rates were lowered, job-creating real investments would become relatively more attractive, and vice versa. Thus, Keynesian macroeconomic management could smooth the business cycle and prevent demand deficient unemployment; while union wage policy, where it could be used for macroeconomic purposes, was able to control inflation. At the same time, government regulation and collective-bargaining controlled the conditions of production. Since all competitors could be required to produce under the same regimes, the costs of regulation could be passed on to consumers. Hence, the return on investment was not necessarily affected by high levels of regulation and union power; capitalist accumulation was as feasible in the union-dominated Swedish welfare state as it was in the American system of free enterprise.

During these 'golden years' the industrial West European nations could develop their own capitalist welfare states – and their choices were remarkably different (Esping-Andersen, 1990). But despite these differences, all were quite successful in maintaining and promoting a vigorous capitalist economy, while also preventing the destruction of particular social, cultural, and/or ecological values (Scharpf, 1991a; Merkel, 1993). But market-correcting policies depended on the state's control of its economic boundaries. Once this capacity was lost, through the globalization of finance and the transnational integration of markets, the 'golden years' came to an end.

Now, the minimal rate of return that investors can expect is determined by global financial markets, not national monetary policy. And real interest rates are generally about twice as high as they were in the 1960s. If a government now tries to reduce interest rates below the international level, the result is no longer an increase in job-creating real investment, but an outflow of capital, devaluation, and a rising rate of inflation.[1] Similarly, once the capacity to control the boundaries of markets for goods and services is surrendered or lost, the state can no longer ensure that all competitors will be subject to the same regime. So if the costs of regulation or collective-bargaining are increased nationally, they can no longer be passed on to consumers. Instead, imports will increase, exports decrease, profits will fall, investment decline, and firms will go bankrupt or move production abroad.

Under these conditions, countries are forced to compete for locational advantage in the form of a Prisoner's Dilemma game (Sinn, 1993; 1994). If nothing else changes, the 'competition of regulatory systems' that is generally welcomed by neo-liberal economists and politicians, may well become a downward spiral of competitive deregulation. But there is a hope, at least among unions and the political parties close to them, that what is lost in national regulatory capacity might be regained at the European level. Against these hopes, however, stands the institutional asymmetry of negative and positive integration.

In theory, the desirability of negative integration or liberalization is not seriously challenged in the EU member states. The basic commitment to create a 'Common Market' was certainly shared by the governments that signed the Treaties and the national parliaments that ratified them. It found its legal expression in the 'primary law' of Treaty provisions requiring the elimination of tariff and non-tariff barriers to trade and the promotion of undistorted competition. But what may not have been clearly envisaged then was the effect of the doctrines of direct effect and supremacy of European law established early on through the decisions of the ECJ. Once these were accepted, the Commission and the Court could promote negative integration without involving the Council of Ministers.[2] At the same time, under the 1966 Luxembourg Compromise, measures of positive integration could be blocked in the Council by a single member state veto. This is not the case under national constitutions where market-creating and market-correcting measures are, in principle, equally legitimate, and both depend on the mobilization of political support.

The text of the Treaties of Rome did not actually require the Community to abolish the constitutional parity between the protection of economic freedom and market-correcting intervention (Joerges, 1991; 1994a). But via the supremacy of European law, the four economic freedoms and injunctions against distortions of competition have gained constitutional force

(Mestmäcker, 1994: 270). Meanwhile, options for European social and economic intervention have been impeded by the high level of intergovernmental consensus required for positive integration.

## POSITIVE INTEGRATION: THE LIMITS OF INTERGOVERNMENTALISM

While negative integration was advanced, as it were, 'behind the back' of political processes, measures of positive integration require explicit political legitimation. As long as the Luxembourg Compromise was applied, indirect democratic legitimacy was derived from the necessary agreement of all members of the Council. The price of unanimity was, of course, a sclerotic decision process. The Single European Act (SEA) of 1986 was supposed to change this by returning to qualified-majority voting (QMV) for harmonization decisions – 'which have as their object the establishment and functioning of the internal market' (Art. 100A). In consequence, it is now no longer necessary to bargain for every last vote (Dehousse and Weiler, 1990). However, voting strengths and rules in the Council are set so that groups of countries united by common interests can rarely be outvoted. In any case, the veto remains a last resort for even individual countries; and unanimity still applies to a wide range of Council decisions. In sum, the need for consensus remains very high for positive integration measures.

Nevertheless, the Community *is* actively harmonizing national regulations in key areas such as health and industrial safety, environmental risks, and consumer protection (Joerges, 1994b; Majone, 1993). Indeed, it began to do so long before the SEA; and these regulations are defining high levels of protection (Eichener, 1993; Voelzkow, 1993; Héritier *et al.*, 1994). How can this be explained given the high consensus requirements in the Council of Ministers?

Unanimity or QMV rules institutionalize veto positions; and the existence of multiple veto positions reduces the capacity for political action (Tsebelis, 1995). But whether this actually results in blockages depends on the constellations of interests at play. If these are harmonious ('pure coordination games') or at least partly overlapping ('mixed-motive games'), unanimous agreement and effective solutions should be possible. Blockages are most likely in constellations of *conflicting* interests – and even then, agreement may be achieved if the losers can be compensated by side payments or package deals (Scharpf, 1992b). If positive integration in Europe runs into insurmountable barriers, the likely explanation will be conflicts of interests that are too intense to be settled within the EU's institutional framework.

Such conflicts do in fact exist. But they are not everywhere, and there is no reason to think that they are always virulent in areas of positive integration. In order to show this, I will concentrate on regulatory policy and on conflicts between economic and political interests. It is assumed for this purpose that rationally self-interested governments will consider three criteria in evaluating proposed European regulations: the extent to which the mode of regulation agrees with their own administrative routines; the likely impact on the competitiveness of industries and employment at home; and – where these are politically activated – the demands and apprehensions of their electorates.

The boundary separating consensual and conflict-prone constellations can be roughly equated with the conventional distinction between product-related and process-related regulation (Rehbinder and Stewart, 1984, 10). In the case of product-related regulations, the persistence of different national quality and safety requirements would perpetuate the fragmentation of EU markets. Since all countries agreed to the creation of the single market, it can be assumed that the common economic interest in unified European standards outweighs divergent interests. Thus, while countries might differ in their substantive and procedural preferences, agreement on common standards is likely to be reached. But this is not true for process-related environmental and safety regulations;[3] and it is even less so for social regulations (Leibfried and Pierson, 1992; Lange, 1992) which increase the cost of production.

In the case of product-related regulations, the interest constellation is shaped by the institutional framework: under Art. 30 of the Treaty, 'quantitative restrictions on imports and all measures having equivalent effect' are prohibited between member states. Under Art. 36, however, such measures are allowed if they are 'justified on grounds of public morality, public policy or public security; the protection of health and life of humans, animals or plants ...'. In other words, if national regulations serve one of the purposes specified in Art. 36, the default outcome, in the absence of a common European regime, would be continued fragmentation in European markets. Even if no country favours this outcome, the member states will still differ with regard to the level of EU regulation they desire. Rich countries will generally prefer higher levels of consumer and environmental protection than poor countries. Thus, the resulting constellation of interests is likely to resemble the 'Battle of the Sexes' game (Figure 8.1) in which negotiated agreement is generally difficult, but not impossible to achieve.

Moreover, even when European regulations have been harmonized, Art. 100A (4) allows countries wanting high levels of protection to introduce more stringent regulations. This changes the default outcome in favour of high-regulation countries and boosts their bargaining power. Thus, it is not wholly surprising that the harmonization of product-related regulations has achieved the 'high level of protection' envisaged for 'health, safety, environmental protection and consumer protection' in Art. 100A (3) (Eichener, 1993).

But the institutional framework and interest constellations are very different for *process*-oriented regulations. These do not affect the useability, the safety or quality of products produced. Steel from furnaces with high sulphur dioxide emissions is indistinguishable from steel produced with expensive emission controls. The same is true for cars produced by workers with or without paid sick leave in firms with or without codetermination. So there is no way in which Art. 36, or any other Treaty escape clause, could justify excluding, taxing, or discriminating against, products produced under conditions differing from those in the importing state.

Thus, in the absence of common European regulation, all member states may find themselves in a Prisoner's-Dilemma constellation and tempted to reduce process-related rules, and cut back on welfare, to improve competitiveness. This would clearly facilitate the adoption of common European

Rich Countries

|  | | High | Low |
|---|---|---|---|
| Poor Countries | High | 2      3 | 1      NA |
|  | Low | 1      1 | 2      NA |

*Figure 8.1* Preference for high or low EU standards in product-related regulations. NA = non-agreement

standards. And the Prisoner's Dilemma loses its pernicious character if binding agreements are possible. Since this is assured in the EU, European reregulation at the level desired by member states should be possible. Yet it is here that the difficulties begin. There are, firstly, differences in national regulatory style. These are likely to produce 'battle-of-the-sexes' games (in which member states would prefer EU agreement on levels of regulation but differ on style) superimposed on the Prisoner's Dilemma which, by itself, would not prevent agreement. Greater difficulties arise from ideological differences. Some governments may not share 'social democratic' or 'green' preferences for high levels of regulation, and may even welcome external competitive pressures to help them achieve domestic deregulation. Such difficulties may vary from one election to the next. But conflicts of interest arising from different levels of economic development are more deeply-rooted.

The EU includes some of the most efficient economies in the world alongside others barely above the threshold level, manifest in large differences in (average)[4] factor productivity. If the less developed countries are to remain competitive in the EU's internal market, their factor costs – in particular wage, non-wage labour and environmental costs – have to be lower as well. Industrial labour costs in Portugal and Greece are, respectively, one-sixth and one-fourth of those in Germany;[5] and differences in social-security levels and environmental costs are of the same magnitude (Ganslandt, 1993). If harmonization raised these costs to the level of the most productive, the competitiveness of the less productive economies would be destroyed. If exchange rates were allowed to fall accordingly, the result would be higher domestic prices and hence, impoverished consumers. If exchange rates were maintained (for example, in a monetary union), deindustrialization and massive job losses would follow – as in Eastern Germany when subjected to West German regulations under a single currency. The more enterprises are subject to international price competition,[6] the less politicians in the poorer countries could agree to cost-increasing harmonization.[7] And in contrast to relations between East and West Germany, rich EU countries would not be willing (or able) to compensate them with massive transfer payments.

Agreement would be no easier if the costs of social or environmental regulation were financed through higher income or consumption taxes rather than by firms. As long as average incomes in the poorest EC countries are less than a fifth of average incomes in the rich, the former must defend themselves against EU environmental and welfare harmonization. And unlike East Germany in the process of German unification, these countries are fully aware of their own best interests and the EU's constitution gives them an effective veto. The resulting interest constellation is represented as a game matrix in Figure 8.2.

Take the case of controls on industrial emissions. Highly industrialized and polluted rich countries are likely to prefer high EU standards (cell 1), which would also protect their own industries against 'ecological dumping'. They would least like to have common (and binding) low standards (cell 3). But for the poor countries, high standards (cell 1) would endanger less-productive firms. Even common rules imposing uniformly low standards (cell 3) would be unattractive, since their less-productive firms would then be exposed to competition from deregulated competitors in high productivity countries. So, for them, the best outcome would be non-agreement (cells 2 and 4) which would also be the second-best outcome for the rich countries. As a consequence, the status quo is likely to continue.

To summarize, positive integration has achieved remarkable progress in the harmonization of product-related regulations. But the harmonization of process-related environmental and welfare regulations is proving much more difficult. Meanwhile, negative integration is restricting national capacities for dealing with the problems created by market integration. Solutions to this dilemma can be sought in two directions – by increasing European problem-solving capacities or by enabling member states to protect their own interests in a transnationally integrated market.

Rich Countries

|  | | High | | Low | |
|---|---|---|---|---|---|
| | | (1) | 3 | (2) | 2 |
| | High | | | | |
| | | 1 | | 3 | NA |
| Poor Countries | | (4) | 2 | (3) | 1 |
| | Low | | | | |
| | | 3 | NA | 2 | |

*Figure 8.2*  Preference for high and low EU standards in process-related regulations. NA = non-agreement

SOLUTIONS I: INCREASING EUROPEAN PROBLEM SOLVING
CAPACITY?

Given pervasive conflicts of interest, problem solving at the EU level
might be facilitated either by institutional reform to improve conflict
resolution or by finding ways of making that conflict more manageable.

**Majoritarian Solutions?**

Obviously, conflict resolution would be most directly assisted if the EU
continued the move towards majority voting. If decisions could be reached
by simple majority, high-productivity countries could impose high standards on the rest of the Union – provided they can agree among themselves. But constitutional changes in the EU depend on unanimity: the
near foundering of the EU's Northern enlargement on the voting issue
shows that potential losers are unlikely to agree to a regime in which they
might be consistently outvoted. In this regard, the 'joint decision trap'
(Scharpf, 1988) is still in good repair.

Moreover, further moves towards full majority voting would generate a
fierce debate about the 'democratic deficit'. As long as the legitimacy of
EU governance rests primarily on the agreement of democratically
accountable *national* governments, those citizens whose governments are
outvoted have no reason to consider such decisions legitimate. In fact,
even the cautious expansions of QMV in the SEA and at Maastricht have
triggered debates so critical of majority decision making that future
progress will need to be based on more solid foundations of legitimacy.
Creating these above the nation state is problematic, for more is needed
than simply an increase in the formal competencies of the European
Parliament. Representation and majority rule will assure legitimacy only if
the body politic allows the imposition of sacrifices on some members of
the community in the interest of the whole; if there is the possibility of a
public discourse over which sacrifices are to be imposed for which purposes and on whom; and if the leaders are accountable to the public and
able to exercise effective power. But the lack of a common language is a
major obstacle to the emergence of a European-wide public discourse:
thus, we have no EU-wide media, no EU-wide political parties, and no
political leaders with EU-wide visibility and accountability.

For the time being it is unlikely that institutional reforms could greatly
increase the capacity for EU-level conflict resolution. Weiler's (1981)
diagnosis holds: in contrast to the legal processes defining and enforcing
the supranational law of *negative* integration, the political processes

required for *positive* integration will remain intergovernmental and easily blocked when national interests diverge. But what of European strategies to *minimize* conflict?

## Regulation at Two Levels?

A range of such strategies are in principle available (Scharpf, 1994). For example, in the harmonization of product-related standards, agreement has been facilitated by restricting Council involvement to the formulation of 'principles', while the details are left to corporatist standardization bodies. Moreover, in process-related *environmental* regulations, Art. 130T now allows any member state to maintain or introduce more stringent protective measures, provided they are 'compatible with this Treaty' (that is, with negative integration).

This opens up the possibility that the obstacles to agreement on process-related regulations might be reduced by a variant of 'variable geometry'. The Prisoner's Dilemma game that European countries are forced to play is not played with equal intensity among them all. Regulatory competition is most acute between countries that produce the same type of goods at similar levels of productivity and production costs. But countries producing at very different levels of productivity and costs do not usually compete with each other in the same markets. Thus, the failure to adopt single European standard would imply that two Prisoner's Dilemma games are being played: one among the most efficient countries that compete on productivity, the other among the less efficient that compete on costs.

From this analysis, the solution seems obvious: while preventing competitive deregulation requires the harmonization of process-related regulations, there is no need for a single, uniform standard. Instead, an explicit agreement on two standards offering different levels of protection at different levels of cost would suffice. The rich countries could then commit themselves to high standards, while the poor could agree to lower standards that would protect them from ruinous competition. As their economies grow, the lower standard could be raised and brought into line with the higher.

Compared to the difficulties of reaching agreement on EU-wide uniform standards, negotiations on double standards should be much easier (Figure 8.3). Moreover, in contrast to other proposals for a two-speed Europe, the club of high-regulation countries would have no interest in excluding applicants who feel able to conform to their levels. The most difficult choice would be faced by 'middle' countries, like Britain or Italy,

Rich Countries

|  |  | High | Low | Double |
|---|---|---|---|---|
| **Poor Countries** | High | 4 / 1 | 2 / 3  NA | 2 / 3  NA |
|  | Low | 2 / 3  NA | 1 / 2 | 2 / 3  NA |
|  | Double | 2 / 3  NA | 2 / 3  NA | 3 / 4 |

*Figure 8.3*  Process-related regulations with the option of a double standard.
NA = non-agreement

who would need to decide whether they dare compete on productivity or must compete on cost.

## But What if Institutions Matter?

So far we have looked only at negotiations between rich and poor countries, and have assumed that within each group agreement should be relatively unproblematic. But this applies only to process-related *environmental* regulations. In the case of industrial-relations and social-welfare regulations, even two-level harmonization would encounter enormous difficulties because qualitative and institutional differences are more salient.

Sweden and Switzerland, for example, are among the most highly developed countries in the world; and yet they differ greatly in the share of GDP they devote to public welfare transfers and services. And while Germany and Britain have similar levels of union density, they have quite different structures of union organization and collective bargaining. Moreover, German industrial relations are embedded in highly developed systems of labour, collective-bargaining and co-determination law; while British labour relations have developed under the maxim of 'free collective bargaining'. So quite apart from any cost considerations or possible side payments, an EU legal regulation of industrial relations is likely to be unacceptable to both British employers and unions. Whereas unions in Germany – and elsewhere in the EU – rely strongly on the legal effectiveness and enforceability of state regulations (Crouch, 1993).

Thus, in social welfare and industrial relations, even among the advanced countries, constellations of interest will not produce benign 'battle-of-the-sexes' games. Instead, with two qualitatively different types of institutional arrangement, we would have a constellation in which both sides might prefer non-agreement to a harmonized system (Figure 8.4).

Institutional differences between member states are politically salient either because powerful interest groups defend the status quo or because they are part and parcel of social and political identity. This is clearly the case where sectors have been sheltered from market forces by the state. These 'sectors close to the state' (Mayntz and Scharpf, 1995) include education and basic research, health care, radio and television, telecommunications, transportation, energy and water supply, waste disposal, financial services and agriculture where state protection from the market has produced quite different institutional arrangements. But practically all of them – from the Commissions' point of view – could be considered non-wage barriers or distortions of competition. And the logic of negative integration

Type 1 Countries

|  | | 1 | | 2 | |
|---|---|---|---|---|---|
| 1 | | 3 | | 2 | |
| | | 1 | | 2 | NA |
| 2 | | 2 | | 1 | |
| | | 2 | NA | 3 | |

Type 2 Countries

*Figure 8.4* Harmonization of welfare and industrial-relations regulations among countries of a similar level of development, but with different institutions. NA = non-agreement

implies their removal – as is currently happening in telecommunications, air transportation and financial services.

However, some of these restrictive institutional arrangements may be justifiable, so that – under Arts. 36 and 100A, or Art. 76 – their harmonization might be more appropriate. But how could the Council reach agreement on a common system of financing and delivering health care to replace the British, Italian and Swedish tax-based, public health systems as well as those of France, Germany and Austria which combine compulsory health insurance and private health care? Old-age pensions are similarly problematic. Here, the move from the German pay-as-you-go insurance system to a common system based, say, on the British two-tier model – combining tax-financed basic pensions and supplementary private insurance – is practically impossible. For the now active generation would have to pay twice – once for the present generation of pensioners under the old system, and again for their own life insurance under the new.

In short, there are important sectors where EU-wide harmonization may be infeasible. But should negative integration be allowed to run its course where institutional structures are seen as restricting trade or competition? If so, existing balances of values and interests will be upset. In some sectors, these costs have been considered politically acceptable – but there is no reason why this should always be so. Where it is not, negative integration will either be forcefully resisted or it may lead to social disintegration and political delegitimation, as in East Germany after the destruction of indigenous institutions.

## SOLUTIONS II: RESTORING NATIONAL BOUNDARY CONTROL?

We need, therefore, to think about how the advance of negative integration can be constrained. This is not a problem where liberalization has to be achieved through decisions in the Council of Ministers. Governments concerned to maintain existing institutional structures are still able to block Commission initiatives. But they have no formal power to prevent the Commission from proceeding against nationally privileged 'undertakings' by way of directives under Art. 90 (3) of the Treaty.[8] And they have even less control over the Commission's power to issue 'decisions' against individual governments under the same article, or to initiate infringement procedures before the Court under Art. 169. Moreover, given the doctrine of direct effect, any individual or corporation could challenge national arrangements before a *national* court, which could then obtain a preliminary ruling from the ECJ under Art. 177.

Thus, political controls will not work – or more precisely, they will only work asymmetrically. As long as the Council must proceed via QMV or even unanimous decisions, a small minority will be able to block positive action. But large majorities, or even unanimous votes would have to be mobilized to correct any extension of *negative* integration through the decisions of the Commission or the Court. The question then is whether it may be possible to limit legally the capacity of the Commission and the Court to extend negative integration beyond what the Council would also find politically acceptable.

At Maastricht, it is true, governments took care to exclude the Court from 'common foreign policy and security policy' and 'cooperation in the fields of justice and home affairs' (Article L). This is, surely, an indication that the Court's power to convert Treaty obligations into supranational law, and to interpret their meaning beyond the original intent, is now a matter of political concern. This may also have contributed to the inclusion of a 'subsidiarity clause' in Art. 3B (2) of the EC Treaty. If that was the case, however, restraining the Court is unlikely to be achieved through the clause itself (as opposed to the change in the political climate which it symbolizes).

By restricting subsidiarity to 'areas which do not fall within [the Community's] exclusive competence', negative integration is left untouched. Moreover, the subsidiarity clause is unlikely to have much legal effect on positive integration (Dehousse, 1993). Given the heterogeneity of member state conditions and capacities, it is inconceivable that a court could strike down any European measure that was supported by a qualified majority by denying that 'the objectives of the proposed action cannot be sufficiently achieved by the Member States'. It is probably more realistic to see the clause primarily as a political appeal for self-restraint directed at the Council of Ministers.

What might make a legal difference, for negative as well as for positive integration, is indicated by the most important decision favouring negative integration. In *Cassis de Dijon* (120/78 ECR, 1979, 649), the Court did not hold, as is sometimes assumed, that the 'mutual recognition' of products was an unconditional obligation of member states. Before Germany was ordered to admit the French liqueur, the Court examined the claim that the German requirement of a higher alcohol content was justified as a health regulation, and found it totally spurious (Alter and Meunier-Aitsahalia, 1994: 538–9). If that had not been so, the import restriction would have been upheld under Art. 36 of the Treaty which permits quantitative restrictions 'justified on grounds of public morality, public policy, public security, the protection of health and life of humans, animals or plants ...'.

Thus, the Treaty *itself* recognizes certain national policy goals that override the dictates of market integration. Admittedly, the Commission, and the ECJ even more so, have done their best to assure the priority of negative integration by applying extremely tough tests before finding that a national regulation is neither discriminatory nor a disguised restriction on trade. In fact, the Commission has followed a consistent line, according to which product-related national regulations either will be struck down, under *Cassis*, because they serve no valid purpose, or must be replaced by harmonized European regulations under Art. 100A (Alter and Meunier-Aitsahalia, 1994). What matters here, however, is the reverse implication: national regulations restricting imports, that serve one of the valid purposes listed in Art. 36, must be allowed to stand unless, and until, European harmonization is achieved.

For product-related regulations, therefore, negative integration does not take precedence over positive integration, and the competency gap mentioned in the introduction is in fact avoided. However, that is not true of *process*-related regulations which, since they do not affect the quality or safety of the products themselves, would never justify exclusion under Art. 36. Moreover, such regulations must also not violate the rules of European competition law (Arts. 85ff), must not insulate public service agencies against competition (Art. 90), and must not amount to competition-distorting state aid (Art. 92).

If this state of affairs is considered unsatisfactory, one may need to go further in the direction indicated by those provisions contained in Arts. 36, 48 (3), 56 (1), 66 and 100A (4) which allow restraints on the free movement of goods, persons and services if they serve one of the 'police-power' purposes of public morality, public policy, public security, public health, and so on. In practice, however, none of these exceptions is still of great importance, since the Commission and the Court have interpreted them in extremely restrictive fashion. The de facto priority of negative integration over national policy preferences has generally been re-established through judicial interpretation.

It remains to be seen whether the same fate awaits the even more explicit reservation clauses introduced by the Maastricht Treaty – for instance Art. 126 (1) which permits the Community only a very limited entry into the education field, 'while fully respecting the responsibility of the Member States for the content of teaching and the organization of education systems and their cultural and linguistic diversity'. By its language at least, the clause will only set limits to the narrowly circumscribed educational competencies of the Community: it will not offer immunity against charges that national education systems might represent restraints on trade and distortions of competition in the market for educational services.

If national policy preferences and institutional traditions are to survive, it seems that more powerful legal constraints are needed to stop the imperialism of negative integration. A radical solution would be to abolish the constitutional status of European competition law by taking it out of the Treaty altogether, leaving the determination of its scope to the political processes of 'secondary' legislation by Council and Parliament. This would create a constitutional balance at the EU level among competing policy purposes, as is true in national systems. In addition, it might be explicitly stated that national legislation remain in force unless, and until, it is shown to be in clear conflict with a specific provision of European legislation. This is the *de facto* state of European law with regard to product-related regulations in the market for goods. It could and should be extended to the markets for services, and in particular to transportation and financial services. These would be changes which, unlike the subsidiarity clause, would really make a difference. In addition, it might be worthwhile to specify in the Treaty itself those policy areas for which member states will retain primary responsibility. The most plausible candidates would be the areas discussed above – education, culture, the media, social welfare, health care, industrial relations and, of course, political and administrative organization.

As I have argued elsewhere, this would give the constitution of the Community a bi-polar character, similar to the 'Dual Federalism' which the American Supreme Court read into the US Constitution before 1937, or to the case law of the German constitutional court protecting the *Kulturhoheit* of the Länder (Scharpf, 1991b; 1994;). There is, of course, no hope that a clear demarcation line between European and national areas of policy responsibility could be defined. But an explicit dualism would force the Court and the Commission to balance the claims for the economic perfection of market integration against equally legitimate claims for the maintenance of national institutional integrity.

But would any of this make any real difference? The EU must, after all, remain committed to the creation of a common market; and so it must retain also legal instruments to defend free access to markets against protectionism. Thus, prohibitions against trade restrictions would need to be retained. What could change is the degree of perfectionism with which restrictions are defined. Even more important: constitutional changes could protect, or re-establish, the powers of national governments to take certain sectors out of the market altogether, or to organize them in ways that modify the market. If that implies a loss of economic efficiency, it should not be the business of the Community to prevent Member States from paying that price.

## SOCIAL REGULATION IN ONE COUNTRY?

But even if the legal straightjacket of negative integration could be loosened, that would not reverse the changes occurring in the political economy of capitalist welfare states. National economies are largely exposed to transnational competition, capital has become globally mobile, and enterprises are freely able to relocate production throughout the EU. And as factor mobility has increased, national capacity to reduce the rate of return on capital investments below the international level, either by lowering interest rates or by imposing additional costs on firms, has been lost (Sinn, 1993). In that sense, there is certainly no path that would lead back to the post-war 'golden age'.

From the point of view of political democracy, it would be dangerous to deny the existence of such constraints; but their significance should not be exaggerated. It is true that Keynesian macroeconomic management is no longer possible at the national level, and is not yet available supranationally. It is also true that the rate of return from productive investment, which capital owners can claim, has increased considerably. Any attempt, by governments or unions, to reverse these losses by redistributive programmes in a national context would fail.

Beyond that, however, the basic relationship between capitalist economies and democratic states is still the same. As pointed out above, even in the post-war period, the symbiosis of capitalism and democracy was only successful because the costs of the welfare state were borne by workers and consumers, rather than by capitalists. If this 'impossibility theorem of redistribution' is accepted, the loss of national regulatory capacity reduces itself to the relatively technical question of where the costs of (new)[9] regulation should be placed. If they are placed on firms that are exposed to international competition, and if all other conditions remain the same, there will be a loss of international competitiveness and a fall in profits, investment and employment. But, of course, other conditions need not remain the same. The rise in the costs of regulation could be compensated through wage concessions, through a rise in productivity or, as long as the European Monetary Union does not yet exist, through devaluation. In effect, these compensatory measures would, again, shift the costs onto workers and domestic consumers.

However, the same result could be achieved more directly and with much greater certainty if the costs were not imposed on firms at all. If new social regulations, such as the German disability-care insurance, were financed through taxes on incomes and consumption, rather than through payroll taxes, enterprises would stay competitive and investments profitable. One example is provided by Denmark, where 85 per cent of social costs are financed from general tax revenues. Since the international competitiveness of Danish enterprises is not affected, the (very costly) welfare state does not play any role in discussions about the competitiveness of the Danish economy.[10] Of course, consumable incomes will be reduced, but this is as it would, and should be in any case.

I do not wish to claim, however, that all objectives of social regulation in the post-war decades could also be obtained in the future without endangering international competitiveness. Even less would I suggest that the growing tax resistance of voters would be easy to overcome.[11] Compared to the post-war decades, the range of choices available to national democratic political processes has certainly been narrowed. But it is not as narrow as many contributions to the current debate suggest. Moreover, it can be widened to the extent that countries and regions succeed in developing their comparative advantages so as to exploit niches in increasingly specialized world markets. But this depends on a high degree of policy flexibility, and a capacity to respond to specific locational conditions and changing market opportunities at all levels of policy making – as well as in management and industrial relations.

Thus, the European economy may indeed need the larger market, and hence common rules, to keep up with American and Japanese competitors in areas where economies of scale make a difference. But Europe will certainly fall behind if negative integration paralyses national and subnational problem solving; and if only unsatisfactory compromises can be reached after long and difficult negotiations at the EU level. To succeed in the global economy, Europe depends on more effective European policy making with better democratic legitimation. But it depends equally on the autonomous problem-solving capacities of national and subnational polities. While the debate about subsidiarity may help limit the perfectionism and the rigidities of positive integration, we also need a debate on limiting the perfectionism of negative integration. Only if we succeed in both can we combine the efficiency of the larger market with enhanced EU problem-solving capacity and the preservation of national – and subnational – democracy.

## NOTES

* This chapter is a revised and modified version of an article that appeared in G. Marks, F.W. Scharpf, P.C. Schmitter and W. Streeck, *Governance in the European Union*, London: Sage Publications, 1996.

1 Conversely, national monetary policy does have the power to attract capital, by setting national interest rates above the international level. But in doing so, it will raise the exchange rate, which decreases the international competitiveness of the national economy.

2 Negative integration was and is pursued by the Commission primarily through 'decisions' and 'directives' under Arts. 89 and 90 and through action against national infringements of Treaty obligations under Art. 169. Of the same practical importance is the direct application of European law in ordinary legal disputes before national courts and the possibility, under Art. 177, of preliminary rulings of the ECJ at the request of any (even inferior) national court. Again, the Council is not involved, and governments will typically appear before the Court only in the role of defendants.

3 Streeck (1993: 10) correctly points out that process-related environmental and safety regulations may create obstacles to trade in the market for machine tools and production plants. Thus he includes these in his definition of 'market-making', as distinguished from 'market-correcting', regulations.

4 Naturally, Portugal and Greece (just like eastern Germany) also have islands of above-average productivity, especially in new plants of multinational corporations.

5 According to surveys conducted by the Swedish employers' association (SAF), overall costs of a man-hour in industry ranged in 1993 between 33 Swedish krona in Portugal, 56 krona in Greece, and 204 krona in Germany (Kosonen, 1994).

6 Of course, the intensity of price competition varies between sectors. For example, in agriculture, 'Southern products' hardly compete with 'Northern products'.

7 Thus, it is not only the opposition of enterprises that stands in the way of a European social policy (Streeck, 1993). Governments in economically weaker states must, on their own account, anticipate and try to avoid the exit option of capital.

8 On the other hand, governments which, for domestic reasons, might not wish to agree to a Council directive may actually prefer deregulation by way of Commission directives and decisions.

9 Presumably, if an economy has been viable so far, its regulatory costs are reflected in current prices and exchange rates.

10 The major threat to the viability of the Danish model, incidentally, comes from European plans to harmonize VAT rates.

11 Here, in my view, is the real reason for the current crisis of European welfare states. Given lower rates of economic growth, rising costs of environmental protection, continued mass unemployment, and a growing retirement population, the willingness of blue- and white-collar voters to bear an ever rising tax burden has become the critical constraint on all policies dependent on democratic legitimation.

REFERENCES

Alter, K.J. and Meunier-Aitsahalia, S. (1994) 'Judicial Politics in the European Community. European Integration and the Pathbreaking Cassis de Dijon Decision', *Comparative Political Studies* 26, pp. 535–61.
Crouch, C. (1993) *Industrial Relations and European State Traditions*, Oxford: Clarendon Press.
Dehousse, R. (1993) *Does Subsidiarity Really Matter?*, Florence: EUI Working Paper, Law No. 92/32.
Dehousse, R. and Weiler, J.H.H. (1990) 'The Legal Dimension' in W. Wallace (ed.), *The Dynamics of European Integration*, London: Pinter, pp. 242–60.
Eichener, V. (1993) 'Soziales Dumping oder innovative Regulation? Interessenkonfigurationen und Einflusschancen im Prozess der Harmonisierung des technischen Arbeitsschutzes', in W. Süss and G. Becher (eds.), *Technologieentwicklung und europäische Integration*, Berlin: Duncker u. Humblot, pp. 207–35.
Esping-Andersen, G. (1990) *The Three Worlds of Welfare Capitalism*, Cambridge: Polity Press.
Ganslandt, H. (1993) 'Das System der sozialen Sicherung in Griechenland', in G. Lottes (ed.), *Soziale Sicherheit in Europa. Renten- und Sozialversicherungssysteme im Vergleich*, Heidelberg: Physica, pp. 185–203.
Héritier, A., Mingers, S., Knill, C., and Becka, M. (1994) *Die Veränderung von Staatlichkeit in Europa. Ein regulativer Wettbewerb: Deutschland, Grossbritannien und Frankreich in der Europäischen Union*, Opladen: Leske and Budrich.
Joerges, C. (1991) 'Markt ohne Staat? Die Wirtschaftsverfassung der Gemeinschaft und die regulative Politik', in R. Wildenmann (ed.), *Staatswerdung Europas? Optionen für eine Europäische Union*, Baden-Baden: Nomos, pp. 225–68.
Joerges, C. (1994a) 'Legitimationsprobleme des europäischen Wirtschaftsrechts und der Vertrag von Maastricht', in G. Brüggemeier, (ed.) *Verfassungen für ein ziviles Europa*, Baden-Baden: Nomos, pp. 91–130.
Joerges, C. (1994b) *Rationalisierungsprozesse im Vertragsrecht und im Recht der Produktsicherheit: Beobachtungen zu den Folgen der Europäischen Integration für das Privatrecht*, Florence, EUI Working Paper, Law No. 94/5.
Kapteyn, P. (1991) 'Civilization under Negotiation'. National Civilizations and European Integration: The Treaty of Schengen', *Archives européennes de sociologie*, 32, pp. 363–80.
Kosonen, P. (1994) *The Impact of Economic Integration on National Welfare States in Europe*, Helsinki: University of Helsinki.
Lange, P. (1992) 'The Politics of the Social Dimension' in A.M. Sbragia (ed.), *Euro-Politics: Institutions and Policy making in the 'New' European Community*, Washington, D.C.: Brookings, pp. 225–56.
Leibfried, S. and Pierson, P. (1992) 'Prospects for Social Europe', *Politics & Society* 20, pp. 333–66.
Majone, G. (1993) 'The European Community Between Social Policy and Social Regulation', *Journal of Common Market Studies* 31, pp. 153–70.
Mayntz, R. and Scharpf, F.W. (eds) (1995) *Steuerung und Selbstorganisation in staatsnahen Sektoren*, Frankfurt: Campus.

Merkel, W. (1993) *Ende der Sozialdemokratie? Machtressourcen und Regierungspolitik im westeuropäischen Vergleich*, Frankfurt/M.: Campus.

Mestmäcker, E-J. (1994) 'Zur Wirtschaftsverfassung in der Europäischen Union', in R.H. Hasse, J. Molsberger, and C. Watrin (eds), *Ordnung in Freiheit. Festgabe für Hans Will-gerodt zum 70. Geburstag*, Stuttgart: Fischer, pp. 263–92.

Rehbinder, E. and Stewart, R. (1984) *Environmental Protection Policy; Integration Through Law. Europe and the American Federal Experience*, Vol. 2, Berlin: de Gruyter.

Scharpf, F.W. (1988) 'The Joint Decision Trap: Lessons from German Federalism and European Integration', *Public Administration* 66, pp. 239–78.

Scharpf, F.W. (1991a) *Crisis and Choice in European Social Democracy*, Ithaca: Cornell University Press.

Scharpf, F.W. (1991b) 'Kann es in Europa eine stabile föderale Balance geben? (Thesen)', in R. Wildenmann (ed.), *Staatswerdung Europas? Optionen für eine Europäische Union*, Baden-Baden: Nomos, pp. 415–28.

Scharpf, F.W. (1992b) 'Koordination durch Verhandlungssysteme: Analytische Konzepte und institutionelle Lösungen', in A. Benz, F.W. Scharpf and R. Zintl, *Horizontale Politikverflechtung. Zur Theorie von Verhandlungssystemen*, Frankfurt/M.: Campus, pp. 51–96.

Scharpf, F.W. (1994) 'Community and Autonomy: Multilevel Policy-making in the European Union', *Journal of European Public Policy*, 1, 2, pp. 219–42.

Sinn, S. (1993) 'The Taming of Leviathan. Competition Among Governments', *Constitutional Political Economy* 3, pp. 177–221.

Sinn, H-W. (1994) 'Wieviel Brüssel braucht Europa? Subsidiarität, Zentralisierung und Fiskalwettbewerb im Lichte der ökonomischen Theorie', *Staatswissenschaften und Staatspraxis* 5, pp. 155–86.

Streeck, W. (1993) *From Market Making to State Building? Reflections on the Political Economy of European Social Policy*, University of Wisconsin: Madison.

Tinbergen, J. (1965) *International Economic Integration*, (second edition) Amsterdam: Elsevier.

Tsebelis, G. (1995) 'Decision Making in Political Systems: Veto Players in Presidentialism, Parliamentarism, Multicameralism, and Multipartism', *British Journal of Political Science*, 25, 3, pp. 289–326.

Voelzkow, H. (1993) *Staatseingriff und Verbandsfunktion: Das verbandliche System technischer Regelsetzung als Gegenstand staatlicher Politik*, Discussion Paper 93/2, Köln, MPI für Gesellschaftsforschung.

Weiler, J.H.H. (1981) 'The Community System. The Dual Character of Supranationalism', in *Yearbook of European Law* 1, pp. 257–306.

Weiler, J.H.H. (1994) 'A Quiet Revolution. The European Court of Justice and Its Interlocutors', *Comparative Political Studies* 26, pp. 510–34.

# 9 Globalization, Labour Markets and Welfare States: A Future of 'Competitive Corporatism'?

Martin Rhodes

## INTRODUCTION

The relationship between globalization and welfare states has neither been adequately theorized nor empirically investigated. Much of the literature assumes a convergence among European welfare states on a 'lean welfare model', given external competitive pressures and unsustainable domestic commitments, while, in the absence of a strong European industrial relations system and social dimension, the collapse of corporatist structures alongside the fragmentation of labour markets is inevitable (for a survey, see Rhodes, 1996). Despite much controversy in the literature over the origins of these changes in national institutional structures, it does seem to be the case that developments in international capitalism are reducing the ability of states to control their economic 'borders', in part because, as Cerny argues, the scale of goods and assets produced and exchanged has diverged from the structural scale of the nation-state, making it increasingly more difficult to provide and control particular public goods (Cerny, 1995). At the same time, these developments have altered the balance of power in domestic settings, shifting influence in favour of capital and giving it an effective veto power in certain cases through enhanced exit options via relocation to foreign markets.

This article does not seek to deny the relevance of the globalization argument: indeed, its central purpose is to try and identify some ways in which globalization interacts with domestic institutional developments. Its central argument is that state steering capacity is being constrained by developments beyond national borders, but that this does not necessarily mean a loss of state control or convergence in a 'neo-liberal' direction, in terms either of institutional change or policy objectives. Indeed, reforming labour market regulation and recasting welfare states may require in most European countries a search for a new type of 'corporatism' rather than its abandonment and, rather than an Anglo-Saxon deregulation of the labour market, a readjustment of the 'continental' model to accommodate market pressures with the preservation of social protection and social consensus. Successful economic adjustment, including greater flexibility in labour markets and the organization of welfare states, may require, in turn, a flexible form of 'market' or 'competitive' corporatism rather than attempted moves in a neo-liberal direction.

Nevertheless, these developments will have important consequences for the organization of welfare states: greater flexibility in the labour market means greater wage flexibility and wage dispersion, increased flexibility in the funding of programmes linked to labour costs and greater flexibility in the design of social security systems. Inevitably, the nature of the 'social contract' will change in the process, involving the greater centrality of the firm, both as an actor and model for socioeconomic organization (see Chapter 11 by Colin Crouch), and the tailoring of social intervention more closely with the demands of competition. As a result, although it may be possible to prevent a convergence on a 'Hobbesian order' of the kind predicted by Bill Jordan (Chapter 12), the low levels of income inequality that have been a feature of the northern continental European welfare states in the past will prove difficult to preserve. Nevertheless, it is the contention of this chapter that those countries most successful in adjusting their economies to the new demands of the global era will be those which simultaneously make the operation of their labour markets and product markets more efficient, while also preserving social cohesion and trust.[1]

## EXTERNAL PRESSURES; DOMESTIC RESPONSES

Two major external pressures have important implications for industrial relations in western European countries and, potentially, also for welfare states. First, more intense *international competition* and *globalization* are placing pressure on both wage and non-wage costs and creating the conditions in which 'social dumping' within western Europe and relocation to countries outside western Europe becomes a potential threat to the status quo. The new international division of labour within large transnational firms and the introduction by multinationals of 'alien' elements into national bargaining arenas causes adjustment problems especially for centralized systems. Cross-class 'flexibility' alliances have undermined 'social corporatist' systems and induced a shift to a more sectorally-based form of bargaining, as in some Scandinavian countries,[2] while employers in all systems are searching for greater company and plant level flexibility in three areas:

- internal (or functional) flexibility in the work place;
- external (or numerical) flexibility *vis-à-vis* the wider labour market;
- and greater pay flexibility at local levels.

Second, and at the same time, the *creation of the single market* and *movement towards EMU* are also placing greater pressure on wage cost competition given the difficulty of competitive devaluation. This again focuses effort on adjusting costs to rapidly changing competitive situations and the focus of employers turns naturally to their capacity for adjusting firm level costs through a combination of flexibility strategies – producing greater freedom from regulatory pressure in the areas of pay, hiring and dismissals and the deployment of labour within the firm.

The above pressures lead, therefore, to attempts to *decentralize* in industrial relations systems. But, although this might suggest that pressures are all focused on decentralizing and deregulating labour markets, there are two important counter-pressures. First, also in response to competitive pressures, and the diffusion of new forms of 'best practice' management and work organization, manufacturers – and also certain service-sector companies – are embracing the principles and techniques of flexible specialization, lean production and total quality management. This implies the creation or maintenance of *co-operative labour relations* and a *high-trust internal firm environment*. The optimal world of internal flexibility in this environment is, therefore, built not by unilateral management action but on team work and low levels of hierarchy within firms. It also depends not just on high levels of skills but also on high capacities for skills acquisition. At the same time, building and sustaining high levels of trust within the company/plant demands not a high degree, but a moderate degree of external flexibility, in other words the capacity of entrepreneurs to adjust their quantity of labour. Too high a level of external flexibility destroys trust and undermines internal flexibility. This trade off – producing a productive form of 'regulated co-operation'[3] – is a critical one for sustaining both competitiveness *and* consensus in European labour markets.

At the same time, both cost competitiveness and stability require more than simply a deregulatory strategy at the level of the firms: they also require a means of preventing wage drift and inflationary pressures from building up in the labour market. This has focused the attention of governments in countries where trade unions are still significant actors on *centralization* on the broad priorities of national wage bargaining, both as a means of keeping inflation in line with Maastricht convergence criteria and preventing rising wage costs from damaging competitiveness and creating more unemployment.

In sum, there are pressures for both a decentralization and a centralization (in some cases a recentralization) of industrial relations systems. An 'optimal' solution would combine some form of incomes policy or national wage co-ordination with pay flexibility within certain margins at the level of the firm, as achieved, for example, in the Dutch system of 'centralized decentralization' (see below). However, such systems clearly also have negative consequences. The building of high trust, internal firm environments with an accent on flexible skills acquisition, alongside a degree of pay flexibility, may do little for labour market 'outsiders' and will increase wage differentials. A more variegated labour market seems inevitable, as does the spread of 'discontinuous' life-work cycles, implying the adjustment of social security systems to cope.


## INSTITUTIONAL ADJUSTMENTS

This chapter does not wish to suggest that the above pressures will lead to direct, and predictable institutional changes in labour markets and industrial relations systems, nor that the outcomes of change will be in the direction of convergence in employment systems or welfare state organization. Research in recent years on the changing configurations of work, employer-employee relations and welfare attest to the persistence of differences, due to the continued importance of the 'societal effect' – that is, the complex relationships between key elements of national economic systems which make them resistant to change and critical in the mediation of any external pressures, be they technological or political/institutional (such as the promotion of an EU social policy) (Maurice, 1995; Jones and Cressey, 1995). Yet given the nature of the 'external environment', which is considerably more constraining and less tolerant of national distinctions than in the past, some responses will more successfully accommodate these pressures than others.

In theory, a west European country's political/institutional structure must accommodate the following pressures without jeopardizing its socioeconomic/political stability if it is to retain its competitive position in a globalizing economy:

- the need to sustain or enter onto a 'high quality' adjustment path (competition based on quality rather than 'price') for key parts of its industrial structure;
- the need for co-operative, competition-oriented labour relations within plants;
- the need for controlled labour costs and prices;
- the capacity for complex trade-offs between external and internal flexibility in the labour market.

As already stated, this does not imply a micro-level convergence in institutions. As shown by recent research on employment and labour market policies, quite different institutions may be functional for different types of firm-market relationship. It would make little sense, for example, to transfer the German training model to a country or region with a quite different system of production with different needs and requirements, regardless of the fact that the German system may be more 'functional' for German industry than, say, Italy's training system for Italian industry (Regini, 1995). But at the more general level of broad institutional relationships, only a limited range of institutional configurations are available to meet the objectives outlined above or solve the problem of their non-delivery. This is why this chapter refers to 'optimal' institutional arrangements and combinations of different types of flexibility. Similar arguments have been used in the past to compare countries in terms of their capacity for controlling unemployment and inflation (the combination of which has been referred to as the 'misery index'). The well-known U-curve model of Calmfors and Driffill, for example, postulated that either highly centralized systems of wage bargaining or highly decentralized systems were capable of delivering the desirable result of low inflation and low unemployment, but that countries in the middle would suffer substantial collective action problems in achieving either (Calmfors and Driffill, 1988). By contrast, this chapter argues that neither highly decentralized systems in Europe nor highly centralized systems are capable of responding to the multiple challenges identified above. Instead, although they are not without their dangers, pragmatic and flexible social pacts involving the social partners – even if they are only moderately well organized and if they include significant elements of decentralization – are best suited to allow a flexible form of adjustment to external challenges.

Successful 'convergence', if it were to occur, would be on some form of 'competitive corporatism' which would be rather different in form in several major ways from the 'social corporatism' of the Scandinavian type that has absorbed the attention of most analysts in the past:

- it would not necessarily involve concertation between centralized peak organizations with a monopoly of coverage, on either the employers or trade union side, since in the post-Fordist, post-Keynesian era such structures have been undermined even in those countries where historical trajectories once favoured them;
- it would rather involve much weaker organizations, each seeking to defend their own organizational cohesion by engaging in concertation with each other and governments, the latter being the most likely instigators (as proven by recent experience) of 'social pacts';
- it would not involve redistributive/equity-linked, labour-market/welfare politics of the Scandinavian 'social corporatist' type but rather only weak components of this type;
- it would rather involve the negotiated adjustment and restructuring of labour market regulation and labour-market-linked welfare programmes, especially pensions funding and entitlements and social security arrangement, while also aiming to achieve, to some extent, two of the more traditional objectives of 'social corporatism' – macro-economic stability and higher levels of employment (although this may be through a combination of measures to defend the existing employed and provide new opportunities for the unemployed);
- it would involve, to a greater or lesser extent depending on the country, negotiating shifts along the external/internal flexibility continuums (see figure 9.1) – involving quite important regulatory reform in some countries;
- and it would be a convergence only within broad parameters: the space for national diversity in institutional arrangement will narrow, but the 'societal effect' will remain important in shaping particular policy structures and outcomes.

In spite of the differences between them, the underlying logic of 'social' and 'competitive' corporatism is in a crucial sense the same: the search for a meaningful form of political exchange in which certain 'goods' are bargained. In the market for political exchange of the 'social corporatist' type, the goods are much more predictable and less subject to negotiation themselves than in the 'competitive' corporatist type, and the costs of entering and exiting the latter type of market are much lower. This suggests that 'competitive' corporatism will be much less stable and more subject to periodic break down and frequent renegotiation. The terms of the bargain may change from one set of negotiations to the next. But before examining this issue closer by looking at a number of examples of recent western European social pacts, what of the politics of flexibility that lies at the heart of these new types of concertation?

RECASTING EUROPEAN LABOUR MARKETS

Although the rhetoric of 'flexibility' is frequently deployed by either employers or trade unions in a highly politicized, if not ideological, way, 'flexibility' in labour markets must be taken seriously if we are to understand the adaptability of countries to new demands of competition in a globalizing economy. If we refer to Figure 9.1, we can see, roughly, how different European countries compare, both among themselves and with their international competitors, along two dimensions of labour market flexibility – internal flexibility and external flexibility.

**Moderately Flexible Internal and External Labour Markets**

The area between the upper part of quadrant three and the lower part of quadrant four is identified as the optimal location for countries wishing to respond to the external challenges mentioned above. It combines a high degree of internal flexibility (based on redeployable skills, high levels of skill acquisition and trust) with a level of external flexibility which is not incompatible with the preservation of trust within the firm. The network of labour institutions that underpins these relationships in the labour market are essential for providing a stable framework for investment, growth and an equitable distribution of the costs and benefits of economic adjustment.[4] A degree of pay flexibility (which is not accommodated within Figure 9.1) within a broadly co-ordinated system is also, as already stated, essential for countries at this intersection of the two quadrants if they are to accommodate themselves to the demands placed on them by European economic integration (both the single market and monetary union). Some are better equipped in this regard than others. Germany appears to be a case *par excellence* of a system that is able to accommodate both cost pressures and new 'best practice' managerial and technological developments with, so far, little change to established working practices, labour relations and methods of labour deployment (Lane, 1994).

Essentially, it is the argument of this chapter that either movement towards this 'optimal' location, or remaining within it, requires a particular institutional structure, and one which approximates 'competitive corporatism'. All of the countries in this area of the diagram have moderately well organized employers and trade unions and average membership density levels. France is the exception, and it is certainly the case that France currently faces the greatest adjustment problems in this group because its trade unions are incapable of organizing a significant portion

FLEXIBLE EXTERNAL,
RIGID INTERNAL
LABOUR MARKETS (1)

EXTERNAL
FLEXIBILITY

FLEXIBLE INTERNAL
AND EXTERNAL
LABOUR MARKETS (4)

HIGH

USA
(1990s)

ASIAN
TIGERS

JAPAN
PERIPHERY

BRITAIN
(1990s)

USA
(1970s)

IRELAND
(1990s)

NETHER-
LANDS

THIRD
ITALY

IRELAND
(1970s)

GERMANY

INTERNAL
FLEXIBILITY

LOW

HIGH

ITALY
(1990s)

FRANCE

JAPAN
(CORE)

BRITAIN
(1970s)

SPAIN
(1990s)

ITALY
(1970s)

SWEDEN
DENMARK
(1990s)

PORTUGAL

SPAIN
(1980s)

GREECE

SWEDEN
DENMARK
(1970s)

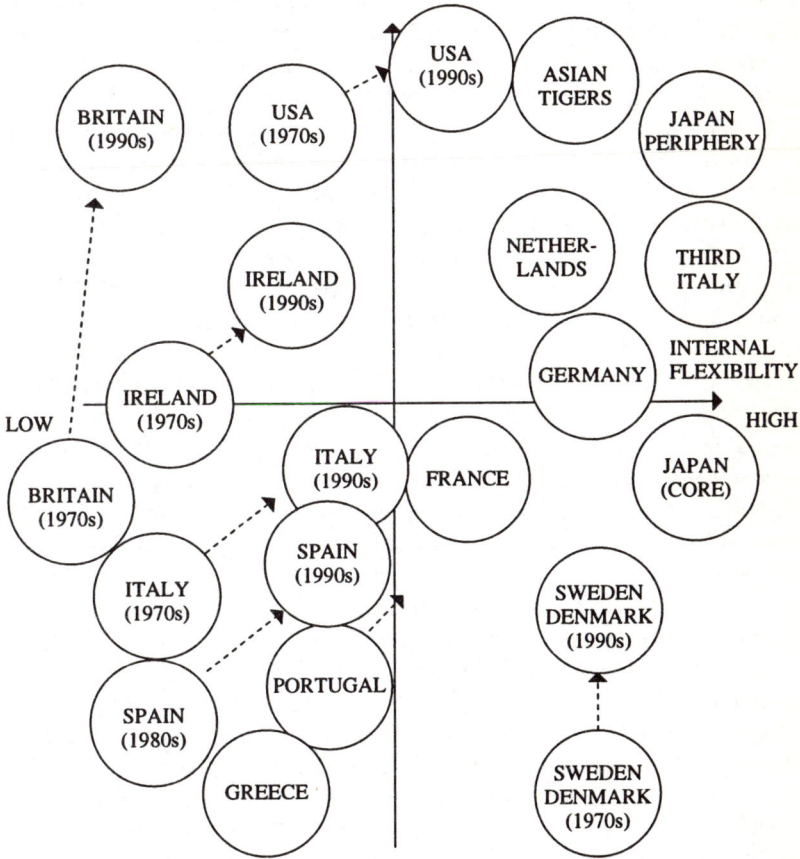

RIGID INTERNAL AND
EXTERNAL LABOUR
MARKETS (2)

LOW

FLEXIBLE INTERNAL,
RIGID EXTERNAL
LABOUR MARKETS (3)

*Figure 9.1*   Labour Market Flexibility Trends

of the French work force (either of the blue collar or white collar variety)
behind a bargain with government on critical issues at the labour
market/welfare state interface (a contrast of the politics of pension reform
in France and more corporatist Italy is instructive in this regard). This

helps explain why restoring the financial equilibrium of the French social security system is involving a shift from Bismarckian social insurance towards a non-employment-based, state-controlled system (Bonoli and Palier, 1997).

But other countries in this group may face problems as well. The Scandinavian countries, for example, are in a process of transition from a centralized 'social' corporatist system towards a less centralized system, in which the emergence of 'cross-class flexibility alliances' make difficult the stabilization of this system around a new institutional equilibrium (Iversen, 1996). However, present trends in Denmark suggest the preservation of a degree of concertation in industrial policy and a search for a new institutional structure for wage bargaining close to the German model of *tarif autonomie* (independent wage bargaining) within a monetary straight-jacket. Germany is also facing problems, with demands for greater internal and external flexibility from employers and problems in negotiating a reform of Germany's generous social protection system. A downward – but negotiated – adjustment of this system seems inevitable, alongside a greater decentralization of wage setting and work force adjustment flexibility. Highly compressed wage differentials – one of the key components of the German system – are likely to expand, as employers attempt to break with the established practice of bringing skilled and semiskilled workers within similar pay parameters, with unpredictable consequences for worker solidarity. While some – who would also point to the decline in firm membership of employers' organizations as individual employers seek greater pay autonomy – see such trends as the first step towards the collapse of the German system, others see it as essential if the country is to respond more flexibly to competitive challenges. For as Carlin and Soskice (1997) argue, radical deregulation is not the answer to the need for German firms to adjust rapidly in response to changes in world markets. For this would undermine the interlocking set of institutions that provides German companies (and, to a lesser extent, other companies in this group) with comparative institutional advantage – the industrial relations and vocational training system which provides a co-operative and highly skilled work force and a form of corporate governance and inter-company relations which provides patient capital and a capacity for technology transfer (see also Rhodes and van Apeldoorn, 1997). But those firms may, on the other hand, benefit from greater internal flexibility with regard to the pay and career development of skilled workers than is provided under the present system of collective bargaining.

## Flexible External and Inflexible Internal Labour Markets

As Figure 9.1 shows, the trajectory of Europe's neo-liberal example – the UK – is far from being optimal in terms of its combination of 'flexibilities' (quadrant one). This is an interesting trajectory because the major innovation since the 1970s – when the UK was close to the southern European cluster in terms of its rigid labour markets – has been the increase in external flexibility, as employers' ability to hire, fire and recruit on a diverse range of labour contracts has been increased. Many would argue that there has been a simultaneous increase in the level of internal labour market flexibility, especially with the break down of union control over the work place. However, the positive effect of this shift towards greater internal flexibility in terms of employer's unilateral power, has been counteracted by the lack of any substantial increase in levels of trust (except in inward investing Japanese firms which, in some sectors, have revolutionized work organization) and still high levels of hierarchy in most UK firms. At the same time, the traditional fragmentation of employers and trade unions has increased, making the provision of collective goods (such as an effective training system) an impossibility, while also making it difficult for the country to escape its 'low skills equilibrium'.

The flexibility trajectory of British firms is, therefore, in danger of taking them along a 'price-based' rather than 'quality-based' competition path, even if lower levels of unemployment than in other European countries suggest a degree of success in labour market innovation. In this respect too, the UK is moving closer to the US model of job creation, with lower costs allowing the recruitment of greater numbers on lower wages (assisted by the abolition of the old Wages Councils – which imposed a UK equivalent of a minimum wage) and provoking the emergence of a new social category – the 'working poor'. Another problem is that, with a decentralized wage bargaining system, the assumption that employers will be able to contain costs and wage drift may prove to be unfounded (as suggested by the still apparent tendency of inflation to rise with economic growth). But the organizational disarray of UK industrial relations militates against an incomes policy (as does the bitter memory of its failure in the 1970s), and will prevent a Labour government from developing a more organized labour market strategy, even if it should seek to develop one (which seems unlikely).[5]

Ireland is following a rather different course, and is moving much closer to the continental systems, especially in terms of its emphasis on consensus-based labour market policy making. Its 'social pact' of recent years has held, despite strong internal tensions, and provides an interesting case-study of concertation – or 'competitive corporatism' – in a cold climate (see below for further details).

## Rigid Internal and External Labour Markets

The countries in quadrant two – which we can refer to as the 'southern cluster' – are in many ways the most interesting in the context of the present discussion, since, despite their manifold difficulties in making the transition towards an optimal combination of flexibilities, they have made important progress within the framework of new social pacts. Employers in these countries have conventionally had to cope with heavy constraints in both external flexibility and internal flexibility, and – beyond the rhetoric of their disputes with trade unions – this has had important consequences for industrial adjustment and employment. Of course, there has always been considerable flexibility in many of these countries, in the form of extensive black economies, small firms beneath the regulatory thresholds (as in Italy where the 1970 Workers' Charter only covered firms with more than 14 employees) and in the unionized, yet highly flexible small firm clusters of the 'Third Italy' (hence its location in quadrant four). But in many large firms, external flexibility and adjustment has been limited by the rigid nature of collective bargaining and state regulation, while all firms have suffered from problems of high internal hierarchy and low levels of trust, and the absence of effective national training systems.

At the same time, wage inflation has been difficult to contain, and in Italy was compounded by a generous system of wage indexation that was only dismantled in the early 1990s. While labour market reform in some countries has been ineffective and conflict-ridden, provoking perverse outcomes (as in the excessive growth of temporary contracts following their liberalization in Spain in the late 1980s), in others it has been more consensual and bargained through increasingly well-consolidated 'social pacts', those of Italy and Portugal being the prime examples. As a result, innovations in labour market institutions and policies are putting some of these countries on a transition path that may lead them towards convergence on the 'optimal' location at the intersection of quadrants three and four. This depends, however, on the durability of the new 'competitive corporatism' that has been developed in these countries and on their capacity to build some of the institutional attributes of 'regulated cooperation' as it exists in the 'best practice' European countries, namely the Netherlands and Germany. This is not to say that these countries must emulate precisely the institutional design of the latter, but rather that they must achieve some 'functional equivalents' in terms of industrial relations, wage bargaining, training and innovation, while at the same time making their labour markets more flexible to remove the sometimes acute 'insider-outsider' problems that afflict them and improve employment prospects for those excluded from the labour market (in essence, this is the lesson being imparted to these countries by the OECD).

Of course, there is always the possibility that these countries could move towards quadrant one, that is in an Anglo-Saxon direction, in which the 'public goods' associated with a movement towards quadrant three would not be provided by the state, in collaboration with the social partners, but rather would be provided within 'company communities' that create their own support cultures (see Crouch, this volume, and Crouch and Streeck, 1997). In this event, these countries are unlikely to be able to take the high-wage, quality production path of economic development (even if they have pockets of advanced production as a result of foreign direct investment); and social inequality, which has narrowed in some of these countries (notably Spain) in recent years, will increase.


## SOCIAL PACTS AND 'COMPETITIVE CORPORATISM'

In one of the few attempts to link the character of a country's labour market flexibility to its levels of bargaining, Alain Lipietz argues that flexibility and negotiated involvement cannot be combined *à la carte*. In particular, a high level of flexibility (in this case conceived of simply in terms of wage flexibility) is assumed to be incompatible with a high level of negotiated involvement, certainly at the societal level, as in the Scandinavian case, while moderate levels of wage flexibility will be compatible with sectoral level negotiations and a high level of flexibility with individual contracts and minimal union involvement (the USA) (Lipietz, 1997). The recent evolution of the Swedish model, which has seen employers seek greater wage flexibility by pushing bargaining away from the central level, would seem to support this conclusion. It may also be the case that the German system will see greater wage flexibility involve a shift to lower levels of bargaining, in which plant-level works councils take power away from branch-level union negotiators. The combination of flexibility *and* negotiated involvement in the 'post-Fordist' conception of 'flexible specialization', as advanced by Piore and Sabel (1984), for example, is deemed infeasible.

This argument suffers, however, from two deficiencies. Firstly, flexibility is mainly conceived in terms of 'liberal wage flexibility' which effectively excludes consideration of the 'constructive' nature of certain forms and combinations of 'flexibilities' for firms and employees. Second, its relationship of certain levels of bargaining with certain types of flexibility is too restrictive, given the emergence of multiple bargaining levels in many countries as employers, trade unions and governments seek to respond to external and domestic pressures. It is the argument of the analysis in this chapter that recent innovations in a number of countries have witnessed the attempt to combine a societal form of bargaining *alongside* flexibility at lower levels, be they the branch or the firm, in which a general system of co-ordination is sustained. It is this search for new institutional responses to demands for 'flexibility' and 'competitiveness', within the external straight jacket of EMU and greater cost competition, that underpins the recent emergence of new forms of corporatist bargaining in western Europe.

'Social pacts' of one sort or another have been concluded and implemented in recent years in the Netherlands, Belgium, Finland, Ireland, Portugal, Spain (in a limited sense), Italy and Greece. We can illustrate the diversity but also the commonalities of such pacts by taking four examples: Ireland, Italy, Portugal and the Netherlands.[6]

In the Irish case, a rather comprehensive social pact negotiated in 1987, 1990 and again in 1993 built on a tradition of centralized wage bargaining and a trend established in the 1980s to address tax, education, health and social welfare issues as well. The emphasis of all three agreements (the most recent entitled the 'Programme for Economic and Social Progress') has been on macroeconomic stability, greater equity in the tax system, and enhanced social justice – in the form of inflation-proof benefits, job creation (in manufacturing and international services sectors) and the reform of labour legislation in the areas of part-time work, employment equality and unfair dismissal, although the labour market remains characterized by a high degree of rigidity, with unemployment and poverty traps exacerbating the problem of long-term unemployment (Rhodes, 1995). Pay rises have been subject to floor and ceiling levels. In return, the trade unions have delivered industrial relations harmony. A rather sceptical evaluation of these pacts has concluded that they have not delivered much when compared to the 'social corporatism' of the Scandinavian model: main objectives such as employment creation have not been achieved and tax reforms have been only incompletely implemented and there has been little serious consideration of how training is linked to the wage-formation system or to how it should be developed as a collective good (Teague, 1995).

Nevertheless, government commitments across a range of issues have been respected, including increasing resources in education, public housing and health care, while also extending social protection to part-time workers and introducing legislation on unfair dismissal, employment agencies and conditions of employment. The social pacts have also played a major role in securing macroeconomic stability, delivering a high level of economic growth in recent years, compared with its European neighbours, and making Ireland one of the most likely members of EMU, since it now more or less fulfils all of the convergence conditions. Also importantly, industrial peace has been preserved, as has the organizational cohesion of the social partners in a time of upheaval – not to mention the tendency of multinationals to try and avoid the recognition of unions (see below). Still to be addressed, however, is the problem that these agreements have largely been tailored to the demands of the stronger unionized sector (rather than those of small and medium-sized firms facing international competition) and that the emphasis has been on protecting the post-tax income of the employed 'insiders', while showing less concern for the 'outsider' unemployed (Kavanagh *et al.*, 1997).

In the Italian case, negotiations in the early 1990s that initially focused on reforming Italy's automatic wage-indexation system – the *scala mobile* – were extended to include the rationalization of bargaining structures and the reform of union representation in the work place. In the significant agreement of July 1993, the *scala mobile* was abolished and a far-reaching reform of incomes policy and collective bargaining was achieved. Henceforth, biannual tripartite and collective agreements were to set macroeconomic guidelines and establish a framework for incomes policy; sectoral agreements were to be signed at the national level on wages (valid for two years) and conditions of employment (valid for four); and enterprise level agreements were to be concluded for four years and negotiated by workers' representatives. The latter innovation created a new form and level of representation within the firm – *Rappresentanza sindacale unitaria* – in which two-thirds of representatives were to be elected by the entire work force (and not just union members as before) and one-third appointed by representative unions, providing an important link between the work place and higher levels of union organization (Regini and Regalia, 1997).

Apart from contributing to Italy's fulfilment of EMU entry conditions – which it has achieved by effectively taking inflation out of the labour market – this social pact also covered a number of other areas, including new measures to compensate those laid off in restructuring, improvements to the training system (boosting internal flexibility), the legalization of temporary work agencies (improving external flexibility), assistance for the unemployed to enter the labour market, and improving the general performance of Italian industry. But it has also become the forum for bargaining the future of more broader aspects of social regulation. The most significant step in this regard was the agreement signed between the unions and the government on pension reform in May 1995 (the employers abstained) which was put to a referendum in the workplaces by the unions where it obtained a hard-won but significant majority backing. This consensus was achieved at the expense of a more radical reform (it retained the previous pension system for elderly workers and introduced a more rigorous system for less senior workers) but it also avoided protracted industrial dislocation, as occurred in the case of the Juppé reforms in France (Regini and Regalia, 1997), and avoided any adverse knock-on effects on other aspects of the social pact, despite the fact that the implementation of the incomes policy has favoured an increase in company profits at a time of reductions in purchasing power. Whether the system can survive the current challenges – including 'one last push for Maastricht' austerity budgets and discontent in various powerful sections of the labour movement (notably the metal workers) with constrained pay agreements – remains to be seen.

In the Portuguese case, there have been five tripartite pacts since 1987 – the latest was signed in 1996 – focusing on incomes and social and labour market measures. They have been presented from the outset as critical for improving the competitiveness of the Portuguese economy and for integration into EMU. The agreements have been very wide-ranging, covering pay rise ceilings, levels of minimum wages, easing regulations on the organization of work (rest, overtime and shift work) – internal flexibility – and on the termination of employment – external flexibility, and the regulation of working hours. The 1992 agreement was broadened further to cover social security issues, including improvements in health insurance reimbursements and tax relief on housing. The 1996 agreement also implemented an incomes policy, linking wage rises to inflation and productivity forecasts (with scope for variation within margins at lower levels), and union agreement has been secured by a commitment to training and employment placement services, to enforcing various rights for part-timers, and a broad programme of working time reduction, with the introduction of a 40-hour week in two stages. The new agreement also covers numerous social security issues, including the reduction of social security contributions for those employers belonging to employers' associations (a measure also conceived to strengthen organizational cohesion) and the introduction of a minimum income on an experimental basis for those on very low incomes. In addition, income tax for those on low incomes will be reduced and a more favourable tax treatment will be made of a variety of health and education benefits as well as old age pensions.

Perhaps the most interesting developments have been in the Netherlands where, as a result of monetary stability, budgetary discipline and social security, something of a 'model' attracting policy emulation in other countries has begun to emerge.[7] In the Netherlands, the early and mid-1980s witnessed one of the most severe employment crises in western Europe, with unemployment reaching 15.4 per cent in 1984. This was attributable in part to the immobilism in industrial relations between the early 1970s and early 1980s (which followed 20 years of state-led, centrally guided, corporatist governance until 1968), a period during which both trade unions and employers rejected a state-led system of incomes policy. In the 1970s, when the twin oil-price shocks fuelled inflation and rising unemployment across western Europe, the negative consequences for the Netherlands were compounded by a break down in relations between the social partners that helped produce a vicious cycle – referred to as 'the Dutch disease' – in which real labour costs accelerated ahead of productivity gains, profits deteriorated, firms substituted capital for labour or relocated to low labour cost areas, and unemployment rose spectacularly (Hemerijk and van den Toren, 1996).

Since 1982, however, the picture has been quite different. Since the signature of a national social pact between employers and trade unions in November that year, there has been a return to corporatism, but a more flexible and responsive bipartite rather than tripartite version, one involving a considerable degree of decentralization in wage bargaining that is compatible with intensified international constraints. This has provided the basis for industrial relations peace, wage moderation and an ongoing process of labour market *re*regulation that has helped keep wage costs down, prevent increasing inequality and boost employment (above all part-time and temporary contracts) to the point where the present 6.7 per cent unemployed is one of the lowest in the OECD area, and where between 1983 and 1993, job growth (at 1.8 per cent per annum) exceeded both the OECD and EU averages (Hemerijk and van den Toren, 1996). The 1982 agreement was consolidated in 1993 at a time when a new rise in unemployment began to place the consensus under pressure. In the 1993 accord, there is provision for greater decentralization of bargaining to company level within the overall coordinated structure – described by Visser (1996) as 'centralized decentralization'. In addition to wage moderation, over this period, concertation has also produced agreements on social security contributions, work sharing and industrial policy, training, job enrichment, the development of 'entry-level' wages and, most recently, the 1995 'flexicurity' accord in which rights for temporary workers were strengthened in return for a loosening of dismissal protection for core workers. There has also been a recent revival of tripartite corporatism, with the reorganization of Dutch employment services along tripartite lines in 1991 and calls by the tripartite Social and Economic Council (which has been marginalized by the shift to bipartism in recent years) for a renewal of national consensus creation, involving government, employers and trade unions in the face of European integration and international competitive pressures. Most importantly, government intervention has been essential in helping break the blockage in negotiations on social security reform, an area where it has proven much more difficult to find agreement on changes to the amount and duration of benefits.

The Dutch case, then, as Visser describes it, is one of corporatism, but not one that is 'against markets': rather, it is a system of 'corporatism and the market' (Visser, 1996) in which monetary stability, budgetary discipline and competitiveness have been achieved, while also reforming social security and boosting unemployment, and escaping both the increase in social inequality that has occurred in Britain and the break down in consensus and large-scale social unrest suffered by France. *En bref*, it is perhaps the most advanced example of 'competitive corporatism' in western Europe.

## THE ORIGINS AND DURABILITY OF 'COMPETITIVE CORPORATISM'

Despite the diversity of the 'new social pacts', they share a number of common features (*International Labour Review*, 1995):

- governments are usually the instigators and in this respect they are state-led;
- they are special initiatives that create a new layer of industrial relations on top of established routine practice, but gradually the 'special' and the 'routine' have become mixed, providing a degree of institutionalization for the new pacts and the co-operative industrial relations practices that underpin them;
- they seek to introduce new forms of labour market flexibility, but frequently they also include new and negotiated forms of social protection, as in the Irish and Portuguese cases;
- they seek to reduce deficits in public or social spending, but do so in a way that avoids either unilateral decision making or a substantial equity deficit and have also successfully avoided disruptive social protest,

although in certain countries (Italy is currently the major example) the strains are beginning to show;

● and they seek to share the burden of achieving productivity gains and the benefits of growth, although this is much harder to achieve in practice than some of the other objectives.

Why do these pacts work? The main reason seems to be the search for 'least bad' solutions by all partners concerned in hard times. Vulnerability to external forces seems to be a key variable in explaining the adjustment of domestic institutional structures and relationships. Governments need to find partners in achieving broad macroeconomic objectives at a time of difficult adjustment to the demands of European integration – especially the Maastricht convergence criteria for membership of EMU. While on the one hand this period has seen a growing shift in the locus of policy making towards central bankers (which in some cases, as in Italy, have become government leaders), taking inflation out of the labour market requires a policy of co-operation between government and the social partners. In this sense, governments are dependent on union and employer organizations and it is in their interest to prevent the latter from declining in terms of their representational strength. Somewhat paradoxically, as shown by the Italian case, this representational strength should be somewhat less than a monopoly, for where trade unions have enjoyed maximum power resources in this respect (as in the Scandinavian case) this has become increasingly incompatible with the emergence of a post-Fordist, internationalized business system and has increasingly tempted governments to bypass or constrain the actions of the social partners (as in the strategy of the Swedish government in the 1980s in importing wage discipline by tying the Krone to the DM).

As recently argued in the Italian case (but this is also applicable to the other countries where 'new' social pacts have been successfully negotiated), unions which do not have high power resources but are well rooted in the work place and embedded in networks of more or less institutionalized co-operation can successfully be involved in concertation because they provide both a constraint and a resource for their partners (Regini and Regalia, 1997): a constraint because they can still effectively veto many policies to which they are opposed (even if this influence is heavily reduced in a period of tight labour markets and deflationary policies); and a resource, not only because they can deliver the support of their members behind agreements, but because in their absence as effective intermediaries, a more militant, fragmented and undisciplined labour movement would be even more difficult to deal with. This is one reason why employers have not engaged in an anti-union strategy of the British type (where derecognition is increasingly common) and are unlikely to do so if they wish to contain labour costs and promote or maintain co-operative work relations within the firm. Nor, should it be stressed, are they likely to weaken their own associations to a critical degree: even in the German case where employers' associations have seen companies abandon their membership and seek to break away from sectoral wage bargaining, employers' associations remain strong bargaining partners.

But of course, this last point does indicate a major source of union weakness – their loss of membership and fear of a further loss of associational strength. One way of sustaining this strength is to be seen to be capable of delivering results – albeit meagre ones because of the poor economic context – to their members and thereby prevent membership loss. Another is to change orientation and seek, as the Dutch trade unions have done, to make 'precarious' – that is, part-time and temporary workers – a key part of their constituency, negotiating in the Dutch case a 'Flexibility and Security' agreement to accommodate such workers in 1996, a strategy which also helps stem a loss of membership and counter the erosion of union strength (Visser, 1996). As Regini and Regalia (1997) argue, as both resource and constraint for their social partners, unions may discourage both governments and employers from taking unilateral action that would risk confrontation, while they may also be able to convince their rank and file that existing power relations will not allow them to obtain more than the joint regulation of wages and some economic and employment policies. In brief, governments and the social partners need each other to achieve 'least bad' outcomes.

What are the threats to the durability of the new social pacts? One is *external*. For while international competition is one of the factors that may be promoting co-operative labour relations in those countries where unions are well institutionalized in firms, at the same time, internationalization and the operations of multinational companies may menace co-operative labour relations if they break with national industrial relations conventions and undermine the connection between employees and trade unions. This occurs in most countries, but has been particularly notable in those with very high levels of inward investment: a recent survey in Ireland, for example, shows that many multinationals operating in that country have been seeking ways of avoiding dealing with unions.

A second threat is *internal* and may derive from the relatively low exit costs involved in these pacts. Especially in those countries with a prior tradition of worker militancy and weak federal unions, it is much too early to say whether involvement in pacts marks a permanent shift to a more co-operative form of labour relations, or, indeed, whether the incentives for co-operation can be maintained in the medium-term. In the Italian case, for example, the commitment of the trade unions is being strained by the constraints on purchasing power that has resulted from the social pact and by government pressures to proceed further with pensions reform. On the other hand, it may be that the costs of exiting from these pacts is actually quite high, even if they are not deeply institutionalized. The exit costs for employers stem from the consequences of a break down in wage discipline and an inability to control labour costs. The exit costs for trade unions may also be high, for abandoning collaboration also means abandoning influence and perhaps also, a reduction in their own capacity for collective action if they are consequently sidelined by employers.

A solution to both problems may come from the European level. Despite the many problems facing the constitution of 'Social Europe', the recently introduced legislation on European works councils and their implementation in a growing number of transnational companies in Europe may prevent such companies from breaking with national industrial relations practice and from breaking the connection between their workers and unions. As for the problem of exit from these pacts, additional incentives for continued participation must be provided at the national level in terms of a return to productivity-linked wage increases as well as employment creation as soon as there is a return to non-inflationary growth. But the trade off between employment and productivity is probably an insufficient basis for ensuring the durability of such pacts. What is required is a commitment 'to a conception of national competitiveness which gives rise to a joint effort for the full development of human resources' (Marsden, 1995), and in this respect the conclusion of an employment pact at the European level stressing the importance of education and training could play an important role.


THE IMPLICATIONS FOR WELFARE STATES

The innovations demanded in labour market management by the pressures identified in section one above will not prevent the trends already present in labour markets (feminization, the increase in temporary and part-time work), or necessarily solve its problems (including that of long-term – and especially youth – unemployment). All of these in themselves are demanding adjustments to employment policy and social protection systems, if only to offset the increase in 'implicit disentitlement' many of them involve (such as women workers with inadequate social security cover linked to maternity leave), and the problems facing those trapped in the cycle of short-term jobs and periodic unemployment in accumulating entitlements in certain countries. However, where governments are linked to social partners through stabilization or competition pacts, there is unlikely to be an assault on the welfare state of the Thatcher kind because reform will have to be cautious and negotiated if the more general process of concertation is not also to be undermined (where there is no possibility of such a pact, and where the worker rank and file remains militant, as in France, reform will also be slow, but in this case because of policy paralysis). This is important, because governments in these countries are seeking additional legitimacy for welfare reform that they are increasingly failing to find at elections.

Where social pacts have been formed around general macroeconomic objectives as well as specific labour market objectives, it is much more likely that concertation over more general welfare issues can also successfully occur, especially in those cases where the 'emergency' character of such pacts has given way to a more embedded, institutionalized set of relationships, as social pacts have overlapped with parallel and more conventional forms of bargaining and the experience of concertation has altered not just the norms of industrial relations behaviour but also, as in the case of Italy, the institutional make up of the system itself. Under such circumstances, far from the pursuit of an outright neo-liberal strategy, some elements of what has been termed 'progressive competitiveness' or 'incentive compatible egalitarianism' could be put in place in national systems of social protection (Bowles and Gintis, 1995). These might include the following:

- a shift away from legislated or rule-governed labour market regulation towards negotiated labour market regulation, as in minimum wages, which has occurred, for example, in the Irish and Portuguese social pacts;
- the relaxation of high levels of security for full-time core workers, in return for greater protection for temporary and part-time workers, as in the Dutch 1996 central agreement on 'Flexibility and Security';
- a redesign of social security systems to prevent implicit or explicit disentitlements, in relation to two groups in particular: women workers (who are often discriminated against by male bread-winner-oriented social security systems); and those not in permanent, full-time employment who may also be discriminated against in terms of entitlements;

- a parallel redesign of social security systems to allow a guarantee of access to skill acquisition and social services at any point during the life cycle, especially through education and training (as advocated, for example, by Esping-Andersen, 1994);
- and the negotiation of flexible retirement schemes, as successfully achieved in the Netherlands.

There are, however, obvious dangers in linking the future of the welfare system too closely to negotiation based in the labour market. One consequence might be the loss of legitimacy of the parliamentary process if there is a policy bias towards the sphere of organized interests. A second would be an over-burdening and complication of bargaining among organized interests, increasing the costs involved for the social partners. And finally, it may link critical policy choices too closely to particular interests organized along traditional employer-union lines, even if, as shown by the experience of many pacts (including the Portuguese case discussed above) the interests of the socially excluded have also been taken into account. Regardless of interesting examples – such as the Dutch – of unions moving beyond their traditional membership base, in order both to boost membership and engage in a more flexible approach to labour market regulation, the possibility that these may continue to back essentially 'insider' policies, that protect their core clienteles, should not be discounted, as has been the case in Ireland where neither the problem of labour market 'outsiders', nor the employment and poverty traps that exacerbate long-term joblessness, have been directly addressed. Under such conditions, rising trends in poverty are unlikely to be reversed (Van Den Bosch, Chapter 6). Nor should one neglect the fragility and perils of policy making based on concertation if the institutional basis for such a strategy is not secure and if the costs of exit for either of the social partners are low.


CONCLUSIONS

This article began by arguing that a combination of mainly external pressures are reshaping European industrial relations systems and constraining welfare states. These are: international competition in a more liberal world (and internal European) trading order, the path towards and completion of European Monetary Union, and the spread of new modes of work organization (lean production, flexible specialization and total quality management). It was also argued that while the future shape of industrial relations systems will depend in large part on their past and existing institutional structure, three objectives are being (and will increasingly be) prioritized in these countries' adjustment strategies and this will require a degree of institutional convergence:

- greater external flexibility in labour market (such as adjusting the barriers between the firm's internal labour market and the outside world), but only to the point where relations of 'trust' within the firm are not eroded;
- greater internal flexibility in labour markets (dependent not just on the ability of the employer to reorganize the work process, but on higher skill levels, less hierarchy in firms and greater 'trust');
- and – especially under EMU – wage cost containment.

Achieving these objectives requires innovation in bargaining and in the behaviour and institutional configurations of industrial relations systems. The optimal location of these, in terms of the combination of internal and external flexibility, will continue to be at the intersection of quadrants three and four, Figure 9.1. The optimal organizational shape of these systems will be something along the lines of the German or Dutch dual system of representation (with significant variations according to the industrial relations tradition), including a considerable decentralization of bargaining on many issues to company/plant levels, but involving some form of incomes policy or wage co-ordination.

Hence, the future is neither neo-liberal, nor one of 'social corporatism' but, for many European countries one of 'competitive' corporatism, prioritizing competitiveness and macro-economic stability and employment creation and redistribution, but down playing the 'equity' function of more traditional, 'golden age' forms of corporatism. This is a future, then, of pragmatic, productivity-oriented social pacts or coalitions. While the longer-term consequences are unclear, these developments will have both direct and indirect consequences for welfare states: greater internal and external flexibility for firms means greater wage flexibility and wage dispersion, increased flexibility in the funding of programmes linked to labour costs and greater flexibility in the design of social security systems. Whether political and industrial relations systems can sustain this new form of class compromise and social contract, is of course, another question.

NOTES

1    See Dunning (1997) for an extended discussion of the dependence of successful market-based economies on the provision of public goods.
2    On cross-class 'flexibility' alliances in Scandinavia, see Iversen (1996).
3    For a development of this argument, see Marsden (1995).
4    For discussions of the debates on 'flexibilities' and 'rigidities' in European
labour markets, and their implications for innovation and economic growth,
see Villeval (1996) and Foden (1994).
5    On the relevance of incomes policy for the future of the UK economy, see
Kessler (1994).
6    The details come from various issues of the *European Industrial Relations
Review* and from *International Labour Review* (1995).
7    Indeed, in the battle with employers demanding radical welfare and labour
market reform who have been attracted to 'lean' welfare and deregulatory
policies by the success in recent years of the extensively liberalized New
Zealand model, social democrats and trade unionists in Germany and
Belgium, for example, have been deploying the 'Dutch model' as proof that
there is a 'third path' between the high levels of social protection of the
continental European countries and Anglo-Saxon, neo-liberal option. For
two very useful studies of developments in the Netherlands, see Visser
(1996) and Hemerijk and van den Toren (1996).

REFERENCES

Bonoli, G. and Palier, B. (1997) 'Reclaiming Welfare: The Politics of French
Social Protection Reform', in M. Rhodes (ed.), *Southern European Welfare
States: Between Crisis and Reform*, London: Frank Cass, pp. 240–69.
Bowles, S. and Gintis, H. (1995) 'Productivity-Enhancing Egalitarian Strategies',
*International Labour Review*, 134, 4–5, pp. 559–85.
Calmfors, L. and Driffill, J. (1988) 'Bargaining Structure, Corporatism and Macro-
economic Performance', *Economic Policy*, 6, pp. 14–62.
Carlin, W. and Soskice, D. (1997) 'Shocks to the System: the German Political
Economy under Stress', *National Institute Economic Review*, 159, pp. 57–76.
Cerny, P.G. (1995) 'Globalization and the Changing Logic of Collective Action',
*International Organization*, 49, 4, pp. 595–625.
Crouch, C. and Streeck, W. (1997) 'Institutional Capitalism: Diversity and
Performance', in C. Crouch and W. Streeck (eds.), *Modern Capitalism or
Modern Capitalisms?*, London: Sage.
Dunning, J.H. (1997) 'Governments and the Macro-organization of Economic
Activity: an Historical and Spatial Perspective', *Review of International
Political Economy*, 4, 1, pp. 42–86.
Esping-Andersen, G. (1994) 'Equality and Work in the Post-Industrial Life Cycle',
in D. Miliband (ed.), *Reinventing the Left*, Cambridge: Polity Press, pp. 167–185.
Foden, D. (1994) 'Restructuring at the European Community Level: European
Integration, Market Forces and Social Policy in Creative Tension', in
W. Sengenberger and D. Campbell (eds.), *Creating Economic Opportunities:*

*The Role of Labour Standards in Industrial Restructuring*, Geneva: International Institute for Labour Studies.

Hemerijk, A. and van den Toren, J.P. (1996) 'The Resurgence of Corporatist Policy Co-ordination in an Age of Globalization', paper presented to the conference on 'Globalization and the New Inequality', Utrecht, 20–22 November 1996.

International Labour Review (1995) 'Perspectives: Experience of Social Pacts in Western Europe', *International Labour Review*, 134, 3.

Iversen, T. (1996) 'Power, Flexibility, and the Breakdown of Centralized Wage Bargaining: Denmark and Sweden in Comparative Perspective', *Comparative Politics*, 28, 4, pp. 399–436.

Jones, B. and Cressey, P. (1995) '"Europeanization": Motor or Mirage for Employment Systems', in P. Cressey and B. Jones (eds), *Work and Employment in Europe: A New Convergence?*, London: Routledge, pp. 1–27.

Kavanagh, E., Considine, J., Doyle, E., Gallagher, L., Kavanagh, C. and O'Leary, E. (1997) 'The Political Economy of EMU in Ireland', in E. Jones, J. Frieden and F. Torres (eds.), *EMU and the Smaller Countries: Joining Europe's Monetary Club*, New York: St Martin's Press.

Kessler, S. (1994) 'Incomes Policy', *British Journal of Industrial Relations*, 32/2, pp. 181–99.

Lane, C. (1994) 'Is Germany Following the British Path? A Comparative Analysis of Stability and Change', *Industrial Relations Journal*, 25/3, pp. 187–98.

Lipietz, A. (1997) 'The Post-Fordist World: Labour Relations, International Hierarchy and Global Ecology', *Review of International Political Economy*, 4, 1, pp. 1–41.

Marsden, D. (1995) 'Deregulation or Co-operation? The Future of Europe's Labour Markets', *Labour*, 9/2, pp. 67–91.

Maurice, M. (1995) 'Convergence and/or Societal Effect for the Europe of the Future', in P. Cressey and B. Jones (eds), *Work and Employment in Europe: A New Convergence?*, London: Routledge, pp. 28–40.

Piore, M.J. and Sabel, C.F. (1984) *The Second Industrial Divide: Possibilities for Prosperity*, New York: Basic Books.

Regini, M. (1995) 'Firms and Institutions: The Demand for Skills and their Social Production in Europe', *European Journal of Industrial Relations*, 1, 2, pp. 191–202.

Regini, M. and Regalia, I. (1997) 'Employers, Unions and the State: the Resurgence of Concertation in Italy?', *West European Politics*, 25, 1, pp. 210–30 (special issue on *Italy between Crisis and Transition*, M. Bull and M. Rhodes (eds.)).

Rhodes, M. (1995) 'Regional Development and Employment in Europe's Southern and Western Peripheries', in M. Rhodes (ed.), *The Regions and the New Europe: Patterns in Core and Periphery Development*, Manchester: Manchester University Press, pp. 273–328.

Rhodes, M. (1996) 'Globalization and West European Welfare States: A Critical Review of Recent Debates', *Journal of European Social Policy*, 6, 4, pp. 305–27.

Rhodes, M. and van Apeldoorn, B. (1997) 'Capitalism versus Capitalism in Western Europe', in M. Rhodes, P. Heywood and V. Wright (eds.), *Developments in West European Politics*, London: Macmillan 1997, pp. 171–89.

Teague, P. (1995) 'Pay Determination in the Republic of Ireland: Towards Social Corporatism?', *British Journal of Industrial Relations*, 33, 2, pp. 253–73.
Villeval, M-C. (1996) 'Unemployment, Labour Institutions and Innovation', *Labour*, 10/1, pp. 209–36.
Visser, J. (1996) 'Two Cheers for Corporatism, One for the Market: Industrial Relations, Unions, Wages and Labour Markets in the Netherlands', Max-Planck Institut für Gesellschaftsforschung, Cologne, mimeo, December.

# 10 Global and Regional Agencies and the Making of Post-Communist Social Policy in Eastern Europe
Bob Deacon

## INTRODUCTION AND OVERVIEW: GLOBALIZATION AND WELFARE

The contribution this chapter makes to the theme of this book is that the future of welfare states in Europe cannot be understood without looking beyond the West European borders of Europe. Developments in social policy in Eastern Europe and the former Soviet Union (see Chapter 7) will clearly have an impact. More important, however, is the role of global agencies such as the World Bank, International Monetary Fund (IMF), International Labour Organization (ILO) and others in influencing both national welfare systems and the social regulation of economic competition between welfare states.

Rhodes (1996 and Chapter 9) has reviewed the literature that demonstrates that the globalization of the economy pits different kinds of welfare state against each other. Choices are imposed upon governments as to whether they accept the low wage deregulation strategy and dump their welfare responsibilities in the pursuit of investments and markets and jobs or whether they attempt to benefit from the higher productivity associated with larger public investment in education, health and allied social expenditures. Scharpf (Chapter 8) has indicated the problems of constructing a European-wide defence of European welfare and speculated that one option still open to some states is to attempt to combine a strategy that lets business make its profits but continues to secure welfare spending on, for example, income transfers, at the cost of wages. Corporate deals with labour agreeing to trade wages for welfare are still possible if enterprise is not taxed.

One of the points of this chapter is to argue that much of the analysis of the impact of globalism on European welfare possibilities is surprisingly economically determinist and in consequence, pessimistic. There is little attempt to understand in order to influence the emerging globalized political processes that do address the question of the political regulation of global competition. Much of this global political discourse is, of course, hidden from view in the professional exchanges between human resource specialists in the World Bank, ILO, and the newly created World Trade Organization (WTO). Nonetheless, as this chapter demonstrates, there is an emerging global discourse as to the best future for welfare in the light of the globalization of the economy. This discourse embodies a contestation between the Bank and the ILO, for example, and within each agency in terms of disputed possibilities. The subject matter of the contestation embraces how the traditional European model of a state wage related Bismarkian social security system might need to be reformed and what supranational social regulations might need to be put into place (social clauses in the World Trade agreements for example) to prevent the race to the deregulated welfare bottom.

The structure of this chapter is as follows. First, some earlier findings about the role of the global agencies in influencing East European social policy are summarized. Secondly, it sets out a conceptual framework for analysing the link between agency impact and national policy. Here a link between agency policy and welfare regime type is hypothesized. Thirdly, the chapter focuses in detail on the policy advice offered to Eastern Europe and the former Soviet Union by the World Bank in the area of social security and social assistance. And Fourthly, the conclusion is drawn that the present phase of globalization is marked by an inter- and intra-agency discourse about social policy. This discourse embraces models of the future which are similar to the past: USA liberalism, German conservative corporatism, Swedish social democracy and, importantly, models of the future which, it is argued by their defenders, better match the new economic realities. These are a safety net, tax-based, targeted social liberalism, espoused by some in the World Bank and a radical unconditional citizenship income approach espoused by some in the ILO. Finally the chapter reviews recent developments in East European social policy and concludes that two types of tension are being played out in the region. One, where countries are reforming their social policy, is a tension between aspirations towards a European conservative, corporatist policy and a budget and World Bank-backed pull towards a safety net social liberal strategy. The other, where little social policy reform is happening, is a tension between a post-communist conservatism and an emerging reality of welfare neglect and collapse. The future of social policy in Eastern Europe and the former Soviet Union holds the key to understanding the future for welfare in the European Union (EU), unless a determined social protectionist strategy is the chosen future for the EU.

## GLOBAL ACTORS AND POST-COMMUNISM: THE STRUGGLE BETWEEN GLOBAL ACTORS

An initial pilot study of the role of supranational and global agencies in shaping social policy since 1989 in Eastern Europe (Deacon, 1994) was based on a survey of the stated objectives and actual practice of the ILO, the European Commission and the IMF with regard to influencing the future of economic and social policy in a number of countries. An initial review of World Bank thinking and practice was also included. It was concluded that major international agencies are involved in shaping post-communist social policy; the advice of different agencies often pulls in opposite directions; banking agencies (IMF, World Bank, ERBD) differ in their emphasis; advice may depend on the particular consultant used by an agency; conflicts between agencies globally (for example, ILO and IMF) are reflected in internal conflicts within countries; and an element of competition between agencies reflects a global competition between different fractions of global capitalism (for example, the European Commission for Europe and the IMF for the USA).

More generally on the basis of the initial investigation it was provisionally concluded that:

> It is evident that a major ideological struggle is taking place over the shape and content of the social security and income maintenance aspects of social policy in the newly emerging democracies of Eastern Europe. The struggle over what is to replace the social guarantees of forced but available employment for all between a USA style individualist social policy, a European style 'conservative' or 'social market economy' style social policy (with which social democracy is merging), and a futuristic citizenship entitlement to guaranteed income is being articulated and fought every bit as much at the level of the supranational agencies as it is being played out within the confines of intra-state politics. The IMF, European Commission, and the ILO are as important actors as local politicians and local trade union and social movements. The arena of social and political struggle over these issues is now a global one (Deacon, 1994).

## GLOBAL AGENCIES, WELFARE REGIMES AND POLICY INFLUENCE

This chapter draws on a research project that is conceived and structured to test the hypothesis that different global and supranational agencies systematically promulgate advice in the sphere of social policy to countries of Eastern Europe and the former Soviet Union, and that this advice is agency specific (that is the ILO prescribing policy (a) and the EU policy (b)), and moreover, that this advice reflects policy typically associated with different welfare regimes (for instance the EU prescribes social policy typical of *European* welfare regimes). Furthermore the hypothesis extends to include the proposition that different countries are likely to be systematically influenced in the making of their social policy more by one agency than another because of factors which affect the differential capacity of each agency to influence each country. In other words a version of this hypothesis would permit of the proposition that the IMF systematically promulgates social policy typical of a liberal welfare regime and that Poland is most likely to be especially influenced by the IMF because of the degree of indebtedness of Poland (the factor which increases the power of the IMF as an agency to influence policy).

Figure 10.1 outlines the hypothesis in more detail. It should be noted, here that the hypothesis includes the proposition that certain agencies cannot be characterized as typically promulgating one type of policy because of the extent to which policy prescription is known to be in flux. This particularly applies to the OECD and the World Bank. The study is focusing on four countries with which to test the hypothesis. They are Hungary, Bulgaria, Lithuania and the Ukraine.

## THE WORLD BANK: SHIFTING DISCOURSE OF SOCIAL POLICY

Our initial hypothesis that it might prove problematic to characterize the social policy prescriptions of the World Bank is proving justified. In this section we present our initial assessment of the technical advice and policy prescriptions offered by the Bank in the sphere of income maintenance for the countries in our sample. First, the instruments available to the Bank for influencing policy are described together with an account of the extent to which they have been used in the countries in this study. Second, a review

*Figure 10.1*   Agency policy and welfare regime type (hypothesis)

| Agency | Policy Advice Characteristic | Power to Influence Where | Countries in Sample More Open to Influence |
|---|---|---|---|
| International Monetary Fund | Residual | Indebted | All to varying degree |
| European Union | Conservative | Phare technical advice available and aim to join EU | Hungary Bulgaria? |
| International Labour Office | Social Democratic or Conservative Corporatist | Government sympathetic to tripartism and workers' protection | Bulgaria? Ukraine Lithuania? |
| World Bank | Variable and Shifting (Residual\ Conservative\ post-Fordist) | Technical advice available and loans taken up | All to varying degree |

Note: a)   The policy advice characteristic above is based on Esping-Anderson's (1990) typology but in the case of the World Bank it is hypothesized that future thinking within that agency is moving beyond the existing regime types to accommodate social policy appropriate to post-Fordist deconstruction and flexibility. This might also apply elsewhere (see concluding section of chapter).

b)   Esping-Andersen did not include South-East Asian (New Tiger) regimes within his analysis. It is hypothesized that such a regime type (state capitalism with education and public health infrastructure) might provide a model for parts of the former Soviet Union but does not yet have major agency support (except perhaps for the OECD).

c)   At the hypothesis stage it is not clear how to characterize the OECD, and the Council of Europe (C of E).

The instruments available to the agencies under investigation are several and varied. They include 'Social Conditionality' (World Bank lending on condition of social policy change) and 'Economic Conditionality' (IMF lending on condition of economic policy change with social policy implications). The following array of instruments is available to the agencies:

| | |
|---|---|
| Additionality Incentive: | EU provision of grant matched to local resources |
| Legal Regulation: | C of E powers to report shortcomings in member country social policy where party to C of E Social Charter |
| Technical Assistance: | ILO, EU, World Bank, OECD, etc. provision of free technical advice |
| Political Agreement: | EU agreements with associated states |
| Resource Redistribution: | EU Structural Fund (if extended to Central and Eastern Europe) |

This differential array of instruments has given rise to comparative advantage competition between agencies. When asked why the countries of Eastern Europe and the former Soviet Union should take any notice of the policy prescriptions of their agency, officials tend to reply in terms of the comparative advantage of their particular agency. These are:

| | |
|---|---|
| IMF: | Secrecy and speed (six-month turn round of advice) |
| World Bank: | Exhaustive sectoral technical analysis and loans |
| OECD: | Impartiality and absence of loans |
| EU: | European aspirations/cultural affinity |
| C of E: | Legal powers (especially in the Human Rights field) |
| ILO: | Sensitive to social costs and social agreements |

of actual detailed policy prescriptions is presented. Third, the extent to which there is internal debate and controversy within the Bank over appropriate policy advice is analysed.

## Bank Instruments and Activity

Figure 10.2 sets out some of the instruments available to the Bank for shaping policy and the extent to which they have been employed so far in the countries being studied.

The Hungarian case represents the most complete story. The full cycle from an initial country economic assessment, through a social sector study with recommendations, and on to a Structural Adjustment Loan (SAL) tranched so that part of it was conditional upon the government introducing national social assistance legislation has been completed. The World Bank's Operation Evaluation Division (World Bank, 1993c) concluded that: 'The SAL conditions were satisfied on time... A social safety net that provides unemployment benefits and social assistance is now in place, but much more needs to be done to rationalize social expenditure in general to target them to the needy.'

How influential the Bank was in ensuring such a piece of legislation appeared on the statute book and how far the Bank did seek to and effect

*Figure 10.2*   World Bank instruments for shaping social policy

|  | *Hungary* | *Bulgaria* | *Lithuania* | *Ukraine* |
|---|---|---|---|---|
| Initial Country Economic Memorandum with Social Sector comments | ✓ | ✓ | ✓ | ✓ |
| Social Sector study with recommendations | ✓ | (part of above) | ✓ | ✓ |
| Rehabilitation loans | ✗ | ✗ | probably | probably |
| Structural Adjustment Loan with Social Conditionality | – Conditional upon Social Assistance reforms | – Conditional upon Social Policy White paper | | |
| Loan Supervision | ✓ | ongoing | – | – |
| (Operation Evaluation) | Success | – | – | – |

the details of this legislation is not yet clear. This is the subject of ongoing investigation. From the Bank's point of view, however, the Social Conditionality of the SAL was further evidence of its commitment to reduce poverty in the context of its global operations. In its own publication, the World Bank (1993d: xi) notes that: 'The share of adjustment lending that addresses social issues climbed from 5 per cent in Fiscal 1984–86 to 50 per cent in Fiscal 1990–92. In Fiscal 1992, eighteen out of thirty-two adjustment loans included an explicit poverty focus, and fourteen of these adjustment loans had tranche-release conditions.'

**Bank Prescriptions**

An analysis of bank prescriptions in the field of income maintenance has earlier been undertaken for other countries by Milanovic (1992) for the Bank. Reviewing the recommendations in the reports on five countries of the former Soviet Union (Russia, Kazakstan, Kyrghyzstan Georgia, and Lithuania) he concluded that there were several policy areas where a consensus appeared to exist in Bank policy, some areas where a difference in recommendations could be explained by the different circumstances of countries, and some key areas where diverse recommendations reflected implicit or explicit disagreements between Bank officials or between the officials and the consultants employed.

Consensus appeared to exist in four areas:

- *old-age, disability and pensions* (statutory retirement age should be increased and made equal for both men and women; working pensioners should be discouraged, by obliging them to choose between wage and pension or by reducing pension by a given amount for each additional rouble earned; and lowest pensions should be protected against erosion in real terms);
- *sick leave* (shift some costs to enterprises);
- *unemployment* (discontinue benefits for the new entrants);
- *social assistance* (redefine the poverty lines).

Disagreements appeared to exist, however, in the following areas:

- *pension levels*: should they be equal for all – a state flat rate minimum – or continue to be wage-related, continuing to fulfil the implicit past 'insurance' contract?;
- *family allowances*: should they be income tested or universal? The argument against means testing rests for some bank personnel on the

grounds of the continuing narrow range of income differentials, the absence of administrative infrastructure, and the close association of children with family poverty;
- *unemployment benefits*: should they be flat rate or wage related?;
- *universal safety net*: should there be such a strategy or not? In the sample of countries examined by Milanovic the case for a universal safety net/minimum poverty line below which nobody should fall, was put for Russia and Lithuania, not dealt with for Kazakhstan and Kyrghyzstan, and argued against for Georgia;
- *public work (work fare)*: the concept of self-targeted public works programmes – as a substitute for means tested social assistance – is defended for some countries only.

Figure 10.3 indicates the results of a comparable analysis for the four countries of this study concentrating upon the potential areas of disagreement noted above. This can only be a snapshot of policy recommendations at a particular moment in time. The Bank staff and consultants working now in these countries are different from the ones working on the initial assessments. Changes in recommendations might follow. This point is discussed in more detail below.

In terms of pension policy, while there are still differences of emphasis between reports that do not argue against wage-related pensions and those that do and between those that explicitly encourage private pensions and those that do not, there is a discernible drift towards a crisis-driven, short-term, flat-rate strategy. This was also noted by Vodopivec (1992: 8) who continued the work of Milanovic for the Bank by reviewing more recent reports (Armenia, Estonia, Latvia, Ukraine) and concluded that 'all reports under current review also advocate flat-rate unemployment and pension benefit'. The congruence seems to be a fruit of concerted action on the part of the Bank – powerful arguments against a flat-rate benefit reported in Milanovic's note notwithstanding. In fact this issue is by no means settled in the Bank, a point returned to later below. In terms of family allowances there is variable advice which presumably partly reflects actual differences in country policy and differences in the inclinations of report authors and consultants.

In terms of safety net policy, these reports reveal that beyond the common lip service paid to the concept of safety net, the actual analysis and recommendations vary widely. Where the report for Hungary favoured a national means-tested strategy (even though in the event a very locally variable social assistance law has been passed), the report for Bulgaria eschewed this idea in favour of categorical helps (even though in

*Figure 10.3*  World bank prescriptions for social security and social assistance

| Recommendation | Hungary | Bulgaria | Country<br>Lithuania | Ukraine |
|---|---|---|---|---|
| Pensions | Raise pension age. Ceiling on benefit. Encourage private. Retirement income test. | Raise pension age. Reduce scope of public pension. Encourage private. | Raise pension age. Reduce replacement rate. Permit private. Maintain wage-related but short-term-flat rate stop gap. | Raise pension age. Retirement income test. Reduce average. Maintain minimum pension and short-term flat rate. |
| Family allowances | Differentiate by number of children. Means test portion of benefit | Reduce the universal coverage. Needs-based transfer to low-income families. | (Presumably retain means-tested family benefits) | See safety nets? |
| Unemployment Benefit | Shorten duration. Flat-rate for phase II. Reduce benefits for some. | Flat-rate. Restrict to dismissed workers. | Reduce flat rate. Eliminate for new entrants. | Flat-rate. Eliminate for new entrants. |
| Safety Net | Define nation-wide eligibility criteria and means test. | An effective safety net to shield vulnerable groups. Provision in kind or food coupons to needy as alternative to cash benefits at local level. | Define poverty line differentiated between regions. Goal of means-tested system but short-term targeting to groups. Benefit in cash and/or kind. | Pending income testing and poverty levels differentiated by region; benefits to vulnerable groups only. Reduce general subsidy. |

Sources: World Bank 1991, 1992, 1993a and 1993b

the event a national means-tested system has been introduced). However, for the 'less European' countries of the former Soviet Union there does seem to be an understanding now on the part of the Bank officials and consultants that continued partial food subsidy and universal entitlements to population categories known to be poor are preferable to unviable means-tested strategies. This point is returned to later.

The work fare idea mentioned in the earlier review by Milanovic seems to have fallen out of favour as World Bank policy. This, interestingly, is a strategy that is now put forward by the IMF (Ahmed, 1993) and defended strongly by one of its leading advocates inside the Fund on the grounds that means testing in partially monetized and fluid economies is unviable and the dangers of discriminatory practice (such as disallowing access to benefit by prejudiced social workers) cannot happen in a work-fare system. In defence of the work fare strategy, IMF officials also point to the need for the urgent implementation of social protection rescue strategies while longer-term, problematic means-tested administrative capacity is put in place.[1]

## Bank irresolution

The preceding review of World Bank policy prescription in the field of income maintenance has indicated at least two areas – pensions and safety nets – where there is clearly internal dissent and or confusion among Bank officials and consultants. These areas of dissent are now explored more fully because they lead to conclusions that are an important refinement to the conclusion of the earlier study.

Before exploring the substantive content of the dispute about pensions and the lack of clarity about safety nets, it is necessary to offer some contextualization in terms of the Bank's anti-poverty strategy. The World Bank and to a lesser extent the International Monetary Fund had, before the collapse of the state bureaucratic system in Eastern Europe, responded to the earlier criticisms of their policy and practice in developing countries by adopting an anti-poverty strategy. The World Development Report (World Bank 1990) focused on poverty. In 1991 the policy paper 'Assistance Strategies to Reduce Poverty' was published. This was followed by the 1992 'Poverty Reduction Handbook'. However, the events of 1989 overtook this initiative and in a development that had not been foreseen, led to a major focus of the Bank's work on poverty alleviation being the countries of the CIS and Eastern Europe. This meant that the Bank was having to deal with, and make recommendation for, developed industrial economies on the mainland of continental Europe. It was ill-equipped to do this, and in order to undertake the task needed to recruit a significant number of new officials and engage a new tranche of consultants more familiar with the income maintenance systems of developed economics and more sensitive to the social guarantees of the earlier regimes, the Human Resources Sector of the Europe and Central Asia Division of the Bank expanded rapidly.

Whereas the dominant tradition and practice in the Human Resources sectors of the Bank had been one influenced by USA liberalism at home and South American models of private welfare development abroad – combined with anti-poverty thinking appropriate to developing countries – the new influx of talent was engaged in a different discourse. Nicholas Barr, Sandor Sipos, Igor Tomes, John Micklewright, and many others brought an understanding of and commitment to the 'European' tradition of wage-related social security systems and a sensitivity to the guarantees of 'communism'. It is within this context that it can be argued that it is not simply that the World Bank is an important actor in shaping post-communist social policy but that the pre-existing social guarantees of 'communism' have and continue to bite back at the Bank and reshape its understanding and thinking about appropriate social policy. Of course, the factors leading to internal Bank disputes are more complex than this. Also shaping Bank thinking are the 'little miracles' of South East Asia that have demonstrated the case for state infrastructural expenditure on education and health, thus denting the case for liberal fundamentalism. The election of Bill Clinton and the off-the-cuff remark in 1993 that 'I reckon the IMF policies have not been good for Russia. The USA is going to try to relax them with more attention to job creation and the social grief that attend economic reform' (*The Guardian*, 14 October 1993) is also a factor. A further complication is that European conservative corporatism and Scandinavian social democracy are under threat globally by economic competition and subject to severe questioning in terms of their capacity to respond to and handle, in income maintenance terms, the consequences of the post-Fordist restructuring of the economy (Jessop *et al.*, 1991).

If this is the context and background to the disagreements within the Bank, which are reflected in the variable recommendations about social policy for Eastern Europe and the CIS, where have the disputes now reached? Has the issue been settled on pensions or on safety nets? On pensions the Bank is in the unusual position of seeing published at the same time by staff and consultants two differently orientated texts. One of these, a World Bank Policy Research Report on pensions produced under a team led by Estelle James (1994) is based in part on a paper by Louise Fox entitled 'Old Age Security in Transition Economies'. Louise Fox had been the author of the Bulgarian social security chapter (World Bank, 1992) within which she had encouraged the development of a private pension scheme and avoided arguing for a national social assistance scheme. Her recommendations for the countries of the region rely on severely reducing the public pension provision to either a subsistence contributory flat-rate or means-tested flat-rate system funded by pay-role tax or general revenue. In addition a compulsory private pillar is proposed, disconnected from the occupational system.

Nicholas Barr, on the other hand, in his chapter on social insurance in a different World Bank volume (Barr, 1994) sets out a set of policy options much more in keeping with existing practice in mainstream European systems. The common ground is the need to raise pension age, and the protection of minimum benefits. The differences are in the scope for state wage-related pensions and their private alternatives. Barr argues that social insurance contributions should be shared between worker and employer and the relationship between benefits and contributions strengthened. Private pensions should not be introduced until the necessary regulations structure has been put in place. Beyond this he argues that 'policy makers have a choice about the form of public/private mix in pensions'. A mainstream Western European system would have three tiers and would be very much a partnership between the public and private sectors. The foundation PAYG (pay-as-you-go) social insurance pension would have a wider role than mere subsistence and involve only appropriate maxima for contributions and benefits. In addition there would be mandatory regulated private pensions and voluntary additional schemes.

Within the Human Resources section of the relevant country divisions the issue is not settled. An internal meeting in November 1993, while perceived by the 'Europeans' to conclude in their favour, was also perceived by the supporters of the flat-rate public pillar as laying the framework for further work demonstrating the relevance of that strategy. The report of the meeting concluded that 'one strategy may be to select a couple of representative countries on which to focus the region's energies and resources for pension reform' (World Bank, 1994). Subsequently an internal conference was convened to take a rain check on policy advice in this area (and that of social assistance). The convenor is strongly of the opinion that it would be unwise to lock Eastern Europe in to the 'costly mistakes' of West European social security commitments and sees instead the opportunity for 'institutional leap frogging', whereby Eastern Europe might fashion schemes more appropriate to post-Fordist flexible production. He has in mind only minimum means and asset-tested state pensions. The policy debate is likely to be unfolded through case examples on the horizon (for example Lithuania) so that the choice of bank staff and consultants is important.

However, while apparently unresolved within the Human Resources section of the relevant country divisions, the separate Education and Social policy arm of the Bank responsible for the Poverty Strategy was commissioned to produce a paper for the joint Development Committee of the World Bank and IMF on Social Security Reforms and Safety Nets. It argued that 'Chile made a dramatic break with the past when it switched to (a pension system) operated by the private sector', but continues to point out that 'reforms of pension systems along the Chilean lines may be an unrealistic goal for ... countries of Eastern Europe and the FSU. An intermediate approach might be a two or three tiered system, including a public scheme providing only the minimum subsistence pension' (Joint Development Committee, 1993: 71). This approach is endorsed by the paper of the chair of the particular joint development committee meeting at which the issue was discussed (27 September 1993). Thus, despite the continued dispute and the significance of Nicholas Barr's work, Bank policy on pensions might be in danger of hardening in the direction of a residual minimum state pension. The issue is not, however, settled. The World Bank Annual Report for 1996 is on Transition Economies and it is interesting to note that Barr was charged with the task of writing the pensions and public expenditure section instead of Louise Fox who had been another contender for the job. Spokespeople for both 'camps' suggested in 1995 that the initial disagreements were softened. On the one hand there was recognition by all that the infrastructure for a fully-fledged privatization of pensions is far from existing. On the other, the commitment to social solidarity in the state scheme was seen as embodied in only the first tier which could give everybody a 30 per cent of average wage replacement rate. A second state tier based on a 2 per cent pay roll tax could give a further 20 per cent replacement in 20 years. Over and above this there was agreed scope for private provision.

Policy on safety nets remains, however, even at the official level of the Joint Development Committee, unresolved and experimental. The chair concluded that 'there is no general consensus on the correct approach to these (safety net) problems or the detailed solutions appropriate in each case' (Joint Development Committee, 1993: 6). The joint paper does, however, in its discussion of the administrative obstacles to means-tested safety nets, comment that 'public works programs paying low wages may provide a cost-effective, if more limited, alternative with admin-costs reduced through self-selection' (*ibid*. 79). This clearly reflects the influence of IMF thinking mentioned earlier. The Education and Social Policy Department of the Bank was commissioned to produce a report on *The Effectiveness of Social Safety Nets in 1995* which focused on best practice. At the same time there were bids for funds to undertake an evaluation of social assistance strategies in the region from staff associated with the European 'camp'. Both reports are awaited with interest.

## A GLOBAL INTER- AND INTRA-AGENCY DISCOURSE

This chapter has reported a detailed analysis of the work of the World Bank in the region. Similar detailed accounts of the work of the EU, ILO, IMF, OECD, and Council of Europe are provided in Deacon (1996). On the basis of this research it is concluded that there is no strong evidence that each agency is systematically identified with agency specific social policy prescriptions and that these agency specific prescriptions are identifiable with a particular welfare regime type approach to policy. Rather it has been demonstrated that the international discourse about desirable inter- and intra-governmental social policy is shifting and cross-cuts agencies. In other words, for each agency examined we have identified internal disagreements about policy prescription, variability in policy prescription and shifting policy thinking over time. The global discourse or, global ideological struggle over the appropriate social policy in Eastern Europe and the former Soviet Union, *is* continuing apace; but different positions, so to speak, cannot always be equated tidily with different agencies.

The advice flowing from the EU to the East is not systematically European conservative corporatist advice. The struggle between Euro-liberals and Euro-corporatists is reflected in the failure of DG V (Social Affairs) to control advice flowing from DG I which handles the Phare Programme. The competitive tendering in Phare, combined with the power of recipient governments to influence tender outcomes, leads to Phare activity in the social policy sphere sometimes being undertaken by the World Bank, sometimes by the ILO, sometimes by consultants of other policy persuasion. The social policy thinking of the OECD appears to be undergoing a paradigm shift from American liberalism to some form of commitment to socially regulated capitalism. Within the Council of Europe, the Social Affairs Directorate appears to wish to rethink the charter or legal rights approach in the social policy field to engage in a discourse which involves breaking the distinction between income from work and income from benefits. Within the World Bank it is perhaps most evident that a heated and hard fought struggle of ideas and policy prescriptions is under way. Here we identified a 'camp' associated with European wage-related, state-funded social security systems and a 'camp' associated with a flat-rate – possibly means- and asset-tested – residual pensions policy. Within the ILO, there appears to be a conflict of opinion between those in the Central and East European Team who favour a traditional European conservative approach, combining state social security with safety net, means-tested social assistance, buttressed by tripartite forms of governance, and those in the team who have advocated something more like a citizens income approach to replace the guaranteed income from work under the old regimes.

Within this cross-cutting global discourse we have demonstrated that the classic worlds of Western welfare capitalism are present (liberalism, conservatism, social democracy) but we have also begun to show that the existing paradigms of welfare policy and strategy are breaking down in the face of the post-Fordist deconstruction of work and security. Within the World Bank there is clearly an attempt by some, that may not be successful, to leap frog beyond what is conceived of as the doomed and now unsustainable social security structures of Europe to a residual means-tested safety net for parts of Eastern Europe and the former Soviet Union. This strategy – which we are inclined to call 'Social Liberalism' – is not yet clearly articulated. The exact meaning of a universal safety net is not defined and the problems of means testing are not clearly thought through. The IMF inclination towards a work fare/food for work kind of safety net is not shared by the Bank. Perhaps the IMF thinking reported in this paper is a work-fare variant of 'Social Liberalism'. This contrasts with the parallel leap frogging, but in a different direction, that was identified in the thinking of some individuals in the ILO. Here it has been suggested that the social security policy appropriate to a post-industrialist situation in the former Soviet Union should embody a citizen's income, available to all without test of means, which would facilitate the flexible economic participation required. This thinking is not shared by the main body of the ILO which is still strongly conservative corporatist.[2]

In other words we remain convinced that social policy making in Eastern Europe and the former Soviet Union is a testing ground for different western social policy strategies; but that this competition between ideas and strategies now embraces a radical citizenship income and a 'Social Liberal' version of post-Fordist social policy, which sometimes find reflection in agency thinking. In Figure 10.4 we suggest very tentatively the following typology of social policy advice flowing eastwards and the association of particular agencies with the different types of advice.

*Figure 10.4*  Global discourse on the future of social policy

| Type of Social Policy Prescription | Agency sometimes promulgating |
| --- | --- |
| Liberalism (USA historically) | IMF? |
| Conservative Corporatism (German historically) | EU, World Bank, ILO, OECD? |
| Social Democratic (Sweden historically) | – |
| Post-Fordist Social Liberalism<br>Version (a)  Universal (Means Test) Safety Nets | EU, World Bank |
| Version (b)  Universal Work Fare Safety Nets | IMF |
| Post-Fordist Radicalism Citizenship Income | Individuals associated with ILO, Council of Europe. |

## EMERGING TENDENCIES IN POST-COMMUNIST SOCIAL POLICY

It is not possible at this stage to demonstrate systematically the impact of different agencies on post-communist social policy making. At a later stage (Deacon, 1996) four case studies (Bulgaria, Hungary, Lithuania, and the Ukraine) will be used to indicate something of the pattern of impact.

Some tentative generalizations are as follows:

● The more indebted a country, the more IMF budget balancing requirements will lead towards liberal, or social liberal outcomes. This is clearly evident in Poland initially and in Hungary in 1995 where the ex-communist party again in power has embarked upon a welfare austerity package including the means testing of child benefits. The Czech republic has been relatively immune from this pressure.
● The more a country has aspirations towards EU membership, the more internal policy making is undertaken against a back cloth of reference to EU, or Council of Europe 'standards'.
● The greater sympathy shown by governments towards tripartite forms of governance, the more ILO prescriptions are likely to be taken seriously. With the recent return of ex-communist governments, in Bulgaria, Hungary, Poland, Lithuania, and their effective influence in Romania and elsewhere, this is an important consideration. The extent to which the ex-communist party has gone through a radical reform process will, however, modify this influence. Relatively unreconstructed Bulgarian socialists will listen more to the ILO than the Hungarian party.

● The larger a country and the greater the capacity and political will for
  independence from the West, the smaller will be the influence of all of
  the agencies. Russia, and, despite its debt, the Ukraine, seem relatively
  immune at this point.

At a general level it can be concluded that the global policy discourse
identified earlier shapes the thinking of social policy makers as they
engage in internal policy making. The Ministry of Finance appeals to IMF
and World Bank language of targeting, means testing, and safety nets. The
Ministry of Social Welfare (Labour and Social Affairs) appeals to the ILO,
EU, or Council of Europe's concern with social protection, social inclusion, and social solidarity.

Welfare regimes in the West – towards which we might have expected
Central and Eastern Europe to move – have been identified as residualism
or liberalism (USA), conservatism (Germany), and social democracy
(Sweden) (Esping Andersen, 1990). There has been much discussion concerning the usefulness of these categories from the stand point of women's
interests. Lewis (1992) has identified dual breadwinner and single breadwinner regimes. Women's independence has been argued to be a separate
consideration from 'decommodification' (Shaver and Bradshaw, 1993).
However, Siaroff (1994) has demonstrated that if countries are measured
on three criteria – the family welfare orientation of policy, the desirability
of female work, and which parent receives benefits for children – there is
quite a close fit between the Esping-Anderson three-fold typology and the
proposed four-fold typology. The clusters of countries in Siaroff's analysis
fit into a four fold typology: protestant, social democratic, welfare states
(Sweden), advanced christian democratic welfare states (Germany),
protestant liberal welfare states (UK), and late female mobilization welfare
states (Spain).

Earlier (1992) I argued that we might expect the emergence of welfare
regimes of these kinds in Central and Eastern Europe. Hungary, I suggested, for example, was likely to move towards liberalism. In addition I
suggested that a further variant was likely to be observed called post-
communist conservatism within which old social obligations would be
retained. Bulgaria would be one such country. Figure 10.5 captures the
key distinctions between Esping-Andersen's three worlds of welfare capitalism (modified in the light of Siaroff), and the pre-existing world of state
bureaucratic collectivism, and suggests the available futures for welfare
in post-communism.

The import of the analysis of global agency discourse has been to
suggest that the available worlds of welfare capitalism have moved on

*Figure 10.5*   Whither post-communist social policy?

| Welfare Regime | Entitlement Basis of Benefit | Distributional Aspects | Women's Interests* |
|---|---|---|---|
| Liberalism | Commodified (markets) | Inequality | 2 |
| Conservatism | Semi-decommodified (insurance) | Status differential | 2 |
| Social democratic | Decommodified (citizenship) | Redistribution | 3 |
| State bureaucratic collectivism | Decommodified (work-loyalty) | Proletarianized but privileges | 3 |
| Post-communism | Pressures towards liberalism; unviability of social democracy; logic of conservatism either as reform towards insurance systems or as post-communist conservatism (but doesn't fit women's interests?) | | |

* Siaroff uses 3 criteria (see text). The score 1, 2, 3 indicates how many of these criteria are positive to women in the regime type.

since projections of the above kind were made a few years ago. The globalized capitalist economy has entered a post-Fordist phase of flexible production and intensified economic competition. Associated with this and worked out by the World Bank partly in its dealings with Central and Eastern Europe is the emerging world of social liberalism/safety net welfare. The alternative radical scenarios of citizenship income entitlement have yet to be implemented anywhere.

   What can be said at this moment at this level of generality about the emerging world(s) of post-communist welfare? There has not yet been undertaken a systematic comparative description and analysis of post-communist social policy. Götting has usefully compared developments in Bulgaria, Hungary, Czechoslovakia (1994 and Chapter 7). Individual country reports have appeared on Poland (Ksiezopolski, 1993), and the Baltics (Simpura, 1995). A recent account of Russian social policy has been made by Shapiro (1995a). The International Social Security Association has monitored developments (Cichon, 1994). The Child Development Centre of UNICEF in Florence has provided an excellent service in monitoring outcomes of policy in two Regional Monitoring Reports (UNICEF, 1993; 1994). The outcome of the SOCO project into the Social consequences of Transition under the leadership of Zsuzsa Ferge is awaited at the time of writing.

Cichon (1994) claims that there is a general pattern of development in the income maintenance sector leading to the establishment of a three pillared system of social insurance (for pensions, short-term benefits), social support from taxes (for child benefits), and social assistance for those exhausting entitlement to benefit or not otherwise covered. To the extent that this is true – and certainly Polish, Hungarian, Czech, Slovak, Slovene, Lithuanian and Bulgarian policy is moving partly in this direction – then the logic of the transformation of state bureaucratic collectivism to conservative corporatism is being followed through. At issue, of course, is the level of benefits, the extent to which state pensions are wage related or only minimum, flat-rate guarantees, the adequacy at a local level of nominal state commitments to social assistance, and the extent to which the state support system is universal or targeted. Because, in many cases, it is only the minimum pension that is being guaranteed, and because support systems are increasingly means tested, the reality begins to look much more like the new world of social liberalism rather than the old world of conservative corporatism. The struggle between the two tendencies continues.

There is a distinction between those countries that have more readily embraced the Bismarkian social insurance system with independent funds and those that have dragged their feet on this and continue to see a closer link between the state budget and benefit funds. It is the latter type of country that is also more concerned to conserve industrial enterprises, and to temporarily lay off workers without pay rather than establish adequate unemployment benefits. This predicted post-communist conservatism (of Bulgaria, Romania, the Ukraine?) is, however, being encircled within its own borders by a new unregulated, private, semi-legal capitalism that refuses to be taxed. In these countries the tension is not so much between a conservative corporatism and social liberalism but between post-communist conservatism and extreme liberalism.

The extreme version of this tension is being played out in Russia and some other countries of the former Soviet Union. Shapiro (1995a) has demonstrated that the trajectory of Russia in terms of income inequality and in terms of effective social policy making is much more towards a Latin-American scenario of welfare collapse rather than any of the variants of western welfare capitalism. This gloomy picture in Russia in the income maintenance sphere is reinforced by a comparative analysis of health policy and mortality outcomes (Shapiro, 1995a). The life expectancy for males in Russia is now (1994) 57.3 years (Field, 1995).

Even the World Bank's strategy is not working in Russia. As one World Bank official put it 'I would add another item to your classification [of welfare futures]. It is actually a system of social neglect [or disregard] in countries at middling levels where the poor are not a very important constituency [they don't vote or their votes are stolen], the middle class is not big enough [and it has definitely shrunk in Russia], and the role of the state is highly uncertain [meaning that the state can expropriate all contributions, or inflate them away or simply cease to exist]'.

In sum, therefore, we can conclude that diverse welfare regimes can now be found in Eastern Europe and the former Soviet Union. These include the existing western welfare model of conservatism and the new post-communist conservatism which is always in danger of giving way to welfare collapse. A new 'Social Liberalism' (liberalism with safety nets) is also evident and is the World Bank's preferred solution. The implications of this emerging trend for Western Europe in the context of global competition are, as we suggested at the beginning, not unimportant. Any new social contract in the welfare field will have to be struck at a global level between agencies and social movements.

## NOTES

1   The analysis of IMF policy will be the subject of a subsequent paper. It is interesting to note, however, at this stage that Fiscal Affairs thinking within the Fund seems to favour practice more appropriate to Southern developing economies and defends these on the basis of their implementability and sustainability. The developed wage-related state pensions structures, for example, of Northern Europe are regarded as unsupportable.

    In an interesting analysis of pension and family allowance policy in the CIS, Ahmed (1993) notes that pensions in the Russian part of the former Soviet Union were supported by contributions from the Southern Central Asian states. In acknowledgement of this, all union fund/initial CIS proposals included family allowances (used more by the South) in the same budget. However, he argues against the perpetuation of universal generous family benefits in parts of Soviet Central Asia as there is a population policy argument against this. Cutting this element leads to the consequential need to reduce the unsupportable wage-related 'Russian' pensions. Work fare style social assistance (the South's food for work programmes) chimes with flat-rate residualized pensions in the North as IMF strategy for the post-Fordist future of welfare.

2   A recent ILO publication – M. Cichon and L. Samuel (eds.), *Making Social Protection Work* (1995) – combines the sentiments articulated by Michael

Cichon that are positive about the emerging trend in Central and Eastern Europe to re-establish 'social protection systems [that] follow generally the Central European models which already existed [...] until the late 1940s' (p. 45), with those of Guy Standing that, if policy makers wished to maximize social protection (rather than employment), then the realities of high unemployment and unstable work histories for a growing minority of the population must point in the direction of reducing the link between employment and transfer payments (p. 40). See also ILO-CEET (1994a and b).

## REFERENCES

Ahmad, E. (1991) 'Social Safety Nets in Transition Economies', in Tanzi, V. (ed.), *Fiscal Issues in Economies in Transition*, Washington: IMF.

Ahmad, E. (1993) 'Poverty, Demography and Public Policy in CIS Countries', *IMF Working Paper* 93/9, February.

Barr, N. (1994) *Labour Markets and Social Policy in Central and Eastern Europe*, Washington: World Bank.

Cichon, M. (1994) 'Financing Social Protection in Central and East Europe: Safeguarding Political and Economic Change', in ISSA, *Restructuring Social Security in Central and Eastern Europe*, Geneva, pp. 41–60.

Deacon, B. (1992) *The New Eastern Europe: Social Policy: Past, Present and Future*, London: Sage.

Deacon, B. (1994) 'Global Social Policy Actors and the Shaping of Post-Communist Social Policy', in A. de Swaan (ed.), *Social Policy beyond Borders*, Amsterdam: Amsterdam University Press.

Deacon, B. (1996) *Globalism and Social Policy*, Sage, London.

Development Committee (1993) *Development Issues: Presentations to the 47th Meeting of the Development Committee*, 27 September 1993, World Bank.

Esping-Andersen, G. (1990) *The Three Worlds of Welfare Capitalism*, Cambridge: Polity.

Field, G.M. (1995) 'The Health Crisis in the Former Soviet Union: A Reflection of Social Crisis' presented to the Fifth World Congress of Central and East European Studies, Warsaw, 6–11 August.

Götting, U. (1994) 'Destruction Adjustment and Innovations: Social Policy Transformation in Eastern and Central Europe', *Journal of European Social Policy*, 4, 3. pp. 181–200.

ILO-CEET (1994a) 'The Bulgarian Challenge: Reforming Labour Markets and Social Policy', Budapest.

ILO-CEET (1994b) 'Social Protection in Transition Economies: From Improvisation to Social Concepts' (a discussion paper by Michael Cichon), Budapest.

ILO (1995) *Making Social Protection Work: The Challenge of Tripartism in Social Protection Governance for Countries in Transition*, ILO: Geneva.

James, E. (1994) 'Averting the Old-Age Crisis', Policy Research Department, World Bank.

Jessop, B. *et al.* (1991) *The Politics of Flexibility*, Aldershot: Edward Elgar.

Joint Development Committiee (1993), *Report of the Joint Development Committee of the IMF and Wotrld Bank*, Washington: World Bank

Ksiezopolski, M. (1993) 'Social Policy in Poland in the Period of Political and Economic Transition', *Journal of European Social Policy*, 3, 3. pp. 227–235.

Lewis, J. (1992) 'Gender and the Development of Welfare Regimes', *Journal of European Social Policy*, 2, 3. pp. 159–173.

Milanovic, B. (1992) 'Review of Social Safety Net Chapters in Reports on the Former Soviet Union', 11 September 1992, World Bank (unpublished).

Rhodes, M. (1996) 'Globalization and West European Welfare States: A Critical Review of Recent Debates', *Journal of European Social Policy*, 6, 4.

Shapiro, J. (1995a) 'The Non-Making of Russian Social Policy', SPA Annual Conference, Sheffield, 18–20 July 1995.

Shapiro, J. (1995b) 'The Russian Mortality Crisis and its Causes', in A. Aslund, *Russian Economic Reform at Risk*, London: Pinter.

Shaver, S. and Bradshaw, J. (1993) 'The Recognition of Wifely Labour by Welfare States', Social Policy Research Centre, Sydney University.

Siaroff, A. (1994) 'Work, Women and Gender Equality: A New Typology', in D. Sainsbury (ed.), *Gendering Welfare States*, London: Sage, pp. 82–100.

Simpura, J. (ed.) (1995) *Social Policy in Transition Societies: Experience from the Baltic Countries and Russia*, Finnish ICSW, Helsinki.

UNICEF-ICDC (1994) *Regional Monitoring Reports*, Nos. 1 and 2, Florence.

Vodopivec, M. (1992) 'Review of the Labour Market and Social Safety Net Sections of CIS CEMs', 23 December 1992, World Bank (unpublished).

World Bank (1990) *World Development Report 1990*, Washington: World Bank.

World Bank (1991) *Bulgaria: Crisis and Transition to a Market Economy* (Vol. II). [Mission included Louise Fox (social security)].

World Bank (1992) *Hungary, Reform of Social Policy and Expenditures*. [Mission included Robert Holzmann (pensions), John Micklewright (unemployment, family benefit, social assistance)].

World Bank (1993a) *Lithuania: The Transition to a Market Economy*. [Mission included Robert Holzmann (social safety net)].

World Bank (1993b) *Ukraine: The Social Sector during Transition*. [Mission included Teri Bergman (unemployment and cash benefits)].

World Bank (1993c) *Performance Audit Report: Hungary; Structural Adjustment Loan*, Report No. 12 103, June, Operations.

World Bank (1993d) *Implementing the World Bank's Strategy to Reduce Poverty*, Washington: World Bank.

World Bank (1994) *ECA Region: Social Security Regional Review, (3 Nov. 1993): Summary of Plenary Session Discussion, 21 Jan 1994*, Washington: World Bank.

# IV    The Search for a New Social Contract

# 11 The Social Contract and the Problem of the Firm
## Colin Crouch

## INTRODUCTION

The business firm has become a central institution in contemporary society in ways which make it, whether the owners and managers of firms want this or not, a problematic institution for democratic politics, or indeed for any politics at all, and, therefore, for the construction of any new form of social contract. The question has several very diverse aspects, and it is their cumulative effect that makes the issue so problematic. First, increasing weight is placed on the individual firm (rather than a whole industry, or government policy) to find new opportunities for economic progress, which has raised the firm to a position of primacy among the institutions of our societies. Second, large corporations are in certain circumstances able to exercise real power in a manner that is not provided for in either economic or constitutional theory. Third, firms are becoming important institutions of identity for their personnel, partly because the most advanced firms increasingly feel a need to develop a company culture, and partly because this growing strength of firms is happening at a time when, with several other social institutions undergoing crises, people are becoming increasingly dependent on their place of work to satisfy a range of social needs. Fourth, firms have an increasing wider social legitimacy, partly through their role in funding or sponsoring aspects of social life outside the sphere of their market activities, and partly because their forms and practices are coming to be seen as almost the only acceptable ones for running organizations of many different kinds.

I shall briefly explain what I mean by each of these points before going on to consider why I think they create a political problem.

## THE CHANGING POSITION OF THE FIRM IN WESTERN SOCIETY

### Increased Dependence on the Firm for Economic Success

For the first few post-war decades, in most western economies there was a co-existence between autonomous companies (exploring and exploiting niches in the constantly changing and innovating product markets) and government policy (which, whether through demand management, indicative planning, provision of infrastructure, or some other devices, provided a macro-level framework). Although the political rhetoric of the political right stressed a need to reduce the role of government, while that of the left wanted to increase it, governments of all kinds agreed on a basic pattern of this kind. The diversity of approaches was surveyed by Shonfield (1965) in an influential work, and he returned to the subject in later contributions written when this model was already in crisis (1983; 1984).

Since then a number of changes have occurred which have shaken these patterns. There has been falling confidence that demand management of a Keynesian kind can restrain inflation. There have also been various changes which have increased the uncertainty and lack of predictability of product markets in an economy characterized by: rapid technological change and innovation; intensifying global competition; the return to an era of steep trade cycles after the end of the Keynesian interlude; the increased orientation of product and service development towards volatile consumer markets. All this is well known. The implication that is important for the present argument is that the individual company comes to be generally perceived as the only mechanism sufficiently flexible and close to the market to cope with product market uncertainty. While many firms might fail in the attempt, some will succeed and survive; and while they are making the attempt they plausibly demand as much freedom as possible from extraneous constraint.

There is, therefore, an extreme lack of confidence on the part of the public sector that it could play a constructive part in such an environment. This is exacerbated by the prevalence of neo-liberal ideology, but cannot be reduced to it as it has independent causes. In fact, one reason for the popularity of neo-liberalism may be that it recognized a deficiency in public policy of which policy-makers were already aware, and provided them with an alternative. The lack of confidence may not always be justified: such developments as Minitel and the TGV have shown that the state (or at least the French state), has had a capacity to innovate successfully in high-technology, customer-oriented sectors. However, within the industrial world at large a lack of confidence in public capability has to be taken for granted. Governments increasingly believe that the only action they can take is to deregulate, to get themselves out of firms' way (Rose-Ackerman, 1992).

Within the argument about the primacy of the firm there is considerable inconsistency over whether very small or very large companies better embody the scope that firms offer. Until very recently it appeared that new advantages lay with small firms, which are better able to realize the values of innovativeness, fast movement and flexibility (Geroski and Schwalbach, 1986; Acs and Audretsch, 1990; Thurick, 1995). Around the time that the crises within such firms as IBM and Fiat were coinciding with a rapid rise in small computer companies in California or the tiny firms in *la terza Italia*, it was widely argued in the management science literature that the days of corporate giants were numbered. Small firms have been seen as particularly important in the creation of jobs (see for example the affirmation of this in European Commission, 1994, p. 13). But, somehow without disturbing this conclusion, gigantism has come back in favour. A few massive mergers in pharmaceuticals, mass media corporations and elsewhere, the achievement of giant size by Microsoft, have heralded a return to arguments about the absolute need for enormous size, and even for strategic alliances among companies which already individually have enormous size, if firms are to stand any chance in a globalized economy (Hayward, 1995).

Behind these fluctuations some things remain constant. If small firms seem central to economic success, that is taken as a clear demonstration that firms must be given as much entrepreneurial freedom as possible, because no public body could deal properly with small, flexible units. If giant firms seem central to economic success, that is taken as a clear demonstration that firms must be given as much entrepreneurial freedom as possible, because no public body could deal properly with such transnational, trans-sectoral organizations. Or, even if public power of some kind ought to be exercised, it is doomed to be unsuccessful in the global economy of giant corporations and financial institutions (Strange, 1994: ch. 2).

## Large Corporations and Real Power

There have been many periods in the past where large firms have been real power players on the political scene. However, this did not in general occur within societies that had the democratic aspirations of contemporary advanced societies, and with a small number of exceptions (mainly in the UK and the Netherlands) even large firms could not escape national jurisdictions. The new global corporations, especially when they form strategic alliances, have a capacity to regulate world trade, to select among regimes for soft laws on such issues as labour conditions, corruption and taxation, in a manner and with a speed and flexibility that completely outpaces the slow, pluralistic and constitutionally correct practices of cross-national political mechanisms (for example the European Union).

Economic theory, which is accepted on this point by most constitutional approaches, argues that the concept of power cannot be applied to pure competitive market economies, since within the pure market no one actor can affect price or any macro-variable by its own actions alone; all actors are anonymous and non-strategic by the definitional criteria of the perfect free market. Of course, the possibility of monopolies and of collusion among firms appearing in practice is recognized, but laws are then framed to prevent these and uphold the pure competitive model. Contemporary markets, it is then pointed out, are very competitive indeed. Therefore, there is no need to worry about the power of companies; such a phenomenon simply cannot exist, provided we guarantee the competitive order.

There are two weaknesses in this argument. First, a competitive market and a pure market are wrongly treated as one and the same. It is possible for a market comprising only two firms to be ferociously competitive. However, such a market is not 'pure'; it cannot be claimed that the firms in a market with a small number of actors match the criteria whereby markets ensure the impossibility of power (anonymity and lack of strategic capacity). It is only within the pure market of economic theory (multiple actors, none of whom can produce an effect by acting alone) that competition takes a form that can be held to be a sufficient condition for removing all anxieties about concentrations of power within the authority structure of giant firms.

Second, the approach to monopoly within most national jurisdictions is naïve. Although anti-monopoly regimes now usually recognize a concept of market power and not just an accounting measure of monopolistic presence, attention is still primarily concentrated on individual product markets, and generous scope is given to the consideration of substitute goods as diluting monopoly power. (For example, the market in cola drinks comes close to being a global duopoly, but people can drink lemonade or many other substitutes, so it is not as matter for concern). Monopoly law and regulatory practice are very reticent in considering the implications of giant size that is distributed across different product markets and national markets, so long as a firm's presence in any one of these does not itself constitute a monopoly. This ignores the capacity of transnational corporations to marshal global and cross-sectoral resources strategically, outside the conditions internal to any one product market. Such strategic action constitutes an act of power and is not, therefore, confinable within market theory.

For example, the media giant, News International, has recently been using its global strength (extensive newspaper ownership in a number of countries and, a strong presence in the heavily oligopolistic world of satellite television) to subsidize the price of some of its UK newspapers in order to reduce the market share of, and possibly to destroy, some of its competitors. The competitors do not have the same global and cross-sectoral resources as News International and are, therefore, unable to follow its price reductions while holding constant the size and quality of their products. It has proved impossible to have this regarded as questionable behaviour within UK monopoly legislation. In contrast, the privatized British telecommunications corporation, BT, *has* been prevented from using profits from running the main public telephone system in order to subsidize the consumer prices of its telephone equipment, on the grounds that its competitors in this latter field do not have a similar capacity. This has been possible because, as a privatized, formerly state-owned, corporation, BT is subject to special regulatory arrangements. It is the fact that it used to be within the public sector that enables BT to be seen as raising a problem of market power, not the fact of the market power *per se*, that concept being difficult to acknowledge within the purely private sector.

## Companies as Cultures and as Communities

The most advanced firms increasingly feel a need to develop a company culture, or 'whole company' approach, if they are to succeed. This means shaping all their activities, and every possible element that comes within the scope of the firm, in targeted pursuit of competitive success. In particular, their employees and the *personae* of their employees', their characters and the quality of their loyalty to the organization, must be fashioned according to a central, co-ordinated plan. The guiding concept is 'human resource management'.

Although present employment conditions are often dubbed post-Fordist, these developments constitute an extension of Fordism to parts that Taylorism never reached. Although the immediate origins of such practices today are often imitations of Japanese practices, they have an older history, some western firms having long developed the idea that employees should identify with the company and give it a commitment of time, loyalty and affection going far beyond the strict terms of the employment contract. Among German firms in particular senior managerial staff became a kind of private civil service or *Beamtetum*, in imitation of the nineteenth-century German state's demand for such loyalty in exchange for the status honour conferred on its officials (Kocka, 1981).

A second and increasingly more vigorous source, however, derives from the growing relative importance of the various services sectors within the economy. Whereas in manufacturing firms there might be considered to be a distinction between the production process (where the employees are located) and the product (where there are few people), in services the process is the product, and the personality of many employees is engaged as much as their technical performance. It is this characteristic of domestic service that makes that set of occupations particularly humiliating to perform, with extraordinary requirements for personal deference as well as impersonal subordination to authority.

From the point of view of many people in Western societies, the claim of the employer to make demands on a growing number of aspects of personality is a problematic intrusion on private space. Clearly, some people do not feel this, or IBM and many similar companies would never have been able to recruit a work force, but one might expect the supply of such persons to be relatively limited. If large numbers of employees, going beyond the ranks of the self-selected, are expected to act in these ways, and towards private corporations rather than towards the public agency of the state, the situation becomes rather different.

However, this tendency is contradicted by two other central trends in contemporary company practice:

- particularly within the increasingly dominant Anglo-Saxon form of corporate ownership, firms change their identity very rapidly as they engage in take-overs, mergers and frequent reorganizations; it is difficult for such shapeless structures to insist on conformity to a company culture;
- the growing casualization of the work force (including such developments as temporary labour contracts, franchising and the imposition of self-employed status on people who are *de facto* employees) is difficult to reconcile with long-term bonding to a company culture. To some extent of course these two contrasting practices – human resource maximization and casualization – are found in different kinds of firm, or between different types of employee (core versus marginal) within firms.

Both these points raise an interesting question. It might be difficult for a firm whose own identity is subject to fluctuation and fragmentation, and/or whose employment strategy involves casualization, to demand deep personal commitments, but in a world where firms are trying to maximize everything, they might well try.

In this they might be helped by a further development. The growing strength of firms as institutions is occurring at a time when several other social institutions are undergoing crises, and some people are becoming increasingly dependent on their place of work, and therefore on their employing firm, to satisfy a range of needs going beyond work and income. In the majority of advanced societies growing divorce rates have made many families unreliable as social units; crime and the motorization of transport have reduced the role of neighbourhoods and urban public space; outside the USA, religious organizations continue to decline. It may, therefore, be hypothesized that the work place has grown in relative importance as a social as well as an economic resource for many people.

## The Legitimacy of Firms in the Wider Society

Firms have an increasing role in funding or sponsoring aspects of social life outside the sphere of their market activities. This extends the role and – because these are non-market areas with non-market decision processes – the power of firms and their central decision-makers to further areas of society. The extended crisis of public finance in most advanced societies, combined with a political priority on reducing public expenditure in order to limit taxation, is the main cause of this change. The relative role of public funding for many activities has declined. Its place is increasingly taken by the growth of sponsorship, whether from motives of advertising, public beneficence, the desire for immortality, a scheme for reducing taxation obligations or an enjoyment of power. Nearly every non-profit or low-profit human activity that requires financial support now seeks sponsorship by companies. A share in control of the activity is only occasionally, though sometimes importantly, required in exchange. However, there is always an exercise of power in the decision to sponsor one activity rather than another.

This process has two interesting consequences. First, the decision-making power of persons who have authority within firms, within the market sphere, is extended to other spheres – spheres where the rules of professional competence and the market that contain their power in the firm itself do not apply. In particular, they may thereby be able to exercise influence over areas that had been deliberately protected from corporate power and market forces (such as higher education and the arts). In some ways firms hereby acquire a public rather than a private power. This can happen in many ways, but perhaps the most obvious is the practice, originating in the USA but rapidly spreading, of permitting charitable donations to be offset against liability for taxation. If one assumes that the tax revenues thereby foregone result in reduced public expenditure, what has happened is that wealthy corporations (and individuals) have been able, not only to decide which of a number of activities to favour with their own money, but simultaneously to pre-empt public money for the same activities, removing decision-making power from public agencies. Second, through their growing prominence in sponsorship activities companies come to be seen as the most significant and legitimate institutions within society, which makes it more difficult to articulate criticisms of their behaviour. A further consequence of this is that senior managerial personnel are in this way acquiring some of the attributes of a ruling class (see Crouch, 1993).

Of course, it can be argued that public funding for cultural and intellectual activities can be at least as dangerous as funding by rich corporations; at least adding some corporations to the lists of sponsors introduces some pluralism, even if it is the pluralism of a very narrow segment of society. Many examples can be provided to demonstrate the force of this point, particularly with respect to the behaviour of state-owned television channels in several countries. However, as I shall discuss in more detail below, states and citizens in many democratic societies had developed codes and understandings about the permissible limits of government interference. Such codes have often not developed around privately funded activities.

On a different point, because firms are increasingly the central institutions of our societies, their forms and practices are coming to be seen as almost the only acceptable ones for running organizations of many different kinds. Non-firm organizations are losing confidence in their *sui generis* status and believe that they must model themselves on firms, even if this means changing the character of their activities. The argument has been applied in particular to government departments and public services. (Osborne and Gaebler's *Reinventing Government* (1992) is in many respects the key text for this, though it is often forgotten that, as their title implies, the authors were trying to find new, innovative ways in which government could learn from business in order better to carry out its tasks; they were not advocating the privatization or diminution of government.) There may often be efficiency gains from this process, as firms in the market place clearly have better records at caring about the efficient application of means to ends than, say, churches, state bureaucracies or families.

However, the extension of the logic of the firm can be problematic for two reasons. Often, though not always, the reason why an activity has not been treated in this way in the past has been that it has been inappropriate or distorting to do so. Some of the controversies resulting from the imposition of internal markets in health services have this character; many of the transactions involved between teams of health workers are diffuse exchanges governed by an ethic of professional duty and extreme concentration on the goal of patient care (Altenstetter and Haywood, 1991). It is not just high transaction costs which are involved in trying to replace that dense network of co-operation by transparent, quantifiable accounting rules. To counter the danger of distortions from such a process, in some cases public policy prevents the complete acceptance of a corporate logic; however, if it still insists on similar overall outcomes it might simply shift the distortion to a different point. For example, a supermarket chain can improve productivity by closing smaller outlets and building a small number of very large outlets on out-of-town sites. (The loss of trade from previous customers who do not have private cars and cannot reach the new outlet is probably cost-effective, because these will usually have been poor people of low spending power.) Now read those sentences again, replacing 'supermarket chain' by 'local education authority', 'outlet' by 'school' and 'customers' by 'pupils' and one can see why school authorities are not as cost-effective as supermarket chains. However, today education authorities may well be required to achieve the kind of productivity gains found in supermarket chains, while not being able to use that particular strategy.

If firms are the only *sui generis* institutions, then the only valid expertise is that which derives from experience in managing them. Not only does this mean that managers from commercial firms are likely to be placed in authority over many other fields of action, but persons with commercial experience will monopolize advice on public policy. This further extends the power of persons from the firm sector to other sectors of life as discussed above, helping to turn them into a new form of ruling class. Also, of course, it places them in a strong position to protect their own private interests.

To date, the apogee of this process of subordinating other institutions to the logic of corporate structure has been *Forza Italia*, the first political party to be in effect a branch of a corporate giant, with employees taking the place of members – and, for good measure, using the television stations owned by the firm for unrestrained political purposes.

## WHY THESE DEVELOPMENTS POSE PROBLEMS FOR A NEW SOCIAL CONTRACT

Within societies that place considerable and perhaps increasing weight on the containment and scrutiny of public political power, the tolerance of the several extensions of the power of firms (in reality, of a limited number of individuals in key positions in firms) leads to considerable imbalance, since these extensions are largely unregulated, unnoticed and unscrutinized. This imbalance makes it difficult to envisage the corporate sector being brought to the table to agree to a social contract, unless it was very much on its terms in a way that undermined the existing rights of customers, the general public and, particularly, employees.

The imbalance takes primarily two forms. First, firms are able to elude public action because of the greater agility afforded to them by the lack of scrutiny and constraint. (Good examples of this would be seen from a comparison of how the EU sets about introducing a regulation and how a strategic alliance of global corporations reaches agreements on its procedures – which is also a regulatory process.) Second, as we have seen, in a number of different ways dominant individuals from firms increasingly exercise influence and sometimes control over many public and non-firm domains. In this activity too they are not subject to the same procedural rules as public or political actors, even if the scope of their action may sometimes rival these.

Furthermore, at the very moment when the power and scope of the corporate sector is growing, it is in several respects becoming less constrained and less accountable in how it uses that power than in the recent past. Globalization makes possible a certain amount of 'regime shopping', which has in turn led to a wave of deregulation as national governments seek to lower the cost of accepting their jurisdiction and act in fear that any constraints on firms may burden them in international competition. The slack labour markets of the fourth quarter of this century (compared with the third) make possible increasing evasion of obligations to employees.

These tendencies are partly contradicted by a number of developments. In the USA the eagerness of citizens to take legal action against any company (or individual or government department) that deceives them or injures their interests in any way, and the willingness of the courts to respond favourably to these actions, makes firms very cautious and wary about any damage they might cause – at least to sections of the public rich enough to risk taking court action. This imposes some important forms of corporate good behaviour going beyond what is required by statute law.

Europeans and European legal systems have yet to learn to act this way. Further, the growth of ecological concerns almost everywhere in the advanced world has required the imposition of new constraints on enterprises, and some pressure towards 'stakeholder capitalism' – which means essentially the more or less formal recognition of the rights within a company of interests other than shareholders: employees, customers, persons in the environment affected by a firm's operations.

There is, however, an important imbalance here. While it is probably true that the protection of customers and the wider environment against the actions of private corporations has gained considerably in importance in recent years, the protection of those most vulnerable to the actions of corporate management – employees – has stood still or in some cases may even have declined in the search for labour market 'flexibility'. It is certainly the case that these rights are under considerable political pressure on the grounds that they have become associated with high unemployment: once macroeconomic measures for tackling unemployment have been virtually ruled out, there is almost total reliance on company managements for creating jobs. If the price they demand is a reduction in labour standards, there will be strong pressure to accede. In this way the reduction of unemployment has become a rallying call of the political right in several countries, reversing the previous historical pattern. In the western country where the attack on labour rights has proceeded furthest (the UK), the position has been reached that an employee stands a good chance of sustaining a right against an employer only if it can be interpreted as a right of an investor, a member of an ethnic minority, or a woman. (For a discussion of how pension rights in particular have a sound basis only because they can be seen as investor rights, see Davies and Freedland, 1995: 575; see the same authors (pp. 381–5 and 583–5) for an analysis of how the strength of ethnic minority and gender rights in the UK has moved in the opposite direction to employee rights.)

This raises the fundamental problem posed by the neo-liberal state: the sole macroeconomic policy remaining to a state that has accepted the logic of the priority of the company as set out at the beginning of this article is to deregulate the corporate environment as much as possible (Crouch and Streeck, 1996). Universal deregulation is in fact the functional equivalent for the 1990s of Keynesianism or *planification* during the 1950s and 1960s. It is background, macro-level action by the state in support of corporate entrepreneurial activity. The problem with it is that it is like Samson's action in pulling down the temple containing his enemies: it killed him too. Once everything has been deregulated, the state no longer has even a *potentiality* for a capacity to act. The economic fate of the population rests solely with the firms, domestic and transnational, which operate within its boundaries. There can be no assurances that the invisible hand which may enable such an economy to achieve a high level of efficiency will do so in a way which can provide a reasonable and stable standard of living for all persons living within the society. The aspiration for such a standard will, however, remain.

## WHAT IS TO BE DONE?

It is relatively easy to spell out the kinds of measure that could equip firms with a constitutional and legal framework required by their social predominance and consistent with the concept of a renewed and balanced social contract – which is different from, and larger than, what is required to enable them to act as the orderly *economic* actors that they are in most advanced societies.

First, in recognition of the growing dependence of employees on firms, employees' rights as individuals and as groups need to be protected and advanced in such areas as: protection from unfair dismissal, openness and access to information, consultation and codetermination (for example works councils), the effective right to representation by autonomous organizations (such as trade unions). (Trade unions in a world in which individual companies are dominant and many employees engaged in relations of commitment and loyalty to firms' goals need to be rather different from most existing unions – but that is a different question.) Second, the concept of 'stakeholder capitalism', already more easily realized within certain northern European jurisdictions than within Anglo-American company law or southern European practice, has recently become a useful focus of debate, especially in the UK. This could prove a fruitful means of expressing employee, customer and ecological interests. Third, company law needs to take a broader, less purely economic, market-bound view of the concept of corporate power. Experience emerging from the regulation of privatized corporations may well be usefully applied more generally. Further, however, this is not just a matter of regulatory control, but in fact also of policy to guarantee the strength and viability of the competitive order itself, in the full sense envisaged by the original *sozialer Markt*. That is, it requires a broad range of positive measures for the small and medium business sector as much as negative controls on corporate giants.

Fourth, funding and sponsorship of non-market or weak-market activities need to be placed on a more constitutional basis. In the debates of the mid-1980s that led to the rise of private, and decline of public, sponsorship of cultural, sporting and educational activities, a caricature was presented of a dangerously monolithic and political state against a vibrant pluralism of benevolent private donors. In reality, in many countries the state had found creative and successful ways of establishing barrier institutions, relatively impervious to political pressure and more or less pluralistic, for channelling public funds; whereas the world of private, and especially corporate, donors contains much dubious practice and power-mongering. In part, a restoration of the concept of the public sector, mediated through barrier institutions, requires revival and re-energizing before matters have slipped beyond recall. In addition, however, much can be done to reduce the pre-emption of control by the corporate sector. Taxation regimes which grant exemptions for charitable giving, or even which accept sponsorship as allowable business expenditure, need to privilege types of corporate sponsorship and donations that accept constitutional forms. By this I mean forms modelled on the autonomous, self-governing foundation or trust pattern of the Ford Foundation, the Volkswagen Stiftung, and so on, rather than the cruder forms of direct funding that have grown at such an extraordinary pace in very recent years.

Finally, areas of human activity outside the scope of firms and markets – education, culture, health, religion – need to recover self-confidence, self-assertiveness, own definitions of efficiency and procedures for achieving it, and belief in their characteristics *sui generis*.

While one could extend such a list of requirements in a number of other respects, and usefully debate their practicality, one must stop short in order to end with a final reassertion of the difficulty at the present time of most such ideas. Attempts to implement any elements of such a programme encounter two fundamental obstacles. First, Europe is currently experiencing simultaneously a globalization of economic processes but a reassertion of the nation state (against supranational political entities) at the political level. There is, therefore, a growing divorce between the level at which political action needs to be taken and that at which it can be taken. There is an important exception to the decline of supranationalism: policy to deregulate markets. But this is the exception that proves the rule, being an extension of the point made above with reference to purely national polities. The deregulatory part of the European integration project, the pursuit of the European Single Market, has met with universal applause, no government being more supportive than the Conservative, neo-liberal British one which in all other respects was fully opposed to further integration. This is because deregulation is a form of integration that immobilizes the scope for further political action. Second, at a time of economic uncertainty and fears of the implications of growing

competition, there is extreme reluctance to impose constraints on the interpretation of the needs of firms offered by the corporate sector itself, especially given the new prominence that that sector has acquired in
policy-making as discussed above. While discussion of stakeholder capitalism flourishes, firms within, for example, German company law, are
eagerly looking for ways of becoming more like Anglo-American companies, with the flexibility and unencumbered manoeuvrability afforded by
having shareholders as the sole legitimate stakeholders. Paradoxically, it is
at times of relatively easy prosperity, when business is perhaps most
inclined to relax and behave itself, that other social actors are inclined to
take its success for granted and, therefore, to impose rules of behaviour on
it. When times are tough, and firms most likely to explore every avenue,
every kind of behaviour, to achieve success, everyone else is afraid to
question them.

In particular it is very difficult at the present time to argue in favour of
strengthening employees' rights at work. In the absence of any confidence
in macroeconomic measures, the problems of unemployment in European
economies are increasingly seen as amenable to solution only by weakening the rights of employees and strengthening those of managers, so that it
is easier and cheaper to deploy and dispose of workers as management
chooses (see, for example, the central burden of the argument of the
OECD's *Jobs Study* (OECD, 1994).

There are exceptions and counter-trends; in a complex world there
always will be. The EU's policy on works councils has made extraordinary progress, defying several of the expectations of the above arguments;
the sheer scale of the ecological dangers that we are producing often
induces greater public fear than do firms' threats that attempts to regulate
them on these grounds will make them move elsewhere. South Korea and
some other newly industrialized countries are showing how, after a period
of unrestrained corporate dominance, publics do begin to assert other priorities. In general however, for as long as conditions obtain, and in particular for as long as it is difficult for public agencies to produce strategies
for productive job creation and economic advance that do not simply
involve placing more reliance on the individual firm, the new position in
our society that the firm has acquired will remain a major constraint on
any attempts to renegotiate the social contract – unless of course it is to be
one similar to a kind of East Asian model of a company-dominated culture
in which mass citizenship rights in the wider society were much diminished from the current expectations of most western European populations.
That would certainly be new.

# REFERENCES

Acs, Z.J. and Audretsch, D.B. (1990) *The Economics of Small Firms: a European Challenge*, Dordrecht: Kluwer.
Altenstetter, C. and Haywood, S. (1991) (eds.), *Comparative Health Policy and the New Right*, Basingstoke: Macmillan.
Crouch, C. (1993), ¿Una nueva revolución gerencial?, *El Futuro de Socialismo*, No. 7.
Crouch, C. and Streeck, W. (1996) 'L'avenir du capitalisme diversifié', in *Ides* (eds), *Les capitalismes en Europe*, Paris: La Découverte, pp. 11–26.
Davies, P. and Freedland, M. (1995) *Labour Legislation and Public Policy*, Oxford: Oxford University Press.
European Commission (1994) *Growth, Competitiveness, Employment*, Luxembourg: Official Publications Office of the European Communities.
Geroski, P. and Schwalbach, J. (1986) *Enterpreneurship and Small Firms*, Brussels: Centre for European Policy Studies.
Hayward, J. (ed.) (1995) *Industrial Enterprises and European Integration: From National to International Champions in Western Europe*, Oxford: Oxford University Press.
Kocka, J. (1981) *Die Angestellten in der deutschen Geschichte 1850–1980*, Göttingen: Vandenhoeck und Ruprecht.
Organization for Economic Co-Operation and Development (1994), *The OECD Jobs Study*, several volumes, Paris: OECD.
Osborne, D. and Gaebler, T. (1992) *Reinventing Government: How the Entrepreneurial Spirit is Transforming the Public Sector*, Reading: Addison-Wesley.
Rose-Ackerman, S. (1992) *Rethinking the Progressive Agenda: The Reform of the American Regulatory State*, New York: Free Press.
Shonfield, A. (1965) *Modern Capitalism: The Changing Balance of Public and Private Power*, Oxford: Oxford University Press.
Shonfield, A. (1983) *The Use of Public Power*, Oxford: Oxford University Press.
Shonfield, A. (1994) *In Defence of the Mixed Economy*, Oxford: Oxford University Press.
Strange, S. (1994) *States and Markets*, second edition, London: Pinter.
Thurick, R. (1995) *Small Firms, Enterprise and Economic Growth*, Amsterdam: Tinbergen Institute.

# 12 European Social Citizenship: Why a New Social Contract (Probably) Will Not Happen

Bill Jordan

## INTRODUCTION

My title makes it clear that I am sceptical about the possibility of a 'New Social Contract' either within the states that make up the European Union, or in the EU as a whole. The idea of a 'New Social Contract' implies the emergence of social institutions that resolve collective action dilemmas by restraining wasteful competition or conflict, for the sake of mutual advantage. This could happen only through the emergence of new solidarities, based on the collective interests of members (of states and of the Union). But I shall argue that the tendency of welfare states to fragment into smaller, narrower mutualities, that has characterized social interactions in the past 20 years or more, will continue to be stronger than the impetus towards collectivization – especially in the social policy sphere.

The idea of new solidarities seems to imply one of two things: either social movements for collective action in the name of mutual interests (political pressure from below), or social engineering by élites, creating collective interests for the sake of efficiency or equity. I shall argue that there is little evidence of the former (and strong reasons for doubting that such movements will evolve, at least in the short term); and that the latter is now largely beyond the capacities of states, or the EU itself. My scepticism is an unwilling one, since I believe that new forms of social citizenship are in principle available, and would both strengthen and widen solidarities, for the benefit of all. But I am increasingly impressed by the difficulties of implementing the measures, creating the institutions, and hence achieving the purposes of a 'New Social Contract'. Since my mood and my analysis are neo-Hobbesian, and my principles are democratic and participatory, I am driven to the position of a rather pessimistic, marginal commentator on the European scene (that is, the Slovakian standpoint).

From this standpoint (that is outside the EU, and perilously, equidistantly proximate to the Bosnian conflicts and the internal convulsions of the former Soviet Union) it is difficult not to see events through the eyes of Karl Polanyi. It is like a speeded-up version of his *Great Transformation* (1944), with the movement towards free-market utopianism spreading from the West, and countered by increasingly nationalistic, violent, anti-democratic and atavistic movements for cultural social protection from the East. The clash between these two seems likely to produce – as in the first half of this century – Hobbesian conflict, before it can lead to a new social contract.

For Hobbes, the need for such a contract arose from individual striving for power and advantage, and from inter-group competition. Today the underlying needs are much the same – for institutions and policies that overcome the socially undesirable consequences of individualism (Barry, 1991: 276) and the social costs of antagonisms between groups. But globalization and the changes it has wrought within European societies make solutions difficult. When the balance of power between capital and labour shifted – somewhere between the mid-1960s and the mid-1970s – old-style collectivism became much harder to sustain. Although they lost some security and protection through these processes, most citizens of welfare states gained new opportunities for strategic action for their own advantage, increasingly orientated towards international as well as national institutions. Both in terms of *identity* (what they made of themselves), and in terms of *strategy* (how they orientated themselves towards others' actions), there was a shift towards more individualistic or household-based approaches, and away from the older collective identities of labourism and social citizenship. I shall argue that these orientations represent formidable barriers to new solidarities.

In the same period, the power of global economic actors (multinational enterprises and international financial organizations) grew in relation to that of states. This challenged the basic assumption behind welfare states – that national polities are the form of organized collective system best able to overcome the unwanted consequences of individual actions and group strategies. If the characteristic forms of third-party enforcement of the post-war era – mutual insurance systems with compulsory contributions from all citizens – are more problematic, the obvious conclusion is that the collectivization process needs to be further widened (de Swaan, 1988; 1994). European social citizenship appears the logical next step (Leibfried and Pierson, 1994), and this solution seems especially appropriate for those who see globalization as primarily a process of accelerated exchanges between advanced welfare states, which are enabled, rather than hindered, by their social policy institutions (Rieger and Leibfried, 1995). But I shall argue that this analysis misses the central dynamic of social interactions in the final quarter of this century – mobilization within groups of people with similar incomes and tastes. States find it increasingly difficult to overcome this tendency, even when its consequences are collectively perverse (for instance, the experience of Bill Clinton's national health insurance plan). I can see no reason why the EU might find it easier to do so.

It might have been instructive to use the two days of the conference on which this book is based to attempt to reach a new social contract between the participants. I suspect that what would have been revealed is that academics in political and social theory are rather strategic global bargain-hunters, seeking advantage across borders within the whole social scientific world, rather than simply in Europe, and, therefore, rather difficult to pin down with forms of restraint that might constitute Euro-solidarity. Perhaps I am merely generalizing from my own case – a British socialist, robbed of his middle-aged aspirations by Margaret Thatcher, now pursuing a post-modern lifestyle, earning a German salary, paid in Austrian schillings, working in a Slavonic country, while still owning his house (and paying his taxes) in the UK.

Within the scope of this chapter, it will be possible only to sketch my arguments, more fully developed in, *A Theory of Poverty and Social Exclusion* (Jordan, 1996). The method of analysis used here is derived from public choice theory and game theory, and emphasizes that the social costs of individualism and intensified competition are now becoming more visible, especially in those countries which most enthusiastically embraced the new forms of free-market utopianism (the USA and UK); but that the relentless logic of these changes in social relations and social institutions will make them extremely difficult to modify through collective action. In a nutshell, some new form of restraint on costly competition, at present driving down the real incomes of median as well as low earners in those countries, is clearly desirable in the interests of all, but equally clearly unattainable, because it represents a public good that it does not 'pay' any political party to promise to provide, or any interest group to support. Instead, what is proposed (and widely supported) is a form of enforcement directed narrowly against the poor, requiring that they fulfil their 'social obligations of citizenship' (Mead, 1986) in exchange for welfare benefits and services. There is a real danger that the 'politics of enforcement', which have already spread from the USA to the UK (see for instance the moral panic over crime, benefit and fraud and single parenthood that led to a change in criminal justice policy in 1993, and a 25 per cent rise in the prison population since then) will now infect the EU (Jordan, 1995; Jordan and Arnold, 1995). If this is so, the only new social contract available to Europeans will be based on Newt Gingrich and his colleagues' 'contract for America' – a political programme that will intensify and institutionalize social division and exclusion, drive up social costs, and increase inefficiency and inequity. An alternative social contract is conceivable, but not politically available, under these circumstances.

## LABOUR MARKETS, HOUSEHOLDS AND THE DIVISION OF LABOUR

In this first section of my chapter, I shall focus on the emergence of nuclear-family households as the primary collective-action units in contemporary societies, and the economic and political consequences of this development. In order to make my point rather strongly, I shall focus on the case of the UK, but I believe that the same analysis could be made of social interactions elsewhere in the EU. The point of this section is to show how middle-income families have become trapped in a cycle of intensified competition that threatens their living standards; but that the logic of their household strategies makes it unlikely that they would support the collective action programmes that might allow them to escape from this trap by restraining competition.

Seen from the perspective of the world economic system, welfare states were rather successful distributional coalitions (Olson, 1965) that captured the rents associated with advanced industrial production by restraining competition between national capital and labour, allowing them to institutionalize agreements about how to share these advantages. This gave the advanced industrialized countries, notably those of Europe, the opportunity for faster rates of economic growth than those achieved in developing countries in the 1950s and early 1960s. Welfare states in their heyday might be modelled as co-ordination games about economic growth; but after 1965, distributional struggles between capital and labour intensified (Brittan, 1975; Gough, 1979), as the share of wages in welfare states grew and profits fell (Kindleberger, 1967). In Olson's terms, this reflected the more successful mobilization of internal distributional coalitions under conditions of institutional stability (Olson, 1982, pp. 53–75). It led to capital seeking new, international strategies for rent seeking, involving the development of the newly industrializing countries on the peripheries of the advanced industrialized world, the gradual erosion of welfare states, and the crumbling of corporatist methods of national economic management (symbolized by the fall of the Swedish Social Democrat government in 1992).

Middle-income households did well from welfare states, not only because they provided security of income during employment and in retirement, but also because they provided opportunities for incremental careers in public services. From the point of view of national labour markets, welfare states can be seen as systems for 'managed crowding' (Hirsch, 1977), under which the oligopolistic collusions that previously restricted entry to lucrative professions like medicine, the law and education were 'democratized'. State employment not only allowed many more such professionals to get well-paid work; it also extended the benefits of professionalization to other groups, like physiotherapists, nurses, social workers and social pedagogues. In many ways, it allowed the bourgeoisie to enjoy 'job rents' by restraining the competition that would otherwise have threatened to destroy positional advantage – for instance, by subsidizing higher education, and thus effectively providing access to professional employment.

When capital broke free of the constraints of national welfare-state games through new capacities for international mobility, this simultaneously transformed the strategic options open to individuals. Exchanges between individuals, not negotiations between collective actors, became the relevant determinants of outcomes. The shift to more open economies, and the breakdown of the restraints imposed by collective agreements, increased the scope for individual actions. The New Right in the USA and UK pursued policies to accelerate this change, through programmes of deregulation, privatization and narrowing social protection. One outstanding feature of social relations, particularly in these Anglo-Saxon liberal countries, has been the priority given to the household unit over other forms of interdependency, such as wider kinship, community, trade union or political party. It is not that individuals have ceased to belong to these (though active membership of class-based formal organizations in particular has fallen). It is more that choices seem to have become more strongly orientated towards the interdependency requirements of that unit, and less towards those of others. Research suggests that, as actors within the public sphere and as citizens, individuals are conscious of this, and justify 'putting the family first' (Jordan, Redley and James, 1994).

The new international division of labour allowed capital to use unskilled labour more flexibly; this in turn allowed firms to exploit some groups (such as people living in isolated, deprived communities, or immigrants, or home workers) for rents. But gradually skilled groups too began to find their advantages were competed away, as their collective action organizations weakened (only one worker in eight in the USA belongs to a trade union now). Eventually the same processes affected technical and professional workers also. In the USA by 1995 the real incomes of college graduates were falling as rapidly as those of high school graduates, between 1989 and 1993, median family incomes fell by $2737 in real terms (Elliott, 1995).

Thus by prioritizing household strategies over other forms of collective action to protect job rents, mainstream citizens enjoyed improving living conditions in the 1980s, while the situation of the poor deteriorated; but by the 1990s they too had become vulnerable to interactional competition. The strategic combinations of male and female labour supply that had served the middle classes well began to be mutually frustrating, while the poor developed other (often illegal) strategies for self-protection. All these developments gave rise to forms of social organization that differentiated mainstream households from marginal ones, and polarized strategic behaviour as well as incomes (Jordan and Redley, 1994), making any social contract between these groups improbable, and increasing costly social antagonisms.

One puzzle for social scientists about the labour-market patterns that are evident in present-day advanced industrialized societies is why women – who nowadays achieve much the same educational qualifications as men, and also often gain technical and professional qualifications early in their working lives – still occupy relatively badly paid positions, relative to men with similar levels of education and training. They are to be found in subordinate roles, in part-time work, or in employment that does not reflect a good return on their investment in qualifications. Even in countries like Sweden, where female labour-market participation rates are highest, where women have most equal rates of pay in each occupation, and where they are predominantly members of trade unions, women work mainly in the public sector, and in part-time posts. Why do women not take more vigorous political action to seek equality in the world of work, or compete more strongly as individuals with men for positional advantage?

One approach to this issue is to model household decisions as best replies to employers' strategies, and as the outcomes of bargaining games between couples (Ott, 1992). Women seem to choose roles which are 'supportive' (in terms of their predominant share of child care tasks and the role of organizing and running the household) and orientated towards maximizing the incremental advantages that their male partners can gain through their 'careers' (that is pensions, perks and occupational welfare benefits). One way to analyse these decisions is as strategies within a 'battle of the sexes' supergame between the couple, over where to live, when and how many children to have, and what employment each should take. The equilibrium solution is for the woman to sacrifice her career opportunities during their children's dependency in order to maximize the man's, in return for the prospect of better pensions and a higher material standard of living in the later part of their married life through his job assets (Jordan, Redley and James, 1994, Chapters 5 and 7). This still leaves the woman with the option of developing the part-time work she does during the time when she is being 'supportive' of the man's career into a career of her own (with its own fringe benefits) when the children are older – for instance, if he takes early retirement, or if his career founders. The solution to the 'battle of the sexes' supergame thus consists in 'taking turns', not over specific decisions about promotion or geographical moves, but over phases of the life cycle, the first of which favours the man's advantages, and the second the woman's. Although 'dual careers' (that is simultaneous career development by each partner) occurs in some households in cities with good employment opportunities, and where both partners are in certain occupations (such as teaching) this alternation over the life cycle seems to be a much more common pattern all over Europe.

Why then do women not pursue the alternative course of seeking a more reliable (given the prevalence of marriage breakdown) share of men's job rents through collective action. Since the strategy of investing in their partners' careers has only a two in three chance of success (in terms of the survival of marriages in the UK), would it not be a better strategy (that is a better reply to employers' demand for flexible labour power, and men's for 'supportive' partnership) to act collectively in the political sphere to achieve equal opportunities – for example, by campaigning for state-funded child care provision?

But this would require women to compete with men for their share of the benefits from job rents. In this competition they would start as 'outsiders' in the present situation, because it is predominantly men who now enjoy the efficiency wages, training opportunities, promotion prospects, fringe benefits and occupational pension rights that constitute these 'insiders' rents. But if all the qualified women entered the market for full-time 'core' jobs of this kind, they would represent a major alternative source of labour power, and offer employers a whole new strategic option. In competing for their share of rents, they would risk competing them away altogether.

This is the essence of Robert Solow's (1990) model of the labour market as a game between insiders and outsiders. The outsiders know that if they make their labour power available at anything below the going rates of pay (reflecting the rents of insiders), employers may simply offer a reservation wage, just sufficient to clear the market, thus eliminating rents altogether. Outsiders, therefore, opt to restrain competition, and accept low rewards (unemployment benefits, or marginal work) so as not to destroy the rents of insiders. In Solow's game, they wait in the hope that such jobs will eventually become available to them.

But Solow's version is not entirely convincing, because it assumes that outsiders are aware of a collective good (a sustainable stock of insiders' job rents) and restrain competition for a possible future stake in this. But it does not specify the collective action group, or the selective incentives or sanctions, through which such restraint is accomplished (Olson, 1965). Indeed, outsiders constitute precisely the kind of disorganized category of individuals that Olson treats as incapable of taking action for the sake of the benefits of restrained competition (Olson, 1982). To carry conviction, the model needs to identify something in the game that gives actors compelling or persuasive reasons not to compete for rents, in terms of private payoffs in the current situation, or group interactions.

This something can be explained in terms of women's situation. As individuals they would be only slightly better off in terms of personal earnings if they competed away men's job rents; and as partners in households where the man had such a rent they would be much worse off if their actions destroyed these rents. In other words, the relevant collective action unit to restrain competition is the household where the woman has a stake in her partner's job rent. Women have strong incentives not to compete, and strong sanctions against such competition, within their partnerships. Seen from this perspective, unrestrained competition threatens their partner's career and job assets. Thus their best strategy is to accept the *status quo*, be supportive, and take a part-time job, for the sake of their stake in their partner's insider status and its benefits (Jordan, 1989).

It is this that most satisfactorily explains the present configuration of household labour supply as the 'best reply' to employers' strategies for flexibility, with men pursuing rents through careers, and women taking part-time work, usually with little career prospects or fringe benefits. Not all of these are low-paid, even though these well-qualified women could probably earn much more. Furthermore, as surveys repeatedly reveal, levels of job satisfaction for women in part-time employment are high. The strategy seemed successful in the UK in the 1980s, where the household incomes of couples with at least one member in regular full-time

employment rose at quite a steady rate. However, auguries from the USA
are now discouraging, as median household incomes continue to fall; this
suggests that the job rents of more qualified and professional employees
are becoming vulnerable to competition from abroad in a deregulated
labour market (Elliott, 1995; Barker, 1995). Thus the restraint exercised
by women as 'supportive' partners is no longer enough to protect the
incomes of better-paid men.

The relevance of all this to the possibility of a new social contract is that
households have become the most important collective action units in
advanced industrialized societies, and hence household strategies have
become the most significant form of collective action that must be
addressed in any attempt to overcome the principal collective action
dilemmas in our current interactions. The theoretical basis for a new social
contract must either show how new social movements could arise that
might campaign for such a contract, or how a social engineering scheme
for overcoming these dilemmas from above might gain political support.
In the next section I shall argue that such a solution is in principle available, but that the dynamic of household strategies, and the configuration of
polarized economic interests, are against any such movements or support.


## COLLECTIVE ACTION AND THE POOR

In this section I shall analyse the choices facing individuals and households who are unemployed or in irregular, marginal work. These are
people without job rents, some of whom are being exploited by employers
who have gained a monopoly position to extract a rent from their labour.
The aim of this analysis is to explain their actions as best replies to the
strategies of employers, government agencies and each other in this
situation.

Implicit in the model of mainstream households developed in the previous section is the claim that their strategies are aimed at excluding such
people from access to job rents, and from a share of the benefits from such
rents. Because it gives priority to the interdependency between household
members, and is aimed at protecting this social formation by conserving
those rents still available to employees, the mainstream strategy necessarily excludes those others from its benefits. As a collective action unit, the
mainstream household both institutionalizes the sharing of benefits and
costs of men's career development and restrains women from competition
in the labour market that might erode men's job rents; it also mobilizes
electoral support for policy measures that restrain competition from other

outsiders, such as the poor. But I shall argue that it also blocks the formation of a distributional coalition (political pressure group) in favour of redistribution from insiders to outsiders.

In principle there is a third (collective) strategy open to women as an interest group, in addition to the two modelled in the previous section. This is to lead a grand coalition of outsiders in a bargaining game with insiders, that aimed to offer restrained competition for their rents, in exchange for a universal share in those rents (that is a New Social Contract). A coalition between women and the poor would have a clear electoral majority, and the institutional mechanism through which this could be achieved would be something like a basic income scheme (Van Parijs, 1992; 1995; Barry, 1994; Brittan, 1995; Young and Halsey, 1995; Atkinson, 1995). This would give all citizens an unconditional income as an individual entitlement, unrelated to their labour market or household roles (Walter, 1988; Parker, 1989). As a rough approximation, insiders as holders of job rents could be expected to be net contributors to such a scheme and outsiders net beneficiaries. The basic income would provide outsiders with a reliable form of income security, and would give them incentives to participate in labour markets on their current terms, rather than seeking to undercut insiders' rents; their interests would, therefore, be best served by keeping the bargain, and thus a self-enforcing social contract would be reached.

Many social and political theorists (of very different persuasions) have argued that, under present labour market conditions, basic income represents the only feasible inclusive institutional structure for balancing the market-orientated interests of the better-off with the protection of the poor (Dahrendorf, 1989; Jordan, 1989; Purdy, 1994; Duncan and Hobson, 1995). Yet this programme has never been widely canvassed, and no major political party in any advanced industrialized state has ever used it to mobilize electoral support; nor have the poor ever organized around it. I shall also analyse how the poor have responded to the strategies of employers and main stream households.

The defining characteristic of poor households is that the mainstream strategy outlined in the previous section is not open to them. Without access to a career and its attendant possibilities of security and job rents, they must orientate themselves towards the opportunities and incentives of the market for marginal work, the availability and rewards of informal work (including unpaid community work and various forms of illegal activity) and the structure and rules of benefits systems. Their choices of how to combine these reflect their strategic replies to employers in search of flexibility, to the benefits authorities, and to each other.

Unlike in the mainstream, where one lifetime strategy seems to emerge as the dominant equilibrium solution to such bargaining games, the labour supply behaviour of poor households seems far more variable. As seen through the official UK statistics, there are large pools of unemployment, a large flow between unemployment and marginal work, and a large segment of households with one member in regular, long-term, low-paid work and others in part-time or irregular employment. It looks as if there are three groups who have adopted quite different strategies in relation to the same institutional structures of opportunities and constraints – the 'dependent', the 'risky' and the 'steady' households.

However UK research in deprived communities suggests that all these strategies combine elements from the labour market, the benefits system, the informal economy, and communal systems of mutual support, and that households move between these strategies over time (Jordan, James, Kay and Redley, 1992). This is because labour-market deregulation has led to a situation of 'hypercasualization', and means-tested benefits systems respond slowly to changes in household circumstances. The choice between the three strategies depends on what is the primary source of household income at any time. Workers who take low-paid regular jobs calculate that they will do better in these (supplemented by family credit and housing benefits) than through the much more variable earnings available in marginal employment, if they compete with others using that strategy. Irregular workers assess these risks before accepting such offers, and the long-term unemployed assess the wage that would be necessary to make it worthwhile for them to sacrifice the continuity of their claims. All three strategies also include an orientation towards informal work opportunities (cash jobs that are not declared to the tax or benefit authorities), and to the support that is available through networks of kin and friends (Morris, 1992; Morris and Irwin, 1992).

In the UK, the significance of informal work, and especially undeclared cash transactions, reflects the changed structure of incentives that has followed deregulation. As the wages of unskilled workers have fallen, and demands for 'flexibility' have been reflected in more irregular (part-time, subcontract, occasional or short-term) work, formal employment has offered fewer incentives, relative to those from informal work, that can be combined with social assistance claims. Furthermore, the casualization of the labour market has increased informal opportunities, while the decline in trade union membership has reduced collective pressures on workers to refrain from such activities for the sake of solidarity (Jordan, 1996, Chapter 2).

Policy debate has focused on benefits dependency and undeclared work by claimants. Hence policy in the UK, as in the USA, has been aimed at limiting the availability of income maintenance for the poor, while steering them towards the labour market. The government's programme since the early 1980s has been one of 'targeting' assistance on those 'in greatest need', but making it more conditional by stricter eligibility tests. Benefits administration increasingly involves detailed investigation of claimants resources, requirements and behaviour, in order to screen out claimants with adequate means, and those who are not truly incapable of work or 'involuntarily unemployed'.

But these measures also drive up transaction costs for each claim, since the individual investigations required consume large amounts of staff time. One way of counteracting this is to force claimants to bear part of these costs. It has become standard administrative practice to suspend payment of benefits in all cases requiring investigation of eligibility. Stricter testing and more complex assessments also involve delays in processing even standard claims (McLaughlin, Millar and Cooke, 1989). During such periods, it is the claimant who absorbs the costs; the household must survive without assistance, and can get into serious debt, or even become homeless.

Insofar as many potential applicants consider the claiming process too costly (Craig, 1991), these procedures succeed in reducing expenditure. However, experienced claimants develop counter-strategies to resist the effects of official administrative practices. From the claimants' point of view, stricter testing, administrative delays and benefits suspensions all change the relative payoffs of declared and undeclared work, making the latter more attractive. Given that most of the work available in the formal labour market is low-paid and short-term, they reason that the risk of debt or destitution when they are forced to claim again is not worth taking, and prefer to take what work is available on an informal (undeclared) basis. In our research on low-income couples with children, two-thirds of the respondents indicated that they had done occasional small 'cash jobs', and most irregular workers justified this in terms of the transaction costs associated with claiming (Jordan, James, Kay and Redley, 1992, Chapters 4 and 6). They told stories of how they had been unfairly disqualified, or had their payments suspended or delayed, to show that it was incumbent on them as responsible parents to do occasional undeclared work, to secure their children's living standards.

These interactions can be modelled as a prisoner's dilemma game between claimants and staff over transaction costs (Jordan, 1995). The equilibrium solution to the game is mutual defection (claimants always do undeclared work, staff always suspend benefits), because if either cooperates it is to the advantage of the other to defect. It could be argued, of course, that since most claimants are long-term, a one-shot prisoner's dilemma game misrepresents what is a series of interactions. Axelrod's work on iterated prisoner's dilemma games (Axelrod, 1984) suggests that the cycle of mutual defections can be broken by players 'signalling' willingness to co-operate by adopting a strategy of minimal retaliation. But the UK government has signalled just the opposite of this with its well-publicized 'clamp downs' on fraud, and introduction of new restrictions. Policies that try to change the payoffs, by increasing the costs of defection, do not change the equilibrium solution to the game. Yet there is a strong impetus within the game for policy makers to try to increase enforcement, and in doing so to raise enforcement costs also, thus increasing both public expenditure and the impoverishment of those to whom the measures are applied (see also next section).

Furthermore, claimants' resistance to such policies is unlikely to take the form of isolated, individual action. In deprived communities informal activity, including undeclared work, becomes co-ordinated through networks of information, which reduce risks of detection, and allow a culture of resistance to benefits authorities to develop. Such forms of resistance rely on the 'hidden transcripts' of underground communication and covert action, under a cloak of compliance (Scott, 1985; 1990). They are much more difficult to suppress through enforcement measures, because risks are dispersed through anonymity and collusion. Poor people's collective action uses these 'weapons of the weak' to compensate themselves for their exclusion from the benefits of mainstream society, and particularly from job rents. But they leave the poor free to take other collective action, such as riots, if the opportunities and incentives for open resistance become more attractive. The relative success of resistance strategies, including undeclared work and crime, is shown in the discrepancy between income measures of the living standards of the poorest household, and expenditure measures. By income measures the worst-off in the UK have suffered an absolute impoverishment since 1979; by expenditure measures they have not.

The full implications of these developments have only gradually penetrated the policy debate and the social scientific research agenda (Jordan and Redley, 1994). There is now growing recognition of the issues, with a government report estimating an annual £1.4 billion in false claims (BBC Radio 4, *Today* programme, 10 July 1995). Yet this has increased rather than diminished pressure for costly enforcement measures. The government is now introducing new measures, such as bar codes on payment books, to combat fraud; local authorities are trying to counter fraudulent claims of student grants; and the Labour Party leadership has pledged its support for councils which invite residents to inform on fraudulent claimants of housing benefits (BBC Radio 4, *Today* programme, 9 August 1995).

While the poor are able to take these self-compensatory actions, and while political parties are able to mobilize support in mainstream households to suppress them, no coalition for redistributing job rents is feasible, and the basic income proposal will not be put on the political agenda. The poor have come to rely on their own actions and strategies, and have turned away from orthodox political pressure. Like those of mainstream households, these strategies can be seen as individually rational but collectively mutually frustrating. They actually contribute to further casualization of employment, and further falls in wage rates. Furthermore, the divergence between mainstream and poor households' strategies, due to social and economic polarization, is now beginning to produce costly social conflicts. As mainstream households become less secure, and their incomes start to fall, they look for others to blame. In the USA, right-wing politicians have found ready scapegoats among the poor, and especially among black welfare mothers. Elsewhere too the blame for the endemic malaise, the 'feel-bad factor', is settled on the 'enemy within' – immigrants, foreigners, deviants – dividing any potential coalition in favour of a new social contract.

## THE POLITICS OF ENFORCEMENT

The new solidarities needed for a social contract, that could provide the basis for European social citizenship, would require political brokerage at the national and the EU level. Political élites would need to be convinced that they would get good electoral returns on policies for social integration, and new institutions to harmonize the interests of collectivities which are currently antagonistic or divergent in their orientations. In principle, as I have suggested, some such possibility exists, in the form of a programme for a European basic income scheme, guaranteeing every EU citizen a certain level of security, which could then be 'topped up' by member states. But I shall argue that politicians are far more likely to be attracted by the returns on programmes of enforcement, directed against marginal members of society (sometimes in the name of integration), that will drive up social costs, and increase antagonism and resistance.

The politics of enforcement can be seen as the other side of the coin of Tocquevillian democracy. Robert Putnam (1993) has distinguished between the virtuous circle of trust, co-operation, enterprise, prosperity and good government that occurs where citizens are active within a culture of civic involvement and voluntary association, and the vicious circle of mistrust, antagonism, clientelism, patronage, economic stagnation and administrative inefficiency that accompanies a regime of Hobbesian third-party enforcement, vertical bonds and authoritarian social relations. He postulates two long-term equilibria around these alternative systems of social relations, the former creating social capital and generating rapid economic growth, and the latter spawning high social costs and low-level performance. While most analysts of institutional systems associate the USA and Western Europe with the former characteristics (Olson, 1982; North, 1990), there is reason to believe that current collective action dilemmas are shifting political responses towards enforcement, especially against minority groups, and may be generating a move towards more costly and less efficient, as well as less democratic, systems of government.

The most obvious examples of such a change have been around the issues of 'underclass', 'dependency culture' and crime in the USA and UK in the 1980s and 1990s, which peaked with the 'back to basics' stance of the Major government in the autumn of 1993 (Jordan, 1995), and the mid-term election of 1994 in the USA. It is reflected in figures on rising rates of imprisonment in both countries, and in the ascendancy of a political rhetoric of punishment and revenge; in the USA this is accompanied by the escalation in executions, and the reintroduction of archaic practices, such as chain gangs. In California, state spending on criminal justice measures threatens to overtake spending on welfare before the turn of the century.

The movement in the USA towards the 'compulsory integration' of the poor is spread across a number of policy domains. On its analysis, most unemployment is 'voluntary', and caused by unwillingness or inability to recognize the social obligations that accompany guarantees of income and welfare security (Mead, 1986; 1988). Hence the provision of benefits should be more authoritative and conditional, so that applicants are made to accept work disciplines and the duty to provide for children out of earnings. In the European context, of course, the notions of individual responsibility, work obligation and compulsory inclusion are mediated by concepts of social citizenship, social inclusion and full employment. Hence 'workfare' as a form of coercion is not preached or practiced in the manner of the US politics of enforcement. Even so, many of the same theoretical arguments apply to US and European policies for retraining and reintegrating those receiving long-term benefits (Adriaansens and Dereksen, 1993). Ambitious plans for reducing unemployment through the co-ordinated efforts of employers, trade unions and the state have been canvassed by the EU (Delors, 1993), and the idea of a New Social Contract – the Treaty of Louvain – has been widely debated in Belgium (Dettane, 1994). Hence the issue of compulsory integration is an important part of any plan for European social citizenship.

There are circumstances in which workfare and its various derivatives ('trainfare', 'carefare', and so on) can promote efficiency, but these are quite circumscribed. One relates to the buoyancy of the labour market; if there are many adequately-paid jobs for those with skills, qualifications and a suitable personal profile, even quite expensive measures that require claimants to train and equip themselves for these available opportunities will be efficient, because they will overcome supply-side barriers to employment among the claimant population. Such examples can be found in many districts of the western states of the USA and Canada. Another set of conditions occur when unemployment benefits are high, there is a niche in which labour-market intervention can provide training or employment without substitution or displacement, motivated applicants can learn transferable skills, and enough vacancies occur to absorb 'graduates' over time. Research in Belgium (Schatteman, Van Trier and Késenne, 1994) found that various schemes in Flanders achieved efficiency because they met these conditions.

However, as a general rule there are many reasons why it is rare for compulsory employment or training to meet efficiency criteria. Coercion is itself demotivating; even a few disaffected participants can be disruptive and reduce the productivity of others. These forms of forced labour are ideal breeding grounds for cultures of resistance, using the 'weapons of the weak' (Scott, 1985) – petty pilfering, malingering, absenteeism, defection, shoddy workmanship and minor sabotage. Such practices can be well co-ordinated through underground channels of co-ordination, that cost the participants much less than open rebellion, and give the utility associated with revenge. History furnishes many such examples, from the Speenhamland system in England (Wakefield 1831; Polanyi, 1944), to the whole system of labour under the centrally planned economies of the Soviet Bloc. All experienced low and falling productivity, as the resistance practices most common in Central Europe ('we pretend to work, you pretend to pay') were consolidated.

In the USA and UK, the New Right claimed that market-orientated institutional reforms would make efficient and equitable interactions self-enforcing. But these reforms ignored perverse incentives and moral hazard of a collective kind – the discrepancy between the pay-offs for broad, inclusive communal solidarity on the one hand, and narrow, snobbish, exclusive mutuality on the other; or between unskilled formal employment and trade union membership, and irregular, informal economic activity and membership of a semi-criminal network, for example.

Despite its disavowal of social engineering and planned outcomes, liberal democratic governance – even of the Hayekian kind – seeks to minimize coercion by providing a framework of rules for interactions in which citizens' individual and collective decisions produce socially desirable outcomes. Neo-liberal institutions have proved, if anything, less strategy-proof than social democratic ones, because they have produced rational egoists who are designed to be good at self-interested strategies. Whereas participatory democrats would seek to educate and mobilize citizens for collective action in the common interest (Barber, 1984; Oldfield, 1990), neo-liberals can only fall back on measures of enforcement, that raise the price of selfish strategies, but often also raise the social costs of all exchanges, and hence reduce efficiency.

In the absence of opportunities for advantageous, legal economic activity for the poor, or payoffs for inclusive membership and co-operation between communities and groups, it was rational for many mainstream citizens to press for increased authoritative enforcement. Crime costs citizens and firms more, in insurance, taxes and inconveniences, as well as loss and pain. But these conditions rewarded populist politicians who exploited social conflicts, and drew dividends from antagonism, rather than brokering co-operation. One problem for democracy is that there is always a temptation for politicians to use widespread fears (in issues such as crime and 'moral degeneration') through mobilizing the public behind stronger enforcement measures. Populism on such issues can transform the nature of political participation by channelling inter-group conflicts into public policy (Jordan and Arnold, 1995).

The present situation poses two intractable problems to national governments, and thus presumably to the EU also. The first is one of implementation; any potential programme for inclusive social citizenship must appeal to (or coerce) large numbers of convert, risk-sharing 'informal clubs' for semi-legal or illegal activities, generating high returns – for instance from drug-dealing – for their members. This means that policies must either offer larger inducements for labour-market participation than the benefits these clubs supply their members, or break them up through enforcement measures. Small rewards (such as a low level of basic income, plus low and irregular wages) or small individual punishments and sanctions would not be enough to achieve either of these goals, since the payoffs to club members are so high. Poverty and social exclusion have thus already driven up the costs of effective policies of any kind to reintegrate those citizens, because they have provoked them into rather effective collective resistance.

Secondly, there is a problem of political legitimation and support. In a polarized society that has experienced a period of enforcement – orientated policies, it would be particularly difficult to switch to an inclusive orientation, especially one based on a fairly novel concept of social justice, such as the basic income approach. How could unconditional assistance be given to a population previously constructed as morally degenerate? And how could full employment, the sacred cow of Christian Democrats and Social Democrats alike, suddenly be sacrificed? Yet the problem of compulsory inclusion, as the alternative strategy for social citizenship, is the opposite one. The danger is that enforcement measures will develop a logic and a political support of their own, regardless of their contribution to efficiency or equity. Democratic political systems might not be able to contain populist excesses, particularly if minorities are able to build upon existing networks to construct more effective forms of collective resistance. In this situation, it would be difficult to stop the culture of contentment from rushing forward into the politics of punishment and revenge.

## CONCLUSION

A new social contract, based on European social citizenship, is for some analysts the natural outcome of the collectivization process (de Swaan, 1988; 1994), in the new context of globalization. The latter process implies the interweaving of foreign and domestic policies (Parry, 1994), through the acceleration of transnational exchanges of all kinds – of goods, services, finance, people, pollution and crime (Held and McGrew, 1994). For Rieger and Leibfried (1995), effective social policies allow states to throw themselves open to world markets; economic integration between national economies is mainly a relationship between welfare states. The tendency is for economic links to grow fastest between countries with similar values, institutional structures and regulatory principles – in this case the relevant characteristics are political democracy and welfare statism, providing interdependence and institutional integration with a stable foundation. Thus shared domestic notions of social justice and social protection have enabled the faster integration of the EU, and will allow a new European social contract to emerge, and be developed in the next century.

The alternative view, put forward in this chapter, is based on an accelerated replay of Polanyi's *Great Transformation* (1994). The notion of self-regulating markets, promoted within the international sectors of advanced industrialized economies, has a logic of its own that tends towards the creation of a global order, not of integrated blocs of welfare states, but of international institutions to uphold private property and contractual exchange. This in turn provokes various divergent movements for social protection, based on nationalistic, ethnic, religious, regional, class or sectional principles (all of which tend to fragment the rational-legal order of the welfare state era), and on narrower mutualities of like incomes and tastes, which erode the economic basis of collectivization. These tendencies in turn subvert democratic citizenship, and substitute forms of populism and authoritarianism for the inclusive interactions promoted by the welfare state.

If any validity is conceded to my analysis, it points to collective action problems that will afflict the EU as much as its member states. The relative decline of Sweden, the most redistributive welfare state in Europe, and the slower growth of all the Western European economics, raise questions about the competitive implications of extensive social regulation. On the other hand, the escalation of both social conflicts and enforcement costs in the USA and UK point to the difficulties associated with a Gingrich-style authoritarian social contract. Above all, there is a question over how mainstream, middle class voters in all the European countries will respond to slower growth, and the impact of international competition (especially from the dynamic economies of Central Europe). Are the extraordinary costs of USA health care, or the massive 'negative equity' in the UK owner-occupied housing sector, merely specific consequences of policy mistakes, leading to a widespread 'feel-bad' factor among such voters? Or are they the unintended collective outcomes of the household strategies identified in the first part of this chapter?

Far from implying further collectivization in transnational units, globalization might instead signal serious problems for existing collective institutions, at the international as well as the national level, and especially over social policy issues. The global citizen of the next century might be a sovereign bargain-hunter in search of his or her most favoured bundle of collective goods, available through the development of private sites by landlords, in partnership with minimalist local authorities. Such contractual communities (Foldvary, 1994) would allow comfortable households to move between self-selecting, homogeneous income zones, leaving a residuum in 'communities of fate', under the authoritative regime of private contractors of a Benthamite complexion. The result would be a medieval landscape of free (but walled) citadels, separated by a wasteland of panopticons and predation.

What seems to be at stake is thus the possibility of democratic community as the basis of a new social contract. The challenge for the next century is to discover forms of collective action and social institutions that are suited to sovereign, consumption-orientated, diverse and quarrelsome individuals, in a global environment with vastly unequal allocations of resources – a Hobbesian dilemma. As benevolence shrinks to narrower limits (the nasty, brutish, bourgeois, suburban family) social engineering becomes more necessary as well as far more difficult. Neither traditional liberal individualism nor compulsory collectivist socialism now seems feasible or attractive.

Above all, the task is to avoid social policy 'solutions' that block unexpected routes to greater benevolence (the Humean path of J.S. Mill, T.H. Green and liberal communitarianism) and abundance (the Utilitarian roadway of Bentham, Smith and Keynes). Social policy, as it exists at present, would be a barrier to the emergence of a more benevolent and prosperous international order. Democratic community will probably be more technically feasible in the next century, but more politically unattainable. The dynamic that excludes the poor may instead exclude the possibility of prosperity and progress.

# REFERENCES

Adriaansens, H. and W. Dereksen (1993) 'Labour-Force Participation, Citizenship and Sustainable Welfare in the Netherlands', in H. Coenen and P. Leisink (eds.), *Work and Citizenship in the New Europe*, Aldershot: Edward Elgar, pp. 191–204.

Atkinson, A.B. (1995) *Public Economics in Action: The Basic Income/Flat Tax Proposal*, Oxford: Oxford University Press.

Axelrod, R. (1994) *The Evolution of Co-operation*, New York: Basic Books.

Barber, B. (1984) *Strong Democracy: Participatory Politics for a New Age*, Berkeley: University of California Press.

Barker, J. (1995) 'Are Low Wages a Danger?', *The Times*, 28 July.

Barry, B. (1991) 'The Continuing Relevance of Socialism', in B. Barry, *Liberty and Justice: Essays in Political Theory, 1*, Oxford: Clarendon Press, pp. 274–90.

Barry, B. (1994) 'Justice, Freedom and Basic Income', mimeo, London School of Economics.

Brittan, S. (1975) 'The Economic Contradictions of Democracy', *British Journal of Political Science*, 5, 2, pp. 129–59.

Brittan, S. (1995) *Capitalism with a Human Face*, Aldershot: Edward Elgar.

Craig, P. (1991) 'Costs and Benefits: A Review of Research on Take-Up of Income-Related Benefits', *Journal of Social Policy*, 20, 4, pp. 537–65.

Dahrendorf, R. (1989) 'The Underclass and the Future of Britain', Lecture given at St George's House, Windsor Castle, 24 April.

de Swaan, A. (1988) *In Care of the State: Health Care, Education and Welfare in Europe and the USA in the Modern Era*, Cambridge: Polity.

de Swaan, A. (1994) *Social Policy Beyond Borders: The Social Question in Transnational Perspective*, Amsterdam: Amsterdam University Press.

Dettane, J.L. (1994) *Keys for Tomorrow*, Hasselt: Esopus.

Delors, J. (1993) 'The Scope and Limits of Community Action', in K. Coates and M. Barratt Brown (eds), *A European Recovery Programme: Restoring Full Employment*, Nottingham: Spokesman, pp. 45–52.

Duncan, A. and Hobson, D. (1995) *Saturn's Children: How the State Devours Liberty, Prosperity and Virtue*, London: Sinclair-Stevenson.

Elliott, L. (1995) 'US Reaps the Unhappy Harvest of Deregulation', *The Guardian*, 20 February.

Foldvary, F. (1994) *Public Goods and Private Communities*, Aldershot: Edward Elgar.

Gough, I. (1979) *The Political Economy of the Welfare State*, London: MacMillan.

Held, D. and McGrew, A. (1994) 'Globalization and the Liberal Democratic State', *Government and Opposition*, 28, 2, pp. 261–85.

Hirsch, F. (1977) *Social Limits to Growth*, London: Routledge and Kegan Paul.

Jordan, B. (1989) *The Common Good: Citizenship, Morality and Self-Interest*, Oxford, Blackwell.

Jordan, B. (1995) 'Are New Right Policies Sustainable? "Back to Basics" and Public Choice', *Journal of Social Policy*, 24, 3, pp. 363–84.

Jordan, B. (1996) *A Theory of Poverty and Social Exclusion*, Cambridge: Polity.

Jordan, B., James, S., Kay, H. and Redley, M. (1992) *Trapped in Poverty? Labour-Market Decisions in Low-Income Households*, London: Routledge.

Jordan, B., Redley, M., and James, S. (1994) *Putting the Family First: Identities, Decisions and Citizenship*, London: UCL Press.

Jordan, B. and Redley, M. (1994) 'Polarization, Underclass and the Welfare State', *Work, Employment and Society*, 8, 2, pp. 153–76.

Jordan, B. and Arnold J. (1995) 'Democracy and Criminal Justice', *Critical Social Policy*, 15, 2/3, pp. 170–182.

Kindleberger, C.P. (1967) *Europe's Postwar Growth: the Role of Labour Supply*, Cambridge: Harvard University Press.

Leibfried, S. and Pierson, P. (1994) 'Prospects for Social Europe', in A. de Swaan (ed.), *Social Policy Beyond Borders*, Amsterdam: Amsterdam University Press, pp. 13–58.

McLaughlin, E., Miller, J. and Cooke, K. (1989) *Work and Welfare Benefits*, London: Gower.

Mead, L.M. (1986) *Beyond Entitlement: The Social Obligations of Citizenship*, New York: Basic Books.

Mead, L.M. (1988) 'The Potential for Work Enforcement', *Journal of Policy Analysis and Management*, 7, 2, pp. 264–86.

Morris, L. (1992) 'The Social Segregation of the Long-Term Unemployed in Hartlepool', *Sociological Review*, 40, 2, pp. 344–69.

Morris, L. and Irwin, S. (1992) 'Unemployment and Informal Support: Dependency, Exclusion or Participation?', *Work, Employment and Society*, 6, 2, pp. 185–209.

North, D.C. (1990) *Institutions, Institutional Change and Economic Performance*, Cambridge, Cambridge University Press.

Oldfield, A. (1990) *Citizenship and Community: Civic Republicanism in the Modern World*, London: Routledge.

Olson, M. (1965) *The Logic of Collective Action: Public Goods and the Theory of Groups*, Cambridge: Harvard University Press.

Olson, M. (1982) *The Rise and Decline of Nations: Economic Growth, Stagflation and Social Rigidities*, New Haven: Yale University Press.

Ott, N. (1992) *Intrafamily Bargaining and Household Decision*, Berlin: Springer.

Parker, H. (1989) *Instead of the Dole: An Enquiry into Integration of Tax and Benefits Systems*, London: Routledge.

Parry, G. (1994) 'The Interweaving of Foreign and Domestic Policy-Making', *Government and Opposition*, 28, 2, pp. 143–51.

Polanyi, K. (1944) *The Great Transformation: The Political and Economic Origins of Our Time*, Boston: Beacon.

Purdy, D. (1994) 'Citizenship, Basic Income and the State', *New Left Review*, 208, pp. 30–48.

Putnam, R.D. (1993) *Making Democracy Work: Civic Traditions in Modern Italy*, Princeton: Princeton University Press.

Rieger, E. and Liebfried, S. (1995) 'Welfare States and Globalization', paper given at Summer School, University of Bremen, 25 July.

Schatteman, T., Van Trier, W. and Késenne, S. (1994) *De Kloof Dichten: Brengt Let Iets Op? Een Onderzoek Naar de Kosten en Baten voor de Overheid van 'Leerwerkbedrijt'*, Antwerp: SESO-UFSIA.

Scott, J.C. (1985) *Weapons of the Weak: Everyday Forms of Peasant Resistance*, New Haven: Yale University Press.

Scott, J.C. (1990) *Domination and the Arts of Resistance: Hidden Transcripts*, New Haven: Yale University Press.

Solow, R. (1990) *The Labour Market as a Social Institution*, Oxford: Blackwell.

Van Parijs, P. (1992) *Arguing for Basic Income: The Ethical Foundations for a Radical Reform*, London: Verso.

Van Parijs, P. (1995) *Real Freedom for All: What (If Anything) Can Justify Capitalism?*, Oxford: Clarendon Press.

Wakefield, E.G. (1831) *Swing Unmasked*, London: E. Wilson.

Walter, T. (1988) *Basic Income: Freedom from Poverty, Freedom to Work*, London: Marian Boyars.

Young, M. and Halsey, A.H. (1995) *Family and Community Socialism*, London: Institute for Public Policy Research.

# 13 Some Sceptical Reflections on EU Citizenship as the Basis of a New Social Contract
Carlos Closa

## INTRODUCTION

The notion of a social contract has been central to concepts of citizenship both in political theory and constitutional practice. Citizenship has been perceived as inclusive of social rights for guaranteeing individuals' autonomy and self-realization as human beings. The neo-liberal assault on the welfare state has questioned this view but, as a reaction, it has also stimulated the search for new ways of reconstructing the classical notion of citizenship. In this context, European Union (EU) citizenship appears very appealing. Three developments have fuelled expectations:

- the severing of the link between rights and nationality within the EU;
- the development of certain EU social rights;
- the recreation of citizenship at the EU level.

The linkage of the concept of EU citizenship to the idea of a social contract is thus gaining currency in Europarlance, although at the expense of conceptual clarity: for 'social contract' refers both to the classical imperative of legitimizing public power with EU citizens' consent (Neunreither, 1995), as well as to an understanding of the Treaty on European Union (TEU) as a pact among individuals as well as states (Weiler, 1995: 22).

This paper does not aim to produce a new conception of social pact; rather, it presents a sceptical view of the prospects of using EU citizenship as an instrument for rebuilding the old social contract and, specifically, its welfare dimension. But this scepticism should not be interpreted as a negation of the possibility of, or, even less, the desirability of such development. The link between citizenship and contractualism is referred to in the first section in summary fashion. The contents and limits of EU citizenship are established in section two in order to show, in section three, that EU citizenship has been mainly developed through negative integration and that this facilitates a liberal-inspired form of social contract. As a result, it is argued in section four, the prospects for developing EU social rights are slim. However, it is also argued that EU citizenship must be central to any redefinition of a social contract in Europe.

The aim of this study is not to compare EU citizenship with an ideal type drawn from national citizenships. Rather, its conception of EU citizenship is grounded in the context of current EU legal and political practice, identifying concrete and precise problems lying at the interface of EU politics and national citizenships.

## CONTRACTUALIST DOCTRINES AND THE BOUNDARIES OF CITIZENSHIP

The idea of a social contract is part of the notion of citizenship itself. The first theoretical expression of contractualism, the Hobbesian one, referred to a basic social contract in which individuals were held equal as subjects (Baubock, 1994). This conveys an implicit idea of weak citizenship but there is a more important characteristic: the individuals who participate in this social contract play no part in defining it. The contract does not imply a redefinition of the group (although this question is not explicitly addressed in a theoretical way) and is, therefore, premised on the pre-existence of a community as the basis for consensual change. Later models of the social contract built upon this pattern of a basic pact to make it dependent on guarantees of fundamental civic rights (Locke) or on the individual's self-realization through political participation by exercising political rights (Rousseau). The modern understanding of contractualism, as reflected in constitutional practice, has extended the pact to include a wider guarantee of social rights, based on the belief (in parallel to economic Keynesianism) that the self-realization of a member of the community contributes to the improvement of the community as a whole.

Certainly, it could be objected that the latter evolution reflects a rather communitarian understanding of the social contract and that liberal versions of the social contract, theoretically rooted in Locke, differ substantially from this. In the liberal tradition, negative freedoms are predominant and the participation in the public sphere is not an instrument for individual self-realization. However, a possible similarity between both models can be identified: the absence of theoretical inquiry into the boundaries of the contracting group. Regardless of their liberal or communitarian inspiration, all forms of citizenship relied on the existence of a pre-defined human group on which the pact is predicated, and, simultaneously, on a bounded and defined public space in which the status of citizenship is guaranteed. This explains why some authors consider that liberal citizenship theories are implicitly communitarian (Bellamy, 1994).

Obviously the factor that has altered current perceptions of citizenship – mass migration – was not an issue when these theoretical models were developed. In practical terms, nation states served to define these boundaries, both in a communitarian as much as a liberal perspective. It is not just that the nation state provided the framework for free individual and collective action; but also that the new political role of individuals demanded a deeper degree of personal commitment, even to the point of self-sacrifice and, at this juncture, nationalism served to foster people's identification with this role: nationalism and republicanism combined in the necessity to fight and, if necessary, to die for one's country, a transcendent entity which took the place of personal allegiance to the sovereign. As Habermas argues, there was a symbiosis between nationalism and republicanism in this respect (Habermas, 1994: 23). The social contract was not unlimited; citizenship was established within bounded and defined communities, and this automatically created a criterion for exclusion. Exclusion was based on the understanding of the state as an entity whose telos is to express the will and further the interests of distinctive and bounded nations, and whose legitimacy depends on their doing so, or at least appearing to do so (Brubaker, 1992: 28). Nationality became the essential attribute for determining an individual's entitlement to citizenship rights.

This theoretical reasoning does not lead to an automatic deduction of a practical distinction between the status of citizens and aliens. It is true that constitutional texts, independent of their liberal or communitarian inspiration, and beginning with the Declaration of the Rights of Man and Citizen, establish a difference between human rights (granted to everybody within the territory of a state) and citizenship rights (reserved only for certain individuals). But it is also true that state practice through the progressive granting of civil, social and even political rights to formerly excluded individuals or groups has steadily eroded the juridical and conceptual distinction between citizens and non-citizens within most western states. The distinction has been kept only at a conceptual level and regarding certain limited rights: fundamental rights (whatever their content) are granted in general on an equal footing to citizens and non-citizens alike (Hammar, 1990: 83). Accordingly, some authors have revitalize the Lockean concept of 'denizen', which means a lawfully resident alien with the same primary rights of political participation as native or naturalized citizens (Layton-Henry, 1990; Meehan, 1993: 18), while 'metic' would be a resident alien with legal status but enjoying only a limited number of the rights of citizenship.

This severing of the link between citizenship and nationality has required a redefinition of communitarian perspectives on citizenship, since from a purely liberal standpoint it is not, *a priori*, conceptually problematic to give aliens citizenship status. Communitarian views have also evolved to encompass the increasing permeability and inclusiveness of the respective communities as part of their own self-identity. Identity is not only based on historical continuity but is also constructed through an understanding of the morally acceptable current status of other individuals within the community. The horrors of Nazism and totalitarianism and the various forms of dictatorship world-wide have led to a reformulation of the ways in which democratic communities define themselves: widely guaranteed fundamental rights are a normative pre-requisite for the constitution of a democratic community. Thus, an extensive granting of rights to non-citizens has become regular practice in western states.

To recapitulate, social contract doctrines inspired the creation of status of rights guaranteed within the boundaries of the nation state; these rights were progressively enlarged and generalized. The creation of the concept of EU citizenship can be understood as part of the process described above: from a liberal standpoint, there is no contradiction in granting certain rights (such as the right to free movement) to nationals from EU member states as a precondition for the operation of the single market. The acceptance which this redefinition of the privileges of national citizenship requires from the communitarian standpoint is based on the subordination of EU citizenship rights to respect for *national* identities, thereby easing anxieties about the dilution of communitarian citizenships within the member states.


## PREMISES AND LIMITS OF EU CITIZENSHIP

Essentially, EU citizenship is a legal status consisting of a set of positive rights – freedom of movement and residence, voting rights in local and European Parliament (EP) elections, the right of petition to the EP; the right to appeal to the ombudsman and the right to diplomatic protection. Most of these are already present (albeit in an imperfect way) in EC law, to which some add implicit rights and duties. The fundamental characteristic of this status is that it is not an alternative to or substitute for national citizenship; but, rather, it adds a second layer of new rights enjoyed in any member state to the first layer of nationality rights enjoyed *within* a member state (Closa, 1992; O'Keefe, 1994). At the moment, the rights embodied in the notion of citizenship of the Union are strictly limited, even though there is provision for their further enlargement. This limitation creates a clear distinction from national citizenship: Union citizenship is a specific status whose scope is reduced to the effects expressly mentioned in the Treaty and, which is, therefore, distinct from the more generic character of national citizenships (Ruzie, 1994: 10). Citizenship of the Union, as enshrined in the TEU and at its current stage of development, is a guarantee for the enjoyment of certain rights regardless of which member state nationality an individual may possess. Moreover, EU citizenship reflects an indirect link between an individual and the Union, mediated by nationality of a member state.

Not surprisingly, then, there are clear limits to the legal status created by EU citizenship. While it seems possible to create an EU citizenship status based on individual rights, the development of certain other citizenship rights is made more difficult by the absence of a community at the EU level that is equivalent, for the citizen, to the nation state. Political participation in national elections is the example of this: their restriction to the community of nationals (in contrast with voting rights in EP and local elections) reinforces a fundamentally non-communitarian understanding of EU citizenship. It is on these grounds that, some 20 years ago, Raymond Aron argued that multinational citizenship was impossible. For him, the development of a fully-fledged status of rights attached to the notion of citizenship would not be possible if disconnected from a sovereign nation (Aron, 1974). The development of a supranational status of rights has proved him wrong to some extent; but what remains to be seen is whether certain rights, which are central to national understandings of social contract, can be developed at the supranational level on the basis of an implicitly liberal model. And, here, Aron would appear to be right.

It has been argued above that the extension of citizenship rights has depended on redefining national assumptions and perceptions of citizenship. Indeed, the prospects for a 'new' social contract are pre-determined by this. The prevalence of negative integration in the EU (which, in its original economic formulation, refers to the removal of national restraints on trade and distortions of competition) (Tinbergen, 1965: 76) means that the only foreseeable contract will, in any case, have a very liberal profile. The move towards a richer contract in terms of social rights at the EU level is made difficult because the process whereby it would have to be achieved – positive integration (the creation of new social and political institutions and instruments in order to shape the operating conditions of the internal market) – would need to embrace a degree of communitarianism which would be incompatible with the current direction taken by the EU.


## CREATING CITIZENSHIP THROUGH NEGATIVE INTEGRATION: THE PRINCIPLE OF EQUALITY IN A FORMAL DIMENSION

The legal status of citizenship serves the primary purpose of establishing equality among individuals; citizenship serves to overcome inequalities created by cleavages such as sex, age and beliefs. Within the framework of the EU, these cleavages (sex, race, age and so on) are redressed by the catalogue of rights included in national citizenships and/or in constitutionally guaranteed fundamental rights, which the European Court of Justice (ECJ) has incorporated as principles of EC law. Therefore, the only meaningful cleavage which justifies the existence of EU citizenship is the one created by nationality (García, 1993: 15). Thus, in the context of EU citizenship, equality has to be understood as equality among nationalities.

Under EC law, the principle of equality is incorporated into the principle of non-discrimination on the grounds of nationality.[1] Surprisingly, in formal terms, citizenship of the Union is not explicitly grounded in the principle of non-discrimination operating in other areas of Community law. It could be argued that, in practical terms, ECJ judicial activism renders this unnecessary, since a generalized right to equality of treatment of Community citizens can be deduced from it (Lenaerts, 1991: 25–32). The prohibition of non-discrimination, as developed by ECJ case law, covers three situations: all direct or overt discrimination (rules which specifically provide for a different treatment of non-nationals); indirect or disguised discrimination (rules which, although based on a criterion which appears to be neutral in practice, lead to discrimination);[2] reverse discrimination which occurs in situations where a member state discriminates against its own citizens in favour of foreign nationals.

The limitations on constructing a general principle of equality through negative integration can be summarized in three points which presuppose a certain model of contract. Firstly, despite its progressive and flexible interpretation, as manifested in the Cowan case,[3] the ECJ finds a constitutional limit to the prohibition of non-discrimination because of the lack of a precise base of a general character: non-discrimination is applied only within the scope of the EC Treaty. Therefore, an individual claiming equal treatment must establish that he/she is in an area covered by the Treaty (Schockweiler, 1991: 16), and this undermines the general character which the principle of equality among citizens should have. The absence of a provision on non-discrimination on the grounds of nationality as one of the elements of EU citizenship of the Union derives from the interpretation that the Treaty framers had of it: in other words, that it should regulate the functioning of the EC Treaty, particularly its economic dimension, rather than being part of the personal status of individuals. This questions the apparent inspiration behind EU citizenship: severing the link between economic activity and rights within the EU (Closa, 1995: 494).

Secondly, since EU citizenship relies on member states' nationality, the completion of negative integration would have to advance logically towards the creation of a legal regime which removes the inequalities among EU citizens created by conditions to acquire nationality in each member state. This raises two interlinked questions. On the one hand, member states still remain gatekeepers for national citizenship privileges (whatever they are) via nationality laws. The heterogeneity of regimes puts EU citizens in unequal positions according to the country in which they may become naturalized. While the introduction of some harmonization measures seems to be possible, more comprehensive (and radical) solutions, such as multiple or dual citizenship appear to lack legitimacy. Furthermore, EU citizens may be in a situation of inequality *vis-à-vis* third country nationals: some member states soften naturalization requirements with countries or group of countries with which particular solidarity links are assumed; and only Italy has reacted to the creation of an EU citizenship by softening naturalization requirements for nationals from EU states. On the other hand, would-be EU citizens are faced with different requirements for gaining access to EU citizenship because of divergent national legislation. In the opinion of Evans, a general extension of the equality principle would require a reduction of the exclusivity of nationality as a condition for access to equality and to allow for the operation of alternative conditions, notably that of residence (Evans, 1995: 110).

Thirdly, there are explicit Treaty derogations to the application of this principle which seek to preserve the inner core of the communitarian perception of national citizenship from the logic of the market. Thus, the principle is not applicable to those situations where nationality is a prerequisite for the exercise of certain rights or functions from which member states may legitimately exclude Union citizens other than their own. These are the situations covered in particular by Articles 48 (4) and 55 of the EC Treaty. The Court has repeatedly confirmed that certain functions with the objective of safeguarding the state's general interest imply the existence of a particular relationship of solidarity with the state, as well as the reciprocity of rights and duties which are the foundation of nationality.[4] The TEU has not modified this situation and the aforementioned articles remain unchanged. Any change derived from the qualitatively different nature of the citizenship of the Union will, therefore, have to be brought about by ECJ case law, and, in this respect, some authors argue optimistically that it seems reasonable to expect that the Court will further narrow the scope of articles 48 (4) and 55 now that the provisions on citizenship have given a clear political dimension to the EC Treaty (Wouters, 1994: 49).

These objections notwithstanding, it may be asked whether advances in the field of negative integration (which establish some basis for a liberal form of social contract) provide any margin for the reconstruction of the welfare dimension of social contractualism.


## SUBSTANTIAL SOCIAL ENTITLEMENTS: THE CASE FOR EU SOCIAL RIGHTS

Normative as well as theoretical arguments suggest alternatively the desirability or the logical possibility of achieving a positive integration of citizenship rights: in other words, the development of social rights that would influence the allocation functions of the market. From the normative point of view, it is evident that the market-led logic behind the European integration process is bound to deepen existing, or even worse, create new intra-societal inequalities. Social rights have the function of removing the (material) inequalities among individuals created by the market. Therefore, the possible impact of the single market on citizens' material status – for instance, an increase in unemployment (Cinneide, 1994) – might justify the development of redistributive EU social rights. Moreover, if the question of inequality is raised in the framework of the EU, a new horizontal dimension appears: as the result of the functioning of the internal market, individuals and groups of individuals may see inequalities within the EU – and even within their own communities – grow larger. Winners and losers are identified along national lines and not as individuals. Put bluntly, the backwardness of the southern member states, either in terms of comparatively underdeveloped forms of social citizenship (García, 1993: 21–2) or unequal access to economic activity (Magone, 1994), erodes the basic equality of citizenship in material terms, while, at the same time, the constraints on fiscal policy created by convergence programmes makes it harder for certain member states to provide social rights at the highest EU standards. It can, therefore, be argued that if the process of Europeanization is itself creating additional disparities, then there are clear grounds for seeking a remedy to this problem at the EU level (Kleinman and Piachaud, 1993). This argument underpins the principle of economic and social cohesion which, as understood by some of its most authoritative interpreters, refers to the status of individuals: in other words, it is a political concept that establishes the maximum socially acceptable divergence among citizens of the Union (Elorza Cavengt, 1992). The underlying thinking is that responsibility for the reduction of economic disparities has to be assumed by the Union as a prerequisite of its legitimacy.

Part of this normative argument underlies the more general theoretical analysis of rights. In a continuing debate with Marshall, the sociological tradition has linked the process of rights acquisition with the development of the market. If civic and political rights were the logical correlate of individual equality created by the market, social rights – and specifically redistributive rights – were created as an instrument for modifying the logic of the market. There seems little doubt that the market is central to the development of citizenship rights within the EC, which justifies the definition of such rights as 'market citizenship' (Marias, 1994) or 'functionalist' or 'segmented' citizenship (Neunreither, 1995). The most highly developed rights – the freedom of movement and residence – are closely linked to the creation of the single market; indeed, they guarantee its efficiency and this secures a wide consensus for such rights. Following the sociological logic, some reputed scholars, inspired by the catalogue of rights developed previous to the Maastricht Treaty, argue that European citizenship is a possible case of reverse citizenship formation (inverting, that is, the order in which these rights are acquired) (Meehan, 1993). In formal terms, Article 8e of the Treaty provides legal grounds for the development of social rights explicitly linked to the citizenship of the Union even without the necessity of a constitutional revision.

Thus, it seems that a case for EU social rights can be constructed on both theoretical and normative grounds. However, EU citizenship does not explicitly provide specific entitlements for the removal of inequalities provoked by the Union itself, and this creates a certain inconsistency in the legal construction. Certainly, it is increasingly becoming common opinion that EU citizenship rights should not be limited simply to those referred to as such by the Treaty (La Torre, 1995: 117; O'Leary, 1996). In fact, a number of entitlements that can be interpreted as social rights – for instance, the entitlement to receive social benefits – may be identified in EC law. However, since they have not been expressly formulated as citizenship rights, their legitimacy (*raison d'être*) is grounded in the economic activity of individuals. They lack, therefore, the universal character of other citizenship rights. Entitlement to social benefits still varies according to the role played by the claimant in the process of Community economic integration, be it as a worker, a dependant, or an economically inactive individual (O'Leary, 1996). The fact that certain social rights (mainly linked to labour market participation) have been explicitly included in the Social Protocol and Agreement – an annex to the TEU based on an intergovernmental agreement that is not strictly subject to EC law and ECJ jurisdiction – does little to improve this state of affairs. As has been correctly noted, the Social Charter and action programme that preceded it were not concerned with social rights *for citizens* but with fundamental social rights for workers (Kleinman and Piachaud, 1993); and this remains the case under the Protocol.

The difficulties in constructing EU social rights as part of EU citizenship are due to their specific nature. The classical Marshallian distinction merely contrasts them to political and civic rights but it fails to capture more subtle questions. One solution to this is to modify the Marshallian distinction between civil, political and social rights. Ferrajoli (1993) has proposed a different taxonomy of rights, combining two different criteria. The first is the logical structure of rights. According to this criteria, I propose a categorization of social rights as follows: rights to personal autonomy (for instance, right to family reunification following right of establishment); secondly, entitlements can be redefined as rights of personal autonomy (for instance, the rights to education or work may be understood as guarantee of non-intervention or as an active obligation of the state to promote them); and thirdly, material provisions designed to realize entitlements formulated as social objectives. The second criterion proposed by Ferrajoli is to identify the status of the recipient of rights, distinguishing fundamental (attached to legal personality) and citizenship rights.

The importance of both criteria derives from the fact that, in combination, they produce a new conception of rights in practice where social rights are not linked to the status of citizenship. The extension of social rights to 'denizens', for example, has been premised on a socioeconomic situation that has permitted two successive processes: firstly, the transformation of 'expectation rights' into effective entitlements. What permits social rights – understood as a social objectives – to become 'effective entitlements' is the presence of a certain level of socioeconomic development linked to a political programme. Secondly, given the contemporary normative self-understanding of the nation state as an area for effective solidarity, these entitlements have been extended to non-citizens. At this point, the essential element in deciding entitlement is the existence of boundaries which distinguish between members and non-members of the community (Freeman, 1986; Kleinman and Piachaud, 1993). However, the boundaries are not traced between citizens (nationals) and non-citizens (non-nationals) but they separate those 'within city walls' (Faist, 1994: 7) from outsiders. The principle of redistributive justice is applied not only to fellow nationals but to any person within the boundaries of the community.

There are several obstacles to a similar development at the EU level. Firstly, the lack of commonality across the EU presents a problem of identification. Apart from a vague agreement on basic human rights, EU member states present a heterogeneous regime of fundamental rights. There are differences in the way different societies attach social rights to the concept of citizenship or even in their tendency to add or detract from them. The frameworks for creating or eliminating social rights are still very much national cultures and, specifically, the degree to which economic welfare in each member state allows for the material provision which underpins them.

The lack of commonality is obstructed by the lack of channels for the formulation of new values. Whilst social conflict has often characterized the development of systems of rights, the behaviour of social actors has not led to a similar development at the EU level. Rather, the EU has become an additional arena for defending privileged *national* forms of citizenship on the eve of enhanced market competition (Breuer *et al.*, 1994). This is related to the still primarily national character of the social actors and, for instance, the interest of certain 'clubs' (such as German trade unions) has been essential for the development of industrial or labour rights within the EU.

Alternatively, the activism of the ECJ has been decisive, for instance, in enshrining certain rights in the EU's constitution. But those commentators who have enthusiastically championed ECJ judicial activism in the area of social rights seem to ignore that while rights of personal autonomy in the social field may be judicially guaranteed, social *entitlements* require policy to be implemented. Some social rights (and certainly those with a redistributive content), conform to a type of 'expectation rights' that presupposes government action. In the absence of EU policies, social rights judicially guaranteed might constrain national governments to follow policies which imply substantial financial commitments. Therefore, member states may be willing to resist moves in such a direction.

A second, related, question refers to the obstacles for operationalizing social rights. In policy terms, social entitlements can be justified through political programmes based on efficiency, equality or solidarity arguments (Kleinman and Piachaud, 1993). What is important, though, is that the kind of social rights inspired by each of these principles is different. While certain social rights can be satisfied through what Majone calls 'social regulation' (that is intervention whose purpose is to solve problems created by specific types of market failure), substantial provisions necessarily require the development of social policy, based on moral or political reasons (and not in the search for market efficiency) (Majone, 1993: 157). In practical terms, the lack of an EU-wide macroeconomic policy, let alone budgetary or fiscal resources to alter the effects of the single market, limit the possible development of 'social entitlements' provided for by the EU (not to mention the kind of transnational social policy predicated by de Swaan (1994)).

The prevalence of *efficiency* considerations in the emergence of social entitlements at the European level seems to be clear. The policy logic behind European social standards is based on fears of 'social dumping' and, following an old opinion by Advocate General Dutheillet de Lamtothe, aims to assist the establishment of a system by ensuring that competition is not distorted in the framework of the Common Market.[5] The objective of social policy as embedded in the Rome Treaty was not the correction of market outcomes in line with political ideas of social justice, but rather enabling the European labour market to function efficiently (Streeck, 1995: 40). The principle of *equality*, on the other hand, seems to play a role in alleviating horizontal inequality (between member states and their regions), particularly throughout its development of regional and cohesion policies. However, the equalizing concept which underlies the principle of social and economic cohesion is not the provision of individual rights in the forms of entitlements (which would be opposed, in any case, since it would erode competitiveness) but rather interregional redistribution (Leibfried and Pierson, 1992: 346). Moreover, the strategic interpretation of cohesion by some beneficiary governments has moved the locus of interpretation of this principle to a higher level, in an effort to restrict the number of participating countries as well as the possible role for regions (Closa, 1995b).

Finally, *solidarity* is frequently invoked in EU rhetoric. In fact, Article A §3 of the TEU states that (the Union) task shall be to organize, in a manner demonstrating consistency and solidarity, relations between the member states and between their peoples. However, policies promoting solidarity are not listed as Union objectives in Article B. These are the objectives for whose fulfilment the provision of adequate resources is foreseen by Article F(3). The conclusion, therefore, is that the promotion of solidarity, although a declarative principle, is not an objective for EU policies. This line of reasoning has been taken a step further by the German constitutional court. The Court has ruled that the development of policy to achieve this objective is beyond the reach of current Treaty provisions and, therefore, the Union cannot provide itself with the financial means and other resources that it might consider necessary for the fulfilment of its objectives. Following its line of interpreting the member states as the Masters of the Treaty, the Court argues that Article F(3) merely makes a statement of intent to the effect that the member states wish to provide it with adequate resources under whichever particular procedure is necessary.[6] The interpretation that might be drawn from this ruling is that the creation of rights according to a logic of solidarity is not perceived as implicit in the nature of the Union.

Citizenship and solidarity are truly interrelated and address similar concerns when citizenship is understood as an institution for the development of social bonds and the obligation of each person towards society. In this context, welfare provision is produced through a process of social cohesion while also producing greater cohesion through the establishment of a particular set of relationships (Spicker, 1991). Although some authors have argued that the development of a Union social policy (and, specifically, redistributive rights) can help to produce greater solidarity (Cinneide, 1994) and, in this sense, to create a community, it seems, in fact, that solidarity is rather a prerequisite for developing redistributive social rights. While they underpin and structure systems of solidarity, redistributive rights also seem to be part of a community's self-perception and identity (Preuss, 1991). The delicate value judgements about the appropriate balance of efficiency and equity, which social policy expresses, can only be made legitimately and efficiently within homogeneous communities (Majone, 1993). It must be recalled that the development of national welfare states in Europe was promoted by a relatively strong perception of a common (mostly male-constructed) citizenship, moulded by identity-shaping experiences such as wars and grounded in an underlying social homogeneity (Leibfried and Pierson, 1992). Redistributive social rights (and a hypothetical 'state of revenue sharing') would imply parallel duties (such as taxes directly raised from citizens) (Leibfried, 1994: 15), accepted either as part of Union citizenship or as a non-discretional duty of member state nationality. Whatever option, the grounds for such developments seem, at present, to be non-existent.

## ALTERNATIVES TO EU CITIZENSHIP AS A FRAMEWORK FOR SOCIAL CONTRACT

Despite the sceptical argument presented above, EU citizenship remains the most meaningful basis for reconstructing a social contract at the EU level. If by citizenship is meant merely a commitment to the shared values of the Union as expressed in its constituent documents – that is, a commitment to the duties and rights of a civic society covering discrete areas of public life (Weiler, 1995) – then the concept of EU citizenship is, of course, unnecessary. These commitments are already implicit in the acceptance of EC law which is directly applicable for nationals. Rather, the value of EU citizenship depends on its ability to protect individuals, via legal status, against the challenges that the EU legal order poses to values incorporated in *national* concepts of citizenship and contract, such as solidarity, cohesion and redistribution.

Critical commentaries on the implications of Union citizenship, however, warn against the exclusionist character which is intrinsic to the notion of citizenship itself (d'Oliveira, 1995: 77–82), claiming even that the European integration process poses a challenge to the established distinction between fundamental rights of general availability and fundamental rights available to individuals in relation to nationality (Evans, 1995: 104). This objection seems to be based on a mechanistic identification of national citizenship with EU citizenship and misses a fundamental difference between the two: the gatekeeper of citizenship privileges is nationhood (and its legal repository, nationality). No European nationality matches European citizenship and, therefore, whatever entitlements are included under European citizenship, member states retain full discretion in determining who their nationals are even for the purposes of EC law. Therefore, regarding EU citizenship as a new banner for privilege is untenable, as long as it depends on nationality, the real banner for citizenship privileges. *A priori*, there is no reason why member states should not generalize EU citizenship rights to all individuals.

A more subtle line of reasoning seeks to subsume the question of EU citizenship rights under the broader question of human rights. In short, it is assumed that individual rights are better served through fundamental rights, and that human rights are a superior normative entitlement. In this argument, the juridical analysis reacts to the sociological tradition which, from Marshall onwards, has referred the whole ensemble of rights (civil, political, social and others) to the status of citizenship. Although the evidence of the process of rights acquisition justifies sociological postulates, the latter identify citizenship, in reductionist fashion, as the main and almost only channel for individual entitlements to rights. From a juridical point of view, the concept of legal personality offers an alternative status for entitlement to fundamental rights (Ferrajoli, 1993), in which all civil rights and some social rights are included. State practice confirms that these are granted to all individuals within the boundaries of a political community.

The normative case for incorporating human rights and fundamental freedoms within the EU Treaty is undisputable, as is the case for generalizing social and civil rights to all individuals regardless of their citizenship status. But the strength of the normative case is somehow weakened by two possible obstacles to its practical development.

Firstly, human rights are a normative category with no self-evident, precise, practical manifestation. Each constitutional order institutionalizes human rights by providing specific contents for fundamental rights listed in declarations and conventions (Bellamy, 1994). Since differences on the understanding of basic human rights are not uncommon among member states, the creation of fundamental rights at the EU level through a political process of creating common standards would be essentially similar to the process of developing EU citizenship. The conceptual disagreements would be purely nominal; but the obstacles identified above would still be a problem, regarding either fundamental or citizenship rights.

Secondly, this line of argument seems to be unaware of an underlying value-option. This is because the objective is, specifically, the improvement of individual judicial protection *vis-à-vis* community law, particularly in face of the ECJ tendency to balance this protection (provided that the substance of the right is not altered) against the Community's objectives. A practical remedy to possible ECJ 'excesses' is posed by national constitutional courts, as the German court reminded it in its Maastricht Ruling. Another possible remedy would be an explicit, enforceable and general Treaty provision on the respect of human rights. In this case, substituting the process of rights creation within the sphere of EU citizenship (whatever its limits) by the institutionalization of human rights would certainly confirm the ECJ as the main actor in the creation of rights. Incidentally, it would also open the way to a notion of social contract which is based on negative rights, judicially secured – in essence, a liberal version of the social contract. It would be liberal in a double sense: first, citizenship status would result from market interaction (negative integration and efficiency-oriented social rights) although with a universally high level of protection (the one set by human rights). Second, and in contrast, rights (either political or social) aimed at correcting the functioning of the market would have to be explicitly introduced through political decision. Redistributive rights – which may be 'inefficient' from a market perspective – have as their only possible justification the democratic will of the citizens (Streeck, 1995: 35). Therefore, these rights would appear to require the democratic political process as a prerequisite. In this case, though, it would be necessary to overcome the widespread belief that rights associated with various manifestations of that 'over-arching evil' in EU politics – the European superstate – are illegitimate.

## CONCLUSION

The prospects for reconstructing the social content of contemporary European national contracts at the EU level seem to be slim. A market-based form of EU social contract has begun to emerge; but national identities still pose a formidable obstacle to its full development. While using EU citizenship as a means for developing a richer form of social contract are normatively well grounded, it is difficult to put into practice. Alternatives to EU citizenship, however, do rely on the partial liberal contract described above. In this context, the development of a European public sphere in which notions of public good can be discussed and identified, becomes a prerequisite for the institutionalization of any form of social contract.

## NOTES

1    In the Allué case, the Court designed the principle of non-discrimination on the grounds of nationality as a principle of equality of treatment. Case Pilar Allué et Carmel Mary Coonan contre Universitá degli Studi di Venezia Case 33/88 Rec. (1989) 1591.

2    In the Allué case, the Court held that the principle of non-discrimination forbids any disguised forms. The argument was repeated by the ruling in the Italy case. Commission des Communautés européennes contre République italienne Case C 3/88 Rec. (1989) 4035.

3    Case C 186/87 Cowan v. Trésor Public (1989) ECR 195. The Court interpreted that the prohibition of non-discrimination can be extended to the recipients of services such as tourists and nationals from a member state in another member state. The plaintiff, Mr Cowan, was, therefore, entitled to receive financial compensations established by national law for nationals in the case of assault.

4    Case 149/79 Commission des Communautés européennes contre Royaume de Belgique Rec. (1980) 3881. Case 66/85 Deborah Lawrie-Blum v. Land Baden-Württemberg Rec. (1986) 2121.

5    Case 43/75 *Defrenne v. Sabenna* [1976] ECR 485.
6    Brunner v. the European Union Treaty. Cases 2 BvR 2134/92 & 2159/92 [1994] 1 CMLR 57.

## REFERENCES

Aron, R. (1974) 'Is Multinational Citizenship Possible?' *Social Research*, 41.

Baubock, R. (1994) *Transnational Citizenship: Membership and Rights in International Migration*, London: Edward Elgar.

Bellamy, R. (1994) 'Tre modelli di cittadinanza', in D. Zolo (ed.), *La cittadinanza: Appartanenza, identità, diritti*, Roma: Laterza, pp. 223–61.

Breuer, M., Faist, T. and Jordan, B. (1994) 'Club Theory, Migration and Welfare States', Centre for Social Policy Research, University of Bremen, ZeS-Working paper No. 15.

Brubaker, R. (1992) *Citizenship and Nationhood in France and Germany*, Cambridge, Mass.: Harvard University Press.

Cinneide, S.O. (1994) *The European Union: Citizenship, Exclusion and Entitlements*, Paper for the XVIth World Congress of the IPSA, Berlin, August.

Closa, C. (1992) 'The Concept of Citizenship in the Treaty on European Union', *Common Market Law Review*, 29, pp. 1137–1169.

Closa, C. (1995) 'Citizenship of the Union and Nationality of Member States', *Common Market Law Review*, 32.

Closa, C. (1995b) 'National Interest and Convergence of Preferences: A Changing role for Spain in the EU?', in C. Rhodes and S. Mazey (eds.) *The State of the European Union Vol. 3: Building a European Polity?*, Boulder: Lynne Rienner.

Elorza Cavengt, F. (1992) 'Cohesión económica y social', *Gaceta Jurídica de la CE*, D–17.

Evans, A. (1995) 'Union Citizenship and the Equality Principle', in A. Rosas and E. Antola (eds.) *A Citizens' Europe*, London: Sage, pp. 85–112.

Faist, T. (1994) 'A Medieval City: Transnationalizing Labor Markets and Social Rights in Europe', Centre for Social Policy Research, University of Bremen, ZeS-Working paper No. 91.

Ferrajoli, Luigi (1993) 'Cittadinanza e diritti fondamentali', *Teoria Política* 9, 3, pp. 63–76.

Freeman, G. (1986) 'Migration and the Political Economy of the Welfare State', *Annals of the American Academy of Social Sciences* 485, pp. 51–63.

Garcìa, S. (1993) 'Europe's Fragmented Identities and the Frontiers of Citizenship', in S. Garcìa (ed.) *European Identity and the Search for Legitimacy*, London: Pinter, pp. 1–29.

Habermas, J. (1994) 'Citizenship and National Identity', in B. van Steenbergen (ed.), *The Condition of Citizenship*, London: Sage.

Hammar, T. (1990) 'The Civil Rights of Aliens', in Z. Layton-Henry (ed.), *The Political Rights of Migrant Workers in Western Europe*, London: Sage, pp. 74–93.

Kleinman, M. and Piachaud, D. (1993) 'European Social Policy: Conceptions and Choices', *Journal of European Social Policy*, 3, 1, pp. 1–19.

La Torre, M. (1995) 'Citizenship: a European Wager', *Ratio Juris*, 8, 1, pp. 113–23.

Layton-Henry, Z. (1990) 'Citizenship or Denizenship?', in Z. Layton-Henry (ed.), *The Political Rights of Migrant Workers in Western Europe*, London: Sage, pp. 186–195.

Leibfried, S. (1994) 'The Social Dimension of the European Union: En Route to Positively Joint Sovereignty?' *Journal of European Social Policy*, 4, 4, pp. 239–262.

Leibfried, S. and Pierson, P. (1992) 'Prospects for Social Europe', *Politics and Society*, 20, 3, pp. 333–66.

Lenaerts, K. (1991) 'L'égalite de traitement en droit communautaire. Un principe unique aux apparences multiples', *Cahiers de Droit European*, 27, 1, pp. 3–41.

Magone, J. (1994) 'Peripheral Citizenship in the European Union: Some Preliminary Political and Sociological Considerations on Southern Europe', 2nd ECSA-World Conference: Federalism, Subsidiarity and Democracy in the European Union, Brussels, 5–6 May.

Majone, G. (1993) 'The European Community Between Social Policy and Social Regulation', *Journal of Common Market Studies*, 31, 2, pp. 153–70.

Marias, E. (1994) 'From Market Citizen to Union Citizen', in Marias, E. (ed.), *European Citizenship*, Maastricht: EIPA, pp. 1–24.

Meehan, E. (1993) *Citizenship and the EC*, London: Sage.

Neunreither, K. (1995) 'Citizens and the Exercise of Power in the European Union: Towards a New Social Contract?', in A. Rosas, and E. Antola (eds.), *A Citizens' Europe*, London: Sage, pp. 1–18.

O'Keefe, D. (1994) 'Union Citizenship', in D. O'Keefe and P. Twomey (eds). *Legal issues of the Maastricht Treaty*, London: Wiley, pp. 87–108.

O'Leary, S. (1996) *European Union Citizenship: The Options for Reform*, London Institute for Public Policy Research.

d'Oliveira, J.H.U. (1995) 'Union Citizenship: Pie in the Sky?', in A. Rosas and E. Antola (eds), *A Citizens' Europe*, London: Sage, pp. 58–84.

Preuss, U. (1991) 'El concepto de los derechos y el estado de bienestar' in Olivas, E. (ed.), *Problemas de legitimación en el estado social*, Madrid: Editorial Trotta.

Ruzie, D. (1994) *Citoyenneté et nationalité dans l'union européenne*, Paper for the 2nd ECSA-World Conference: Federalism, Subsidiarity and Democracy in the European Union, Brussels 5–6 May.

Schockweiler, F. (1991) 'La porteé du principe de non-discrimination de l'article 7 du traité CEE', *Rivista Diritto Europeo* 30, 1, pp. 3–24.

Spicker, P. (1991) 'Solidarity', in Room, G. (ed.) *Towards a European Welfare State?*, Bristol: SAUS, pp. 17–37.

Streeck, W. (1995) 'Neo-voluntarism: a New European Social Policy Regime?', *European Law Journal*, 1, 1, pp. 31–59.

de Swaan, A. (1994) 'Perspectives for Trans-national Social Policy in Europe: Social Transfers from West to East', in de Swaan, A. (ed.), *Social Policy Beyond Borders*, Amsterdam: Amsterdam University Press.

Tinbergen, J. (1965) *International Economic Integration*, Amsterdam: Elsevier.

Weiler, J., Haltern, U. and Mayer, F. (1995) 'European Democracy and its Critique', *West European Politics*, 18, 3, pp. 4–39.

Wouters, J. (1994) 'European Citizenship and the Case-Law of the Court of Justice of the European Communities on the Free Movement of Persons', in E. Marias (ed.), *European Citizenship*, Maastricht: EIPA.

# Index

Note: Page numbers in **bold** print indicate tables and figures.

This book is to be returned on
or before the date stamped below

UNIVERSITY OF PLYMOUTH

PLYMOUTH LIBRARY

Tel: (01752) 232323
This book is subject to recall if required by another reader
Books may be renewed by phone
CHARGES WILL BE MADE FOR OVERDUE BOOKS